STAYING VERTICAL

a daily exploration

Dr. Stephen Trammell & Jared Richard

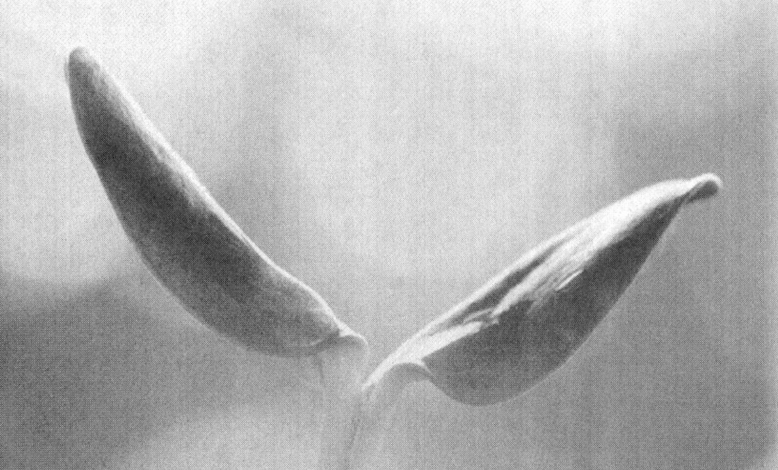

STAYING VERTICAL

a daily exploration

DR. STEPHEN TRAMMELL & JARED RICHARD

Published in the United States by Champion Forest Baptist Church,
Houston, TX
www.championforest.org

Book design by Jacque Sellers

Cataloging-in-Publication Data

Trammell, Stephen & Richard, Jared

Staying Vertical : a daily exploration/
by Stephen Trammell & Jared Richard

384 p. 22 cm.

Summary: 365-day devotional designed to enhance the reader's daily walk with God.

ISBN 978-0-982-6630-4-2 (pbk.)

1. Devotional Calendars. 2. Devotions, Daily.
3. Devotional Literature. 4. Spiritual Growth. 5. Meditations.
6. God-Meditations. 7. Discipleship. 8. Prayer Books and Devotions.
I. Title.

242.2 –dc22

DEDICATIONS

To Tonya, Tori, and Austin
for the joy of living out our faith together.

~Stephen

To my incredible wife, Jordan, who makes me want to be a better follower of Christ so that I can be a better husband to her, and to my parents, who instilled in me at a young age both a love for the Lord and for His Word. Thank you for your Godly, yet humble example.

~Jared

FOREWORD

For over a decade I have had the honor and privilege to call Dr. Stephen Trammell and Jared Richard dear friends and brothers in the faith. God allowed me to serve alongside these two men when I first surrendered to the call of vocational ministry. They have played pivotal roles in my spiritual development, and I could not have imagined, those 11 years ago, the depth of love and admiration I would develop for them both.

I have never served under a more humble and Spirit-led pastor than Dr. Trammell. God has used him in my life again and again as my greatest spiritual mentor other than my earthly father. He has modeled Jesus for me in every aspect of life from marriage and parenting to pastoring. I was blessed to learn the foundations of ministry from a man whose foundation was Jesus.

There has never been a friend and brother in Christ as dear to me as Jared. We have walked through many highs and many lows in our journey of friendship, and I cherish every step along the way. Jared's passion for the Word of God has spurred me on to be a better husband, pastor, and follower of Jesus. Every time I am in need of a Christian brother to encourage me in the faith, he is the one I turn to.

Both of these men pour their lives into the spiritual discipleship of those around them. They don't just write about being a fully devoted follower of Jesus, they live every word. I pray that God would use the Holy Spirit and the words of this book to bring you closer to the image and likeness of Jesus Christ. I pray that as these men have done for me, they will also do for you by leading you to the cross of Jesus Christ to find full acceptance and love there. May you allow these men to speak into your life, and may your life never be the same.

Travis Boyd
Minister of Worship,
McGregor Baptist Church

ACKNOWLEDGMENTS

When you decide to keep your "yes" on the altar, you get to experience the adventure of joining God in His activity. I want to thank God for paving the way for this devotional book to become a reality. We are so blessed to have a godly senior pastor, Dr. David Fleming, here at Champion Forest Baptist Church. His spiritual gift of leadership permeates the vision and focus of being a church on mission with God to fulfill the Great Commission. Pastor David and I became best friends when we met over two decades ago during our days of pastoring in Louisiana and obtaining our degrees from New Orleans Baptist Theological Seminary.

This devotional book is extra special in that I have had the privilege of co-authoring this project with one of my Timothy's in ministry, Jared Richard. I met Jared over 10 years ago while I was pastoring in Baton Rouge, Louisiana. Jared served as the president of the Baptist Collegiate Ministry at LSU and soon thereafter joined our church staff. For the past five and half years, Jared has been with me here at Champion Forest Baptist Church serving as our teaching pastor and minister to young adults. God has given Jared a brilliant mind and a passionate heart for the pursuit of God's truth. You will enjoy his devotionals throughout this book.

As you know, it takes a team to publish a book. I am so grateful for the dream team God assembled. I want to thank my wife, Tonya, for our twenty-three years of marriage and for her willingness to spend hours editing this manuscript and putting her special touch on each page. I want to thank Jacque Sellers for her incredible display of God's creativity in designing the book cover and adding special features on each page. Jacque has leveraged her giftedness for God's glory in each of my devotional book projects and I am so grateful. Our media pastor, Chris Todd, has been a continual source of wisdom and a pleasure to serve with in this project implementation and he knows how to do just about anything. When I have a question, I usually call Chris. Our support services pastor, Joey Mouton, is always leaning in ready to mobilize his team to make concepts become tangible. I appreciate his servitude and contagious enthusiasm.

My heart overflows with gratitude for the entire staff and church family here at Champion Forest Baptist Church. Thank you for your devotion to the Lord.

STAYING VERTICAL
INTRODUCTION

The odometer for my journey with God indicates thirty-four years. I became a follower of Jesus Christ on March 28, 1979, when I transferred my trust from myself to Jesus alone for salvation. That divine transaction impacted my eternal security and my eternal destiny. I was adopted into God's forever family!

Being saved and growing in your salvation are uniquely different. Once I received the gift of eternal life, I had to learn how to grow in my love relationship with the Lord. Paul shared with the church at Philippi, "Therefore, my beloved, as you have always obeyed, so now, not only as in my presence but much more in my absence, work out your own salvation with fear and trembling" (Philippians 2:12 ESV). As we journey with God, we have to learn how to work out what He has worked in.

What is the key to staying vertical while living in a world full of horizontal distractions? We combat the devil, the world, and our flesh. Staying vertical is a mark of spiritual maturity. The road to spiritual maturity is paved with daily discipline. Making daily deposits into your love relationship with the Lord will help you develop into the fully devoted follower of Christ you were created to become.

I want to invite you into a 365-day journey through God's Word that will help you make those daily deposits and elevate your level of spiritual maturity. As you read the daily devotionals, you will notice the daily Bible readings listed for you. Make room in your daily routine to spend time reading chronological through the Bible this year. Allow God to speak to you through His Word and to grow you into Christlikeness.

Ask God to take you to a new level of intimacy with Him as you journey through the Bible. Allow God to have His way in your life. To maximize your daily time alone with the Lord, consider journaling your journey with God. Write or type daily entries to record your thoughts and your insights gleaned from God's Word.

My prayer is that you will experience God in such a fresh way this year that it will become a major spiritual marker in your life. Enjoy the journey as you encounter God and embrace the benefit of staying vertical for His glory.

Staying Vertical,
~ Stephen

January 1

God's Idea

Chronological Bible Reading Plan: (Day 1: Genesis 1-3)

"Then God said, 'Let us make man in our image, after our likeness. And let them have dominion over the fish of the sea and over the birds of the heavens and over the livestock and over all the earth and over every creeping thing that creeps on the earth.'" Genesis 1:26 (ESV)

You were God's idea. You are not a mistake; you are a masterpiece created by God and for God. So, what on earth are you here for? Why did God create you? Just look to the Bible to discover your purpose. God created you so that you could come into union with Him and continue the ministry of Jesus on the earth. God removed the barrier of sin by providing Jesus as the atoning sacrifice for sin. Turn from your sin and turn to Jesus alone for salvation.

Now that you are in union with God through Christ, enjoy the abiding relationship made possible to you. Commit to spend time in God's Word each day and unhurried time alone with God in prayer. Stay connected to Christ and allow Him to live His life in you and through you to fulfill God's plan. Don't bypass the relationship in order to go do something for God. Focus on the the abiding relationship you have been given with Jesus and allow Him to feature His life through you.

Commit to read through the Bible in one year. If you would be willing to read God's Word for twenty minutes each day, in one year, you will have read through the entire Bible. Make a commitment to start today. I will include a chronological reading plan for you at the top of each daily devotional to help you on your journey.

~ *Stephen*

January 2

Make the Call

Chronological Bible Reading Plan: (Day 2: Genesis 4-7)

"And Adam knew his wife again, and she bore a son and called his name Seth, for she said, 'God has appointed for me another offspring instead of Abel, for Cain killed him.' To Seth also a son was born, and he called his name Enosh. At that time people began to call upon the name of the LORD." Genesis 4:25-26 (ESV)

God pursued Adam and Eve in the garden of Eden and demonstrated His love for them by providing a sacrifice for their sin. God killed an animal in order to provide garments of skins to clothe them. His redeeming love flowed in the garden to rescue Adam and Eve from their sin.

A pivotal moment takes place in Scripture during the time of Adam and Eve's son, Seth, and grandson, Enosh. At that time people began to call upon the name of the Lord. God's pursuit is reciprocated. People began to call on His Name.

The thread of God's redemptive activity can be traced throughout the Bible. When we move into the New Testament and walk through the Gospels to embrace the obedience of Christ on the cross, we can then rejoice in His bodily resurrection and ascension. God came to our rescue! He has made it possible for us to call on His Name!

- *"For there is no distinction between Jew and Greek; for the same Lord is Lord of all, bestowing his riches on all who call on him. For 'everyone who calls on the name of the Lord will be saved.'" Rom. 10:12-13 (ESV)*

What are you doing with the precious gift God has given you to call upon His Name? Are you maximizing the gift by pursuing Him daily and by practicing His Presence moment-by-moment? Call upon the Lord. Seek Him diligently and focus your life on His agenda. Remove distractions. Eliminate idols. Run to Jesus.

~ *Stephen*

January 3

Sign of the Covenant

Chronological Bible Reading Plan: (Day 3: Genesis 8-11)

"I have set my bow in the cloud, and it shall be a sign of the covenant between me and the earth. When I bring clouds over the earth and the bow is seen in the clouds, I will remember my covenant that is between me and you and every living creature of all flesh. And the waters shall never again become a flood to destroy all flesh." Genesis 9:13-15 (ESV)

What's at the end of the rainbow? There's no need to look for a pot of gold. When you get to the end of the rainbow, you will discover the ultimate Promise Keeper. God is keeps His Word! God is trustworthy!

The sinfulness of man had saturated the earth so God chose to saturate the earth in judgment by flooding the earth. Only Noah and his family survived due to God's provision of the ark. Noah joined God in His activity by obeying God's instructions to build the ark and to fill the ark. God accomplished His mission through Noah's obedience.

God produced a visible sign of His covenant relationship with us. He set the rainbow in the cloud as a demonstration of His covenant relationship. God is the ultimate Promise Keeper. God demonstrated His grace by preserving humanity and providing for the salvation of Noah's family.

God has taken the initiative to bring us into the ark of safety by grace alone through our faith in Jesus alone. Our salvation is secure in Jesus because of His completed work on the cross on our behalf. Jesus took the punishment for our sin and satisfied the justice of God.

God has given us His Holy Spirit as a deposit guaranteeing our inheritance (Eph. 1:13-14). Have you entered the ark of God's safety by placing your faith in Jesus alone for salvation? Are you willing to invite others to come to know the Promise Keeper personally?

~ *Stephen*

January 4

Proper Perspective

Chronological Bible Reading Plan: (Day 4: Job 1-5)

"Then Job arose and tore his robe and shaved his head and fell on the ground and worshiped. And he said, 'Naked I came from my mother's womb, and naked shall I return. The LORD gave, and the LORD has taken away; blessed be the name of the LORD.'" Job 1:20-21 (ESV)

Have you ever wondered why God allows bad things to happen to good people? When you read about the life of Job and the severity of the adversity he faced, you come away feeling that life is unfair. Job was upright, blameless, turned from evil, and feared God. He had experienced tremendous familial blessing and financial blessing. Job was a godly man who had it all and then lost it all.

His story is heartbreaking and his response to adversity is inspiring. Instead of being bitter, resentful, and angry, Job chose to praise God in the midst of his suffering. Job demonstrated the value of having a proper perspective when going through seasons of adversity. He acknowledged the frailty of his own humanity and the reality of God's sovereignty. Job declared, "The LORD gave, and the LORD has taken away, blessed be the name of the LORD." Job chose to bless the Lord in the midst of his severe trauma, grief, and loss. Instead of magnifying what he lost, Job recognized what he had left and magnified the Lord.

Job is a model to follow. You don't want to go through what he went through. However, you can respond to adversity the way Job did by living life from God's perspective. Ask God to help you see your circumstances from His eternal perspective. Instead of focusing on your circumstances, focus on the Creator who loves you and who will give you the grace to match what you face. In brokenness and humility, cry out to God and receive His divine enabling.

~ *Stephen*

January 5

Humility University

Chronological Bible Reading Plan: (Day 5: Job 6-9)

"'Truly I know that it is so: But how can a man be in the right before God? If one wished to contend with him, one could not answer him once in a thousand times.'" Job 9:2-3 (ESV)

Have you come to grips with your finiteness? Have you discovered how big God is and how small you are? For a human being to try to grasp the awesomeness of God is like a gnat trying to grasp the awesomeness of a Boeing 747 commercial airliner. We are finite; God is infinite. We are limited; God is unlimited.

Job presents a loaded question, "How can a man be in the right before God?" As Job is navigating the rugged terrain of tribulation, he is contemplating his personal identity in light of God's holiness. Job is cognizant of his own human condition before the Lord Almighty. In humility, Job acknowledges the vastness of God within the velocity of his own personal struggle.

Are you living in light of the reality of God's nature and character? Do you embrace a posture of humility as you consider the wonder and glory of God? When you walk through a season of uncertainty or paddle through tumultuous waters, you will be drawn into contemplating the reality of your existence. You will begin to acknowledge your dependency upon God and your awareness of His holiness will be heightened.

How can you be right with God? What can you do? The bad news is that you cannot be right with God based on your personal effort or personal righteousness. In and of yourself, you will always fall short of the glory of God. The good news is that Jesus has closed the gap that separates you from God. Jesus did what you could not do so that you could benefit from His atonement. In Christ, you are made right with God!

~ *Stephen*

January 6

Life, Love, and Compassion

Chronological Bible Reading Plan: (Day 6: Job 10-13)

"'You have granted me life and steadfast love, and your care has preserved my spirit.'" Job 10:12 (ESV)

Job was in a season of desperation. He knew calamity on a first name basis. Surrounded by an inner circle of friends, Job made a profound statement about God's provision. In the midst of severe adversity and extreme suffering, Job chose to look up even when he was completely down.

Can you echo Job's statement of faith? God has granted you life. You were God's idea. God created you and planted you so that you can bloom for His glory. You are alive today because God has given you life. What are you doing with the life God has given you?

God has lavished you with His steadfast love. You matter to God. Your value has already been established when God gave His only Son to die for you on the cross two-thousand years ago. That's how much God loves you and values you. Don't let the devil stick a clearance label on your life. You have already been purchased by the shed blood of Jesus and the value of your life is priceless!

What sustains you? What keeps you going? God's compassion and tender care preserve you. He is the source of your strength and the reason for your existence. God will see you through the seasons of uncertainty and will help you overcome the obstacles that seek to divert your focus. God cares about you and everything you care about. You are His treasure and He keeps your tears in a bottle. Nothing bypasses God's awareness. He knows where you are and just what you need right now. Will you rest in His care and receive His personal touch ministry?

~ Stephen

January 7

BREVITY OF LIFE

Chronological Bible Reading Plan: (Day 7: Job 14-16)

"'Man who is born of a woman is few of days and full of trouble. He comes out like a flower and withers; he flees like a shadow and continues not.'"
Job 14:1-2 (ESV)

Job confronts his human condition. He acknowledges the brevity of life and the certainty of death. Job identifies the presence of pain and tribulation in this fallen world. In anguish of soul, Job considers his life and weighs the impact of his circumstances.

Sometimes life seems to race by like the flash of a camera and at other times life seems to slow down and emerge at the pace of a canoe on a still pond. The common denominator is the brevity of life. In light of eternity, life on earth is so brief. It is difficult to fathom that a person's life can be condensed to the dash between the date of one's birth and one's death.

- *"Yet you do not know what tomorrow will bring. What is your life? For you are a mist that appears for a little time and then vanishes."*
  Jas. 4:14 (ESV)

Will your dash make an eternal difference? Will you allow God to use you for His glory? You may have a few more decades of living on this earth or you may only have a few months. What will you do with the time you have left? Invest the rest of your life in that which has eternal value. Stop fretting over the things in this life that erode your peace and evaporate your passion for the Lord. Focus on the love God has for you and the love God wants you to express to a lost and dying world through you.

Jesus warned us to anticipate tribulation in this world. Rejoice! Jesus has overcome the world and He lives in you.

~ *Stephen*

January 8

My Redeemer Lives

Chronological Bible Reading Plan: (Day 8: Job 17-20)

"'For I know that my Redeemer lives, and at the last he will stand upon the earth. And after my skin has been thus destroyed, yet in my flesh I shall see God, whom I shall see for myself, and my eyes shall behold, and not another. My heart faints within me!'" Job 19:25-27 (ESV)

When you are going through a season of adversity the natural proclivity is to turn inward. You slide into the posture of being consumed with how you are feeling and how you are doing and drift into self-pity. Pain has the power to redirect your focus.

Job unveiled his inward thoughts and the agony of his soul. He expressed his hurt and his disappointment with his current reality. Job was surrounded by three so-called friends who just didn't get it. They were not a productive source of encouragement and comfort. Job made a decision to shift his thinking. He embraced a healthy and beneficial perspective by declaring, "For I know that my Redeemer lives." Job acknowledged the sovereignty of God and the redeeming love of God.

How desperate is your situation? What has captivated your mind and dominated your emotions? What kind of season are you in currently? Declare by faith that your Redeemer lives. Articulate the reality of God's sovereignty and the certainty of God's redeeming love. God is for you. God knows where you are and what you are feeling right now. Your Redeemer lives. Run from your fear, anxiety, and anguish. Deliberately run to your Redeemer.

Look how far God has brought you. Calculate where you would be without His grace, His mercy, and His persistent pursuit. One day you will see God. One day you will stand before God to give an account for your life. Your Redeemer lives inside of you so that you can join Him in redeeming others.

~ *Stephen*

January 9
Fully Devoted

Chronological Bible Reading Plan: (Day 9: Job 21-23)

"'But he knows the way that I take; when he has tried me, I shall come out as gold. My foot has held fast to his steps; I have kept his way and have not turned aside. I have not departed from the commandment of his lips; I have treasured the words of his mouth more than my portion of food.'" Job 23:10-12 (ESV)

Job was fully devoted to God. Both in private and in public, Job was cognizant of the omniscience of God. Job recognized that God was all-knowing and all-seeing and that nothing escapes God's attention. As a result, Job was conscientious about the paths he took, he was cautious about the decisions he made, and he was committed to the ways of God.

Your decisions determine your direction and ultimately your destination. The decisions you make each day have immediate and eternal implications. Therefore, your decision-making process is vital. Are you doing life God's way? Are you making decisions based on God's will or based on your own personal agenda.

Job did not make decisions in a vacuum. Job had a heightened awareness of God's activity. In revering God, Job lived his life in view of God's purpose and plan. He did not want to make a decision that would violate God's nature and character. Job wanted to live his life consistent with God's will.

God knows the way you take. When He has tried you, will you come out as gold? Hold fast to God's steps. Keep His way and do not deviate from His path. Do not depart from His commandments.

Ask God to show you what you need to stop doing, what you need to continue doing, and what you need to start doing? Be a fully devoted follower of Christ and passionately pursue His will.

~ *Stephen*

January 10

Maintain Integrity

Chronological Bible Reading Plan: (Day 10: Job 24-28)

"'As God lives, who has taken away my right, and the Almighty, who has made my soul bitter, as long as my breath is in me, and the spirit of God is in my nostrils, my lips will not speak falsehood, and my tongue will not utter deceit. Far be it from me to say that you are right; till I die I will not put away my integrity from me. I hold fast my righteousness and will not let it go; my heart does not reproach me for any of my days.'" Job 27:2-6 (ESV)

Your life is like a tube of toothpaste, when squeezed, whatever is on the inside will come out. Adversity has a way of squeezing out fears, frustrations, resentment, and bitterness. By nature, we suppress those things that disappoint us or hurt us. We seek to dodge pain.

Job experienced an intense season of testing that revealed what was on the inside of him. Job was honest about his disappointment and transparent about the resident bitterness within his soul. In spite of the avalanche of adversity, Job chose to maintain his integrity. He made a commitment to not speak falsehood, to not utter deceit, and to not put away his integrity. Job resolved to hold fast to his righteousness and not let it go.

Everybody looks good from a distance. What do you see when you get close enough to see what is on the inside? How are you doing internally? Maintain integrity by staying close to the Lord and clean before the Lord. Surrender to the Lordship of Christ and make sure that the tongue in your mouth lines up with the tongue in your shoe. Hold fast to the righteousness of Christ. You are positionally right before God in Christ. Apply that positional righteousness through practical righteous living.

~ *Stephen*

January 11

ANGUISH AND AFFLICTION

Chronological Bible Reading Plan: (Day 11: Job 29-31)

"'And now my soul is poured out within me; days of affliction have taken hold of me. The night racks my bones, and the pain that gnaws me takes no rest.'" Job 30:16-17 (ESV)

I don't know how much more I can take. Have you ever said that? Have you ever felt that way? Job became weary from his arduous journey with adversity. His soul was now in anguish and his days of affliction had gained more ground. Job's emotional stability had been capsized by the violent waves of pain. His image had been altered and his self-worth had been placed on the clearance rack. Job hit a low point.

Living in a world polluted by sin and infested with our fallen condition generates an environment far from paradise. We live on a broken planet that stems from the Fall of man. The earth is cursed and humanity combats the presence of sin, sickness, and sorrow. God redeems us from our sin and re-creates us to be like Christ so that we can be the salt of the earth and the light of the world. God allows us to remain on this broken planet to join Him in restoring fallen humanity. God entrusts us with the task of sharing the Good News of Jesus Christ. He is our hope, our peace, and our future.

God dispenses grace to match our need. When you spiral down into the depths of despair, God's grace is distributed in proportion to your deficit. The Apostle Paul advanced through adversity by accessing the grace God supplied. "But he said to me, 'My grace is sufficient for you, for my power is made perfect in weakness.' Therefore I will boast all the more gladly of my weaknesses, so that the power of Christ may rest upon me" (2 Cor 12:9 ESV).

~ Stephen

January 12

God's Patience

Chronological Bible Reading Plan: (Day 12: Job 32-34)

"'Behold, God does all these things, twice, three times, with a man, to bring back his soul from the pit, that he may be lighted with the light of life.'"
Job 33:29-30 (ESV)

Elihu had patiently sat and listened to Job and Job's three friends. Elihu was young and somewhat intimidated by these men. In his listening, Elihu burned with anger as he surmised that Job was righteous in his own eyes. His anger increased by his summation of Job's three friends because they had found no answer, yet they declared Job to be in the wrong. Then Elihu articulated profound insight into the patience of God. He affirmed that God is persistent in bringing back a man's soul from the pit so that he may be lighted with the light of life.

Consider God's patience in your life. Take a moment to examine your life and trace the decisions you have made over the years. How many times has God rescued you from the pit of poor choices? How many times has God patiently waited for your compliance to His will? We would have no hope for knowing and doing God's will without His abundant supply of grace and patience. "The Lord is not slow to fulfill his promise as some count slowness, but is patient toward you, not wishing that any should perish, but that all should reach repentance" (2 Pet. 3:9 ESV).

Allow God's patience to generate an attitude of gratitude in you as you join Him in His activity today. Enjoy being a recipient of God's patience and seek to emulate His patience as you interact with others. Make yourself available for God's use as He draws others to Christ through you. Be patient with others just as God has been patient with you.

~ *Stephen*

January 13

Awesome Majesty

Chronological Bible Reading Plan: (Day 13: Job 35-37)

"'And now no one looks on the light when it is bright in the skies, when the wind has passed and cleared them. Out of the north comes golden splendor; God is clothed with awesome majesty.'" Job 37:21-22 (ESV)

As Elihu spoke to Job, he declared the splendor and awesome majesty of God. In our humanity, we have limitations. Our Creator, God, has chosen to reveal Himself to us. In His holiness and righteousness, God made it possible for us to come into relationship with Him through the atoning work of Jesus on the cross. God has made Himself knowable and imparts to us the gift of eternal life.

- *"Though you have not seen him, you love him. Though you do not now see him, you believe in him and rejoice with joy that is inexpressible and filled with glory, obtaining the outcome of your faith, the salvation of your souls." 1 Pet.1:8-9 (ESV)*
- *"Beloved, we are God's children now, and what we will be has not yet appeared; but we know that when he appears we shall be like him, because we shall see him as he is." 1 John 3:2 (ESV)*

Consider the depth of what you currently know about God as a result of your personal relationship with Him through Christ. As you calculate the level of intimacy you enjoy with God, measure the reality of what is yet to come for those of us who know Him personally. One day we will have the awesome privilege to stand before God and obtain the full extent of the salvation of our souls. We will receive our glorified body and enjoy eternal life with God in heaven. We shall be like Him and see Him as He is.

~ *Stephen*

January 14

Measure of a Moment

Chronological Bible Reading Plan: (Day 14: Job 38-39)

"'Where were you when I laid the foundation of the earth? Tell me, if you have understanding. Who determined its measurements—surely you know! Or who stretched the line upon it?'" Job 38:4-5 (ESV)

There are times when God has to remind us that we are not God. When we fail to remember that God is the Creator and we are the created, we position ourselves for a lesson in humility. It is possible to get so busy doing life that you forget the reality of who God is and what He has done.

God had to remind Job of his personal limitations and the shortfall of his humanity. Job made some short-sighted assumptions about God that did not line up with God's nature and character. Job was speaking from his own limited understanding about life. God intervened by speaking to Job and engaging him with some thought provoking questions.

Just after graduating from college, I was asked to preach one of my closest friend's funeral. He died as a result of an aggressive form of cancer at age twenty-two. God placed the following passage of Scripture on my heart to share at Jimmy's funeral.

- *"For my thoughts are not your thoughts, neither are your ways my ways, declares the LORD. For as the heavens are higher than the earth, so are my ways higher than your ways and my thoughts than your thoughts." Isa. 55:8-9 (ESV)*

Are you having a difficult time making sense out of some of the things going on in your life right now? Acknowledge God's supremacy and His majesty. Entrust your life and your circumstances to His redemptive care. God fashioned you for His glory and He will accomplish His plan through you in the midst of your circumstances.

~ Stephen

January 15

God's Will Prevails

Chronological Bible Reading Plan: (Day 15: Job 40-42)

"Then Job answered the LORD and said: 'I know that you can do all things, and that no purpose of yours can be thwarted.'" Job 42:1-2 (ESV)

The chisel of adversity and the hammer of suffering produced an informative perspective within Job to be able to declare that God can do all things. Job acknowledged the power of God and the firm reality of the prevailing purposes of God. Regardless of the trajectory of the circumstances and the momentum of the adversity, God will accomplish His plan.

God allowed Job to experience a journey filled with heartache, loss, grief, and anguish. Through it all, God navigated the path for Job to come to the place of desperation which ultimately led to the place of restoration.

- *"And the LORD restored the fortunes of Job, when he had prayed for his friends. And the LORD gave Job twice as much as he had before." Job 42:10 (ESV)*
- *"And the LORD blessed the latter days of Job more than his beginning. And he had 14,000 sheep, 6,000 camels, 1,000 yoke of oxen, and 1,000 female donkeys. He had also seven sons and three daughters." Job 42:12-13 (ESV)*
- *"And Job died, an old man, and full of days." Job 42:17 (ESV)*

What's your story? Maybe you have gone through an avalanche of adversity or the undulation of uncertainty. What have you learned about God's faithfulness? Have you come to experience the prevailing purposes of God? God has the final say and He is working all things together for your good and for His glory (Rom. 8:28-29).

~ *Stephen*

January 16

God's Provision

Chronological Bible Reading Plan: (Day 16: Genesis 12-15)

"Now the LORD said to Abram, 'Go from your country and your kindred and your father's house to the land that I will show you. And I will make of you a great nation, and I will bless you and make your name great, so that you will be a blessing. I will bless those who bless you, and him who dishonors you I will curse, and in you all the families of the earth shall be blessed.'"
Genesis 12:1-3 (ESV)

Without trust, there is no authentic relationship. Relationships are built on the foundation of trust. As you know, to be trusted one must be trustworthy. Without question, God is worthy of our trust. He is holy, righteous, immutable, eternal, and perfect. God honors His Word. God keeps His promises. God has impeccable timing and matchless integrity.

When God revealed Himself to Abram, the relationship of trust was demonstrated. God commanded Abram to leave his comfort zone and to embrace the unknown. God promised to bless Abram and to make Abram a blessing. At this time, Abram was seventy-five years old and he and Sarai had no children. Even though God's promise did not make logical sense in that Sarai was well along in years and childless, Abram took God at His Word and obeyed Him.

What are you doing with what God has said to you? Have you obeyed what you already know? God blesses obedience. When you obey God, you come to know God by experience. You will discover God's will as you obey God's will. Walk in the light God gives you and watch to see how God unveils the next step that He wants you to take. As you obey, God will show you the way.

~ *Stephen*

January 17
God's Miracle

Chronological Bible Reading Plan: (Day 17: Genesis 16-18)

"The LORD said, 'I will surely return to you about this time next year, and Sarah your wife shall have a son.' And Sarah was listening at the tent door behind him. Now Abraham and Sarah were old, advanced in years. The way of women had ceased to be with Sarah." Genesis 18:10-11 (ESV)

Is the level of your faith determined by the intensity and severity of your circumstances or by the One in whom you are placing your faith? Abraham and Sarah's situation was desperate and seemingly impossible. Abraham was one hundred years old and Sarah was ninety years old and barren.

Don't miss the blessing behind "even when." Even when Abraham was past age and Sarah was barren, God enabled them to become parents because Abraham considered God faithful. God had already made the promise of blessing Abraham with offspring (Gen. 12:2-3).

- *"By faith Sarah herself received power to conceive, even when she was past the age, since she considered him faithful who had promised." Heb. 11:11 (ESV)*
- *"Therefore from one man, and him as good as dead, were born descendants as many as the stars of heaven and as many as the innumerable grains of sand by the seashore." Heb. 11:12 (ESV)*

Instead of focusing on your circumstances, focus on the faithfulness of God. You can bring your burdens to the Lord with openness and transparency. You can bear your soul before the Lord as you navigate the terrain of a fallen world. God formed you and fashioned you for His glory. Your circumstances will not derail the purposes of God from being fulfilled in your life. Trust God to demonstrate His faithfulness to you. Be sensitive to God's activity today in the midst of your circumstances.

~ *Stephen*

January 18

God's Grace

Chronological Bible Reading Plan: (Day 18: Genesis 19-21)

"And the child grew and was weaned. And Abraham made a great feast on the day that Isaac was weaned. But Sarah saw the son of Hagar the Egyptian, whom she had borne to Abraham, laughing. So she said to Abraham, 'Cast out this slave woman with her son, for the son of this slave woman shall not be heir with my son Isaac.'" Genesis 21:8-10 (ESV)

Shortcuts in life can generate adverse consequences. Instead of waiting on God's timing to produce offspring, Abraham and Sarah took a shortcut by utilizing Sarah's servant, Hagar. "And Sarai said to Abram, 'Behold now, the LORD has prevented me from bearing children. Go in to my servant; it may be that I shall obtain children by her.' And Abram listened to the voice of Sarai" (Gen. 16:2 ESV). Sarah got what she wanted, but later didn't want what she got!

Abraham had to make the difficult decision to send Hagar and Ishmael on their way in order to keep marital peace with Sarah. Hagar finds herself in desperation and ready to give up her life and the life of her son, Ishmael, as they wander in the wilderness of Beersheba. She placed Ishmael under a bush anticipating his death as well as her own. Then God intervened:

- *"Then God opened her eyes, and she saw a well of water. And she went and filled the skin with water and gave the boy a drink. And God was with the boy, and he grew up. He lived in the wilderness and became an expert with the bow. He lived in the wilderness of Paran, and his mother took a wife for him from the land of Egypt." Gen. 21:19-21 (ESV)*

God's grace always matches the desperation of our need. God has the final say even in the darkest of moments. When life gets messy, don't hesitate to turn to the Master! God's grace is more than enough!

~ *Stephen*

January 19

Jehovah Jireh

Chronological Bible Reading Plan: (Day 19: Genesis 22-24)

"And Isaac said to his father Abraham, 'My father!' And he said, 'Here I am, my son.' He said, 'Behold, the fire and the wood, but where is the lamb for a burnt offering?' Abraham said, 'God will provide for himself the lamb for a burnt offering, my son.' So they went both of them together." Genesis 22:7-8 (ESV)

Abraham demonstrated absolute loyalty and devotion to God by his willingness to sacrifice his promised son. Abraham and Sarah were beyond child bearing years. Yet, God provided the miracle of Isaac's conception. Now God is asking Abraham to sacrifice that which was promised to him.

- *"And Abraham lifted up his eyes and looked, and behold, behind him was a ram, caught in a thicket by his horns. And Abraham went and took the ram and offered it up as a burnt offering instead of his son." Gen. 22:13 (ESV)*

Is there anything in your life that takes priority over your relationship with Jesus? Are there any allurements sifting your affection away from your devotion to Christ? Do you have an Isaac in your life that you are unwilling to sacrifice?

Could it be that God wants you to sacrifice that Isaac in your life to enable God to have top priority in your life? God wants first place in your daily walk. God wants to be the supreme object of your energy and affection. He not only deserves it, but He demands it.

Spend a few moments taking inventory of your current priorities and identify what is preventing God from being your top priority.

~ *Stephen*

January 20
Leaving a Legacy

Chronological Bible Reading Plan: (Day 20: Genesis 25-26)

"And the LORD appeared to him the same night and said, 'I am the God of Abraham your father. Fear not, for I am with you and will bless you and multiply your offspring for my servant Abraham's sake.' So he built an altar there and called upon the name of the LORD and pitched his tent there. And there Isaac's servants dug a well." Genesis 26:24-25 (ESV)

What kind of impact will your life make on the next generation? What is going to outlive you and outlast you? What deposits are you making into the next generation? In order to leave a legacy, you must live a legacy.

Abraham and Sarah lived out their faith in God before their son, Isaac. They were intentional about handing down the faith and leaving a legacy. Sarah died and was buried. Abraham died years later and was buried in the cave of Machpelah with Sarah.

How did their faith impact Isaac's life? God graciously appeared to Isaac just as He had appeared to Abraham. God affirmed Isaac with His abiding presence and promised to bless him and multiply his offspring for Abraham's sake. Did you catch that? The blessing from God was in honor of Abraham, for Abraham's sake. Isaac responded to this encounter of God by building an altar there and calling upon the name of the Lord. Isaac continued the faith that Abraham and Sarah had modeled before him.

What kind of legacy will you leave? Will those closest to you continue in the faith because of the faith you lived out during your time on the earth? Leave a legacy by living a legacy. Worship God privately and publicly. Serve the Lord with passion and enthusiasm. Be an irresistible influence for the Lord and impact the next generation.

~ *Stephen*

January 21

God Encounter

Chronological Bible Reading Plan: (Day 21: Genesis 27-29)

"Then Jacob awoke from his sleep and said, 'Surely the LORD is in this place, and I did not know it.' And he was afraid and said, 'How awesome is this place! This is none other than the house of God, and this is the gate of heaven.'"
Genesis 28:16-17 (ESV)

Don't miss God! You can be so preoccupied with your life and your plans that you neglect practicing the Presence of God. God is omnipresent. There is nowhere God is not. He is always at work around you. Unless you intentionally look to see where God is at work, you can miss Him. Detecting God's activity requires being sensitive and observant.

As Jacob placed a stone under his head and went to sleep, he had a dream in which he saw a ladder with angels ascending and descending on it. God said to him, "I am the LORD, the God of Abraham your father and the God of Isaac. The land on which you lie I will give to you and to your offspring. Your offspring shall be like the dust of the earth, and you shall spread abroad to the west and to the east and to the north and to the south, and in you and your offspring shall all the families of the earth be blessed" (Gen. 28:13-14 ESV).

Upon reflection of the night's events, Jacob realized that he had encountered God. He named the place, Bethel, which means house of God.

Each time you read the Bible, you are encountering God. Whenever you choose to share your faith with someone, you will encounter God. As you seek to meet needs and continue the ministry of Jesus on the earth, you will encounter God. God reveals Himself to you as you join Him in His activity.

~ *Stephen*

January 22

God's Protection

Chronological Bible Reading Plan: (Day 22: Genesis 30-31)

"So Jacob sent and called Rachel and Leah into the field where his flock was and said to them, 'I see that your father does not regard me with favor as he did before. But the God of my father has been with me. You know that I have served your father with all my strength, yet your father has cheated me and changed my wages ten times. But God did not permit him to harm me.'"
Genesis 31:4-7 (ESV)

Jacob experienced God's protection as he served Laban. Though Laban deceived Jacob in several ways, Jacob found comfort in God's Presence. Jacob recognized God's provision in the midst of the unfortunate treatment Laban inflicted. The instability of the circumstances surrounding Jacob did not penetrate the protective covering provided by God. Jacob rested in the consistent provision of God.

When you are treated unfairly, be encouraged by the reality of God's protection and God's abiding Presence in your life. Even when your circumstances create an atmosphere of uncertainty, you can anchor your faith to the rock of God's nature and character. You can trust God to see you through.

Jesus knew what it meant to be betrayed and to suffer injustice. Jesus was perfect and encountered unfair treatment by those whom God had created.

- *"When he was reviled, he did not revile in return; when he suffered, he did not threaten, but continued entrusting himself to him who judges justly." 1 Pet. 2:23 (ESV)*

Do what Jesus did. Entrust yourself to Him who judges justly. Entrust your life to the One who has given you life and to the One who has the final say in every circumstance you face.

~ *Stephen*

January 23

Walking with a Limp

Chronological Bible Reading Plan: (Day 23: Genesis 32-34)

"And Jacob was left alone. And a man wrestled with him until the breaking of the day. When the man saw that he did not prevail against Jacob, he touched his hip socket, and Jacob's hip was put out of joint as he wrestled with him."
Genesis 32:24-25 (ESV)

As God's workmanship, Jacob came away from the night of wrestling with a limp and a new name. You don't come into close proximity with the living God and leave the same. God gave Jacob the name Israel, which means God prevails. Jacob was known as a deceiver, but God gave him a new name to live up to. Jacob would become the patriarch of the twelve tribes of Israel.

Have you ever wrestled with God? Who won? Wrestling is part of being God's workmanship. Jacob, as God's workmanship, came to know God in a new way after a night of wrestling. Just like in weight training, without resistance there is no growth.

God allows us to go through seasons of uncertainty. God allows us to experience seasons of silence and yes, even seasons of suffering. We wrestle with God in those seasons. Our faith is challenged and often our prayer life is stretched. We come to know God by experience. Sometimes that experience involves pain.

God is for you. He is willing to go to any length to bring you into a vibrant, intimate, and growing relationship that is personal and eternal. God will pursue you and groom you so that you will be conformed into the image of Christ. Your life matters to God. After you encounter the Living God, you may walk with a limp to remind you of His daily provision.

~ *Stephen*

January 24

Reward of Reconciliation

Chronological Bible Reading Plan: (Day 24: Genesis 35-37)

"And Isaac breathed his last, and he died and was gathered to his people, old and full of days. And his sons Esau and Jacob buried him." Genesis 35:29 (ESV)

Isaac was greatly blessed by God and was enabled to finish strong. His sons, Jacob and Esau, experienced a tumultuous sibling rivalry that produced immense family turmoil. Their upbringing was filled with deception, selfishness, and inequality.

The grace of God was clearly evidenced when Jacob and Esau reconciled after years of separation and seething bitterness and resentment. Jacob prepared generously for the day he faced Esau. Jacob feared Esau's retribution, but received restoration instead. "But Esau ran to meet him and embraced him and fell on his neck and kissed him, and they wept" (Gen. 33:4 ESV). Their reunion reflected the grace of God which sustained them through major transitions throughout their lives.

Reconciliation has a tremendous reward. When you choose to restore ruptured relationships, you bring honor to God and you demonstrate obedience to His Word. Reconciliation is a gracious response to God's redeeming work in your life that compels you to make things right with others. You cannot be right with God without being in a right relationship with others. You cannot be in a right relationship with others unless you are right with God.

Is there anyone with whom you need to initiate reconciliation? Do your part to make things right. Experience the power of God as you build a bridge of reconciliation. The peace of God will flow into your life as you practice instant obedience.

~ *Stephen*

January 25

Unveiling Unforgiveness

Chronological Bible Reading Plan: (Day 25: Genesis 38-40)

"Then Midianite traders passed by. And they drew Joseph up and lifted him out of the pit, and sold him to the Ishmaelites for twenty shekels of silver. They took Joseph to Egypt." Genesis 37:28 (ESV)

If anyone ever had reason to be infused with the bile of bitterness, it would have to be Joseph. His brothers were void of mercy and full of hatred and jealousy to the point of selling Joseph into slavery. The brothers even deceived their father, Jacob, by tearing Joseph's coat of many colors and dipping it in blood to portray the possibility of Joseph being devoured by a ferocious animal. We would call this a genuinely dysfunctional family.

The truth is that every family is dysfunctional at some level. Every family has allowed the sewage of unforgiveness to seep into their home for a season and perhaps for a reason. Unforgiveness can quickly become toxic, acidic, corrosive, and radioactive. Many families have been destroyed by the venom of unforgiveness.

Salvation is an event, followed by a process. The event of your conversion took place at the moment you confessed your sin and trusted Jesus as your personal Savior and Lord. Your name was written in the Lamb's Book of Life, you were adopted into God's family, and you were filled with the Holy Spirit. Since that moment, you have been involved in the process of growing spiritually. You have been working out what God has worked in. The process continues until you go to Heaven!

Forgiveness is a process, followed by an event. God does a work in you to give you understanding about the unforgiveness resident within you. How will you respond to unfair treatment? Will you become bitter or better? Unveil unforgiveness and extend forgiveness to bring honor to God.

~ *Stephen*

January 26

God's Instrument

Chronological Bible Reading Plan: (Day 26: Genesis 41-42)

"Joseph answered Pharaoh, 'It is not in me; God will give Pharaoh a favorable answer.'" Genesis 41:16 (ESV)

God uses human instrumentality in His redemptive process. God chooses to involve us in His master plan. Life is not about our story that we invite God into. Life is about God's story that He invites us into. How will you respond to God's invitation?

Joseph had been forgotten by the chief cupbearer and the baker, but not forgotten by God. The Lord was with Joseph when he was in the palace and when he was in prison. As God would have it, the Pharaoh had a vivid dream that no one could interpret, including the chief cupbearer. God then prompted the chief cupbearer to remember Joseph and to let the Pharaoh know how Joseph had previously interpreted both his dream and the baker's dream. That opened the door for Pharaoh to invite Joseph to seek to interpret his dream.

- *"Then Pharaoh said to Joseph, 'Since God has shown you all this, there is none so discerning and wise as you are. You shall be over my house, and all my people shall order themselves as you command. Only as regards the throne will I be greater than you.'" Gen. 41:39-40 (ESV)*

Make yourself available for God's use. Place your "yes" on the altar and be willing to join God in His activity. Practice instant obedience and maintain your integrity. God will promote you in His timing. Nothing escapes His attention. Be faithful to do what God has called you to do and be willing to get out of your comfort zone in order to be used by God for His glory.

~ *Stephen*

January 27

PROCESS BEFORE EVENT

Chronological Bible Reading Plan: (Day 27: Genesis 43-45)

"So Joseph said to his brothers, "Come near to me, please." And they came near. And he said, "I am your brother, Joseph, whom you sold into Egypt. And now do not be distressed or angry with yourselves because you sold me here, for God sent me before you to preserve life." Genesis 45:4-5 (ESV)

Forgiveness is a process, followed by an event. The process includes the pain caused by the offense or neglect or wound. Often, the pain grows into bitterness rooted in unforgiveness. God begins to alert you to the presence of unforgiveness inside of you which produces conviction. Responding to the convicting work of the Holy Spirit, you choose to extend forgiveness in private through prayer to the one who offended you. God enables you to release the unforgiveness you have harbored in your heart.

Once you have received God's forgiveness for your unforgiveness and you have extended forgiveness privately through prayer, then you prepare to go public on your private forgiveness. This moves into the event of forgiveness. After you have spent time with God in prayer, you transition into communicating your forgiveness to the offender.

Joseph experienced the process of forgiveness which prepared him for the event of forgiveness. When Joseph revealed himself to his brothers whom had sold him into slavery, he deliberately extended forgiveness to them. It was apparent that Joseph had forgiven them privately in prayer as he communed with God each day. Private forgiveness enabled Joseph to go public on his forgiveness by saying, "Come close to me."

When you extend forgiveness to others, it splashes Living Water on them and releases and refreshes you. Remember that forgiveness is immediate, once you go public, but trust takes time.

~ *Stephen*

January 28

God, Jacob, and Joseph

Chronological Bible Reading Plan: (Day 28: Genesis 46-47)

"And God spoke to Israel in visions of the night and said, 'Jacob, Jacob.' And he said, 'Here I am.' Then he said, 'I am God, the God of your father. Do not be afraid to go down to Egypt, for there I will make you into a great nation. I myself will go down with you to Egypt, and I will also bring you up again, and Joseph's hand shall close your eyes.'" Genesis 46:2-4 (ESV)

Jacob had endured hardship, grief, and anxiety. He lived for years with the darkness of Joseph's death looming over him, when in fact, Joseph was alive. After God promoted Joseph to second in command over Egypt, and after Joseph revealed himself to his brothers and forgave them, Jacob and his family came to meet Joseph.

Jacob had another encounter with God whereby God spoke to him in visions of the night. God affirmed Jacob with His abiding Presence and comforted Jacob with the assurance of protection and provision. God promised to make Jacob into a great nation and to allow Joseph's hand to close his eyes.

- *"Thus Israel settled in the land of Egypt, in the land of Goshen. And they gained possessions in it, and were fruitful and multiplied greatly. And Jacob lived in the land of Egypt seventeen years. So the days of Jacob, the years of his life, were 147 years."* Gen. 47:27-28 (ESV)

God keeps His word. You can entrust every detail of your life to God's care. He created you so that you can enjoy an ongoing love relationship with Him. God includes you in His redemptive story and invites you to join Him in His activity. Your faith will be refined as you trust God and obey His directives. God will accomplish His purposes and plan through you as you yield to Him. Respond to God with the words of Jacob, "Here I am."

~ *Stephen*

January 29

Forgiveness and Memory

Chronological Bible Reading Plan: (Day 29: Genesis 48-50)

"When Joseph's brothers saw that their father was dead, they said, 'It may be that Joseph will hate us and pay us back for all the evil that we did to him.'" Genesis 50:15 (ESV)

Forgiveness is tested by memory. Only God has the capacity to forgive and forget. We have the capacity to forgive, but we struggle with forgetting what happened to us. Inevitably, something will trigger the memory of the pain of our past.

Remember, Joseph's brothers sold him into slavery and Joseph experienced quite a ride before becoming second in command in Egypt. Joseph had revealed himself to his brothers. He had forgiven them in private before God, then he went public with his forgiveness and even provided for the needs of his family. Their father, Jacob, dies and it triggers the pain of the past. Joseph has already forgiven his brothers for their mistreatment, but they now fear retribution as a result of Jacob's death.

- *"'As for you, you meant evil against me, but God meant it for good, to bring it about that many people should be kept alive, as they are today. So do not fear; I will provide for you and your little ones.' Thus he comforted them and spoke kindly to them." Gen. 50:20-21 (ESV)*

Forgiveness has an Encore. After you have forgiven the one who offended you, wounded you, neglected you, or betrayed you, something may come along and trigger the memory of the pain in your past. Though you do not have the capacity to forgive and forget, by the grace of God and in the power of the Holy Spirit, though you remember, you can choose to forgive.

~ *Stephen*

January 30

Identity Crisis

Chronological Bible Reading Plan: (Day 30: Exodus 1-3)

"But Moses said to God, 'Who am I that I should go to Pharaoh and bring the children of Israel out of Egypt?'" Exodus 3:11 (ESV)

Who am I? Why am I here? These two basic questions are innate in every human being. We long to know who we are and we strive to discover why we are placed on this planet called earth. Our security is proportionate to our understanding of our identity.

God allowed Moses to experience forty years in the palace and then forty years in the desert. God wanted Moses to learn some things about his personal identity through a desert experience that he could not learn in the palace. God was preparing Moses for the purpose of delivering the children of Israel from Egyptian bondage. The burning bush encounter was a life changing experience for Moses. The encounter enabled Moses to come to know God in a personal way. God revealed His holiness to Moses and then unveiled His plan for Moses to embrace.

As you can imagine, Moses could not visualize himself as the deliverer of the children of Israel. They had been slaves for over 400 years. Moses began making excuses and tried to deny his usefulness to God. Moses began to focus on what he lacked and missed the reality of God's ability to do the extraordinary through ordinary people.

Have you ever doubted your usefulness to God? Have you ever tried to convince God that you are not fit for His plan? God is not impressed with our abilities or our inabilities. God is not limited by our limitations. Are you willing to yield to God's control and allow Him to have His way in your life? God is willing to take you through a desert experience to prepare you for His assignment.

~ *Stephen*

January 31

Feeling Inadequate

Chronological Bible Reading Plan: (Day 31: Exodus 4-6)

"But Moses said to the LORD, 'Oh, my Lord, I am not eloquent, either in the past or since you have spoken to your servant, but I am slow of speech and of tongue.' Then the LORD said to him, 'Who has made man's mouth? Who makes him mute, or deaf, or seeing, or blind? Is it not I, the LORD? Now therefore go, and I will be with your mouth and teach you what you shall speak.'"
Exodus 4:10-12 (ESV)

Have you ever felt inadequate? It is an overwhelming feeling. Anxiety intensifies when you feel that your assignment is beyond your ability. Moses felt that way. He had received an assignment from God to deliver the children of Israel out of Egyptian bondage. Moses was to confront the Pharaoh and to forge a path of deliverance for those enslaved by Egypt. Moses began to read off his list of excuses for God to consider. Moses was trying to get God caught up on the deficits that he had been living with all of his life. In others words, Moses was not quick on his feet and he felt inadequate to be God's choice for the task.

God is so patient. He gently reminded Moses of who the Creator is. Who gives man the ability to speak, to hear, and to think? Who makes it possible for humanity to know and to do and to be? God graciously affirmed Moses by saying, "Go, and I will be with your mouth and teach you what you shall speak."

God is your sufficiency. He will never ask you to do anything that He does not equip you for. Will you trust God to provide for your role in His story? God will be your sufficiency. God will compensate for your inadequacy.

~ *Stephen*

February 1

Dealing with Delays

Chronological Bible Reading Plan: (Day 32: Exodus 7-9)

"'But I will harden Pharaoh's heart, and though I multiply my signs and wonders in the land of Egypt, Pharaoh will not listen to you. Then I will lay my hand on Egypt and bring my hosts, my people the children of Israel, out of the land of Egypt by great acts of judgment. The Egyptians shall know that I am the LORD, when I stretch out my hand against Egypt and bring out the people of Israel from among them.'" Exodus 7:3-5 (ESV)

After God announced that He would elevate Moses in the eyes of Pharaoh, the troubling reality of deliverance delays set in. God confirmed that He would continue to harden Pharaoh's heart and that in spite of multiple signs and wonders, Pharaoh would not listen to Moses. That would demotivate the chosen deliverer of Israel and generate a significant level of frustration.

Can you relate to how Moses must have felt? Can you identify a time in your life when you experienced a delay that made no sense? You may have wondered why God would allow such a delay. Moses combated a host of delays embedded in the miraculous plagues of Egypt initiated by God. Each time, Pharaoh would soften up for a moment and announce the release of those enslaved by Egypt, and then quickly go back on his word. Moses had to ride the tumultuous waves of inconsistency.

God has a divine purpose behind every delay in life. Though our view is limited and our understanding is somewhat finite, God has an infinite purpose behind each delay you face in this life. God is sovereign. He rules and He reigns, even when your circumstances do not line up with your understanding. Nothing will thwart God's will and nothing will prevent the purposes of God from being fulfilled. Rest in His sovereignty. God is working out His plan in the midst of the delays you experience.

~ Stephen

February 2

Obedience and Blessing

Chronological Bible Reading Plan: (Day 33: Exodus 10-12)

"All the people of Israel did just as the LORD commanded Moses and Aaron. And on that very day the LORD brought the people of Israel out of the land of Egypt by their hosts." Exodus 12:50-51 (ESV)

God keeps His word. He is the ultimate promise keeper. What God starts, He finishes! God was faithful to provide for Moses and the children of Israel throughout the process of their deliverance from the bondage of Egypt. After sending the nine plagues upon Egypt, the tenth plague was the turning point for Pharaoh and for the people of Israel. God instructed Moses to have the people of Israel sacrifice a lamb for each family and to take some of the blood and put it on the doorposts and lintel of the houses in which they ate the lamb.

- *"'The blood shall be a sign for you, on the houses where you are. And when I see the blood, I will pass over you, and no plague will befall you to destroy you, when I strike the land of Egypt.'" Exod. 12:13 (ESV)*

The grace of God was evidenced as the He did not allow the destroyer to enter the houses of those who obeyed His command. Instead, God chose to passover their houses. The passover is a clear indication that God blesses obedience. God brought the people of Israel out of the land of Egypt.

Do not bypass the grace of God as evidenced by the shed blood of Jesus Christ. If you have not turned from your sin and turned to Jesus alone for salvation, your first step of obedience is to make that decision right now. Don't delay! Trust in Jesus alone for salvation. Place your faith in the completed work of Christ on the cross. He shed His blood for the removal of your sins. Trust and obey and He will show you the way!

~ *Stephen*

February 3

FOLLOWING GOD'S LEAD

Chronological Bible Reading Plan: (Day 34: Exodus 13-15)

"And the LORD went before them by day in a pillar of cloud to lead them along the way, and by night in a pillar of fire to give them light, that they might travel by day and by night. The pillar of cloud by day and the pillar of fire by night did not depart from before the people." Exodus 13:21-22 (ESV)

God makes His Presence known. For the children of Israel, God revealed His Presence through the glory cloud. God would guide the Israelites by the visible manifestation of the cloud during the day and the pillar of fire by night. When the cloud lifted and shifted, the Israelites moved.

The people of Israel followed God's lead and crossed the Red Sea on dry ground. God removed the threat of the Egyptian army by causing the water to cascade down upon them. "Israel saw the great power that the LORD used against the Egyptians, so the people feared the LORD, and they believed in the LORD and in his servant Moses" (Exod. 14:31 ESV).

As God's workmanship, where did Moses learn that kind of sensitivity to God's movement? Did he learn it in the palace during his first forty years on the earth or perhaps during the second forty years of his life as a shepherd in the desert? The burning bush experience obviously made an abiding difference in his sensitivity to God's Presence.

God is always at work. Are you sensitive to His activity? You can experience God's Presence moment by moment as you commune with Him through prayer and feed on His Word. You can experience God's Presence as you maintain a posture of expectation and anticipation. Recognition of God's activity is proportionate to your sensitivity.

~ *Stephen*

February 4

Restructure Your Life

Chronological Bible Reading Plan: (Day 35: Exodus 16-18)

"Moses' father-in-law said to him, 'What you are doing is not good. You and the people with you will certainly wear yourselves out, for the thing is too heavy for you. You are not able to do it alone.'" Exodus 18:17-18 (ESV)

Do you have margin in your life? Margin is the space between your load and your limit. God has designed you to handle a certain amount of His work during your brief stay on this planet called earth. God has given you all the time you need to accomplish His plan.

Moses reached a breaking point due to being overextended and overwhelmed. The masses of people each wanted a piece of him. They wanted his time, his attention, and his decision making prowess. Though serving as judge over Israel, Moses failed to exercise proper judgment over his own life.

God came to the rescue by bringing Jethro into Moses' life. Jethro lovingly spoke into Moses' life to declare, "What you are doing is not good." Moses couldn't see the unhealthy path that he was on. Jethro saw it clearly and succinctly. Jethro was willing to help Moses' restructure his life.

What is overwhelming you right now? Has your load exceeded your limit? What are you giving your life to that is outside of God's will? Step back and evaluate your current reality. You may want to ask someone you know and love and trust to help you examine your life. Allow that person to give you feedback on what they see going on in your world. Their perspective could help you see what you are not seeing.

God uses other people to help us walk in obedience to His will. Pray and ask God to bring a Jethro into your life.

~ *Stephen*

February 5

God Delivers

Chronological Bible Reading Plan: (Day 36: Exodus 19-21)

"'I am the LORD your God, who brought you out of the land of Egypt, out of the house of slavery.'" Exodus 20:2 (ESV)

Moses spent forty years in the palace, forty years in the desert, and then forty years as the deliverer of the children of Israel. God was strategically developing Moses for the special assignment of leading the Israelites out of Egyptian bondage. Before delivering The Ten Commandments, God reminded them of His provision of bringing them out of the land of slavery. God graciously got them out of Egypt, now He was getting Egypt out of them.

God is a God of Relationship. He initiated the love relationship we enjoy with Him. God chose to become like us so that we could become like Him. God took the initiative to develop us in Christ, as a royal priesthood, a holy nation, and a people belonging to Him. Being adopted into His forever family did not come into fruition because of our human effort, but as a result of God's redemptive activity.

If you ever question your value in God's eyes, just look to the cross. God took the initiative to build the ultimate love bridge to you so that you could have harmony with Him and enjoy eternal life. When did you respond to God's offer of salvation? When did you become a follower of Jesus Christ and a recipient of God's unconditional love?

God has delivered you from your sin and brought you into the land of Promise. Now take the initiative to share the gift of eternal life with others. Shine His light and share His love so that others can have the personal and eternal relationship you enjoy with Jesus.

~ *Stephen*

February 6

Moses on the Mountain

Chronological Bible Reading Plan: (Day 37: Exodus 22-24)

"Now the appearance of the glory of the LORD was like a devouring fire on the top of the mountain in the sight of the people of Israel. Moses entered the cloud and went up on the mountain. And Moses was on the mountain forty days and forty nights." Exodus 24:17-18 (ESV)

God deepens relationship with His people by establishing a blood covenant. The covenant relationship is marked by the signature traits of loyalty, devotion, and obedience. God initiates the love relationship and permeates the relationship with His glory. Moses received an invitation from the Lord.

- *"The LORD said to Moses, 'Come up to me on the mountain and wait there, that I may give you the tablets of stone, with the law and the commandment, which I have written for their instruction.'" Exod. 24:12 (ESV).*

Moses encountered God on the mountain forty days and forty nights. He received the law and detailed instructions to bring to the people. God articulates His covenant community rules in the context of relationship. Can you imagine what Moses experienced with God during those forty days and forty nights?

God values intimacy and He paves the way for us to know Him intimately. God has provided the means necessary for us to come into a covenant relationship with Him. The ultimate display of His unconditional love is found in the atoning work of Jesus on the cross. God was willing to build an eternal relationship with us by allowing Jesus to become the only acceptable sacrifice for our sin. God demonstrated His love for us by sacrificing His Son for our sin. Jesus paid the debt He did not owe so that we could know the depth of God's redeeming love. In Christ, we are in a covenant relationship with God on the basis of the shed blood of Jesus.

~ *Stephen*

February 7

The Tabernacle

Chronological Bible Reading Plan: (Day 38: Exodus 25-27)

"'And let them make me a sanctuary, that I may dwell in their midst. Exactly as I show you concerning the pattern of the tabernacle, and of all its furniture, so you shall make it.'" Exodus 25:8-9 (ESV)

God revealed to Moses the architectural dimensions, interior design, and precise function of the Tabernacle. Picture over two million Jews encamped in an area that would take about twelve square miles. If you lived on the outskirts of the encampment, then you would have to walk nearly six miles to bring your sacrifice to the Tabernacle. From the distance, you would be able to view God's glory cloud descending from the sky down into the Most Holy Place.

The Tabernacle was mobile. It was designed in such a way that when God's glory moved, the Tabernacle could be moved to accommodate God's presence. Did you know that you are "the walking Tabernacle" of God's presence? "Or do you not know that your body is a temple of the Holy Spirit within you, whom you have from God? You are not your own, [20] for you were bought with a price. So glorify God in your body"
(1 Cor. 6:19-20 ESV).

God demonstrated in the Old Testament through the Tabernacle that His desire is to dwell with His people. As His Tabernacle, God has chosen to dwell in you permanently. He indwells you by the Holy Spirit. You are His priceless treasure. Are you being a Tabernacle in which His presence is fit to dwell? Have you allowed Him to move into every area of your life? Have you given Him full control of your life, your desires, your ambitions, and your fears?

~ *Stephen*

February 8

THE LORD OUR GOD

Chronological Bible Reading Plan: (Day 39: Exodus 28-29)

"'I will dwell among the people of Israel and will be their God. And they shall know that I am the LORD their God, who brought them out of the land of Egypt that I might dwell among them. I am the LORD their God.'"
Exodus 29:45-46 (ESV)

Moses received specific instructions related to how God would commune with His people. God established the sacrificial system to provide atonement for the sins of the people. God ordained the priesthood so that Aaron and his sons could serve at the tent of meeting. Every detail of the Tabernacle and the ongoing service within the sacrificial system was articulated by God to Moses.

Why would the Creator of the universe go to such lengths to make a way for His creation to encounter Him personally? God took the initiative to enable His people to worship Him. God affirmed His desire to dwell among them and to be their God. He would remind them of His redemptive act of bringing them out of Egypt that He might dwell among them and be the Lord their God.

God's love compels Him to initiate relationship. God created us so that we can know Him personally and intimately. Sin is the barrier that separates lost people from our holy God. There is nothing they can do on their own to remove the barrier. God took the initiative to close the gap between sin and righteousness.

- *"For our sake he made him to be sin who knew no sin, so that in him we might become the righteousness of God."* 2 Cor. 5:21 (ESV)

Jesus makes it possible for us to know the Lord our God. Jesus was the only acceptable sacrifice for our sin. Jesus took on the full wrath of God for our sin, paid our sin debt in full, and removed our sin.

~ *Stephen*

February 9

Intercessory Prayer

Chronological Bible Reading Plan: (Day 40: Exodus 30-32)

"'You shall make an altar on which to burn incense; you shall make it of acacia wood. A cubit shall be its length, and a cubit its breadth. It shall be square, and two cubits shall be its height. Its horns shall be of one piece with it. You shall overlay it with pure gold, its top and around its sides and its horns. And you shall make a molding of gold around it.'" Exodus 30:1-3 (ESV)

Invest a few moments of time in taking inventory of your life. What are you offering up to God? How are you allocating your time and your energy? Are you living to bring glory to God in all things?

The Table of the Bread of the Presence, the Golden Lampstand, and Altar of Burning Incense were located in the Holy Place of the Tabernacle. As you come to this feature in praying through the Tabernacle, begin to worship God and to intercede for others. Present specific requests to God and pray with passion for those God places on your heart.

- *"Let my prayer be counted as incense before you, and the lifting up of my hands as the evening sacrifice!" Ps. 142:2 (ESV)*
- *"Through him then let us continually offer up a sacrifice of praise to God, that is, the fruit of lips that acknowledge his name." Heb. 13:15 (ESV)*

As you pray, your prayers rise like burning incense. As you live out your faith in Christ, your life becomes an aroma pleasing to God. As you offer your body to God for His glory, you are expressing worship to God.

Obedience to God demonstrates your passion to please Him and to honor Him with your life and your lips. Does your conversation honor God? Does your conduct move God's heart?

~ Stephen

February 10

Collaboration

Chronological Bible Reading Plan: (Day 41: Exodus 33-35)

"All the men and women, the people of Israel, whose heart moved them to bring anything for the work that the Lord had commanded by Moses to be done brought it as a freewill offering to the Lord." Exodus 35:29 (ESV)

God instructed Moses on the specific design of the features of the Tabernacle. As Moses spoke to the people of Israel, God moved their heart to respond with a demonstration of generosity. All the men and women whose heart moved them brought various items to contribute to the construction of the Tabernacle including the furnishings. The people were mobilized to bring their assets as a freewill offering to the Lord. Every person was valuable and every gift added value to the project.

- *"Now there are varieties of gifts, but the same Spirit; and there are varieties of service, but the same Lord; and there are varieties of activities, but it is the same God who empowers them all in everyone." 1Cor. 12:4-6 (ESV)*

God has graced you with gifts to honor Him and to benefit others. What will you do with what God has given you? How will you unleash generosity to invest in the work of the Lord? We do better together and God desires that we work together to accomplish His master plan.

There is power in collaboration. When we link hands and arms with fellow believers, we are igniting a bond that honors God and is expressed through serving others. We can come together to model the generous love of God by making personal sacrifices to fulfill His will.

Everybody is somebody in the family of God. God has saved and equipped every child of God to be on mission with God in order to continue the ministry of Jesus. What do you need to stop doing? What do you need to start doing? What do you need to continue doing?

~ *Stephen*

February 11

Intimacy with God

Chronological Bible Reading Plan: (Day 42: Exodus 36-38)

"He made the altar of burnt offering of acacia wood. Five cubits was its length, and five cubits its breadth. It was square, and three cubits was its height. He made horns for it on its four corners. Its horns were of one piece with it, and he overlaid it with bronze." Exodus 38:1-2 (ESV)

When you think about relationships, there are different levels of intimacy. Some relationships are emotionally distant and superficial whereas some relationships have the capacity to be more consistent and feature an element of closeness. Then there are those relationships where the interaction is meaningful, transparent, and magnetic.

The Encarta Dictionary defines the word intimacy as a close personal relationship; a detailed knowledge resulting from a close or long association. One of my favorite definitions of intimacy is: "in to me you see."

God desires intimacy with you. In the Old Testament, the portrait of intimacy was the formation and utilization of the Tabernacle. God made a way for His people to experience intimacy with Him through a religious relationship.

As you enter the Tabernacle, the first item you encounter is the altar of burnt offering. The New Testament equivalent is the cross of Jesus Christ. Jesus became the ultimate sacrifice for your sin. As you pray through the Tabernacle, spend some time at the "altar of burnt offering" to praise God for His ultimate love gift and for Jesus being willing to pay the penalty for your sin.

God took the initiative to provide the way for you to enjoy an intimate love relationship with Him through faith in Jesus. What are you doing with the relationship God has made available to you?

~ *Stephen*

February 12

Moving with God

Chronological Bible Reading Plan: (Day 43: Exodus 39-40)

"Throughout all their journeys, whenever the cloud was taken up from over the tabernacle, the people of Israel would set out. But if the cloud was not taken up, then they did not set out till the day that it was taken up. For the cloud of the Lord was on the tabernacle by day, and fire was in it by night, in the sight of all the house of Israel throughout all their journeys." Exodus 40:36-38 (ESV)

God would guide the Israelites by the visible manifestation of the cloud during the day and fire by night. When the cloud lifted and shifted, the Israelites moved. The Tabernacle was constructed in a way that emphasized ease of mobility. This enabled the Israelites to move when God moved.

As God's workmanship, where did Moses learn that kind of sensitivity to God's movement? Did he learn it in the palace during his first forty years on the earth or perhaps during the second forty years of his life as a shepherd in the desert? The burning bush experience obviously made an abiding difference in his sensitivity to God's Presence.

God is always at work. Are you sensitive to His activity? You can experience God's Presence moment by moment as you commune with Him through prayer and feed on His Word. You can experience God's Presence as you maintain a posture of expectation and anticipation. You always find what you are looking for. If you are looking for the activity of God, you will find it.

Be sensitive to God's activity. Be responsive to His invitation to join Him in His activity. Keep your "yes" on the altar to be available for God's use. Move with God and abide in His perfect will.

~ *Stephen*

February 13

Sin and Sacrifice

Chronological Bible Reading Plan: (Day 44: Leviticus 1-4)

"'If the whole congregation of Israel sins unintentionally and the thing is hidden from the eyes of the assembly, and they do any one of the things that by the Lord's commandments ought not to be done, and they realize their guilt, when the sin which they have committed becomes known, the assembly shall offer a bull from the herd for a sin offering and bring it in front of the tent of meeting.'"
Leviticus 4:13-14 (ESV)

As you read the first four chapters of Leviticus, you detect the theme of sin and sacrifice. God is holy, righteous, and pure. God does not tolerate sin. In His grace, God established the sacrificial system to be implemented by Moses and the priesthood. The system featured specific laws pertaining to specific measures to be taken for specific sins. As you can see, God takes sin seriously.

In order for the people of Israel to enjoy the benefits of their covenant relationship with God, they had to obey the laws established within the sacrificial system. Sin separated them from God. Sin inhibited their fellowship with God and misrepresented His nature and His character. God provided atonement for both sins of omission and sins of commission.

When a person failed to do what God commanded or when a person did something God commanded them not to do, that person sinned. When that sin became known to the person, he would then be required to bring a burnt offering for sins of commission (Lev. 1:3-4) or a sin offering for sins of omission to the entrance of the tent of meeting. The priest would then carry out the process for atonement.

Take a moment to consider your life before our holy God. Ask the Lord to search your heart and to reveal unconfessed sin in your life.

~ *Stephen*

February 14

Bring Your Offerings

Chronological Bible Reading Plan: (Day 45: Leviticus 5-7)

"This is the law of the burnt offering, of the grain offering, of the sin offering, of the guilt offering, of the ordination offering, and of the peace offering, which the Lord commanded Moses on Mount Sinai, on the day that he commanded the people of Israel to bring their offerings to the Lord, in the wilderness of Sinai." Leviticus 7:37-38 (ESV)

God values relationships. Having a right relationship with God and having a right relationship with others is your personal responsibility. God has provided the way for you to be right with Him. Placing your faith in the completed work of Jesus on the cross justifies you before God and places you in right standing. God forgives you of your sin, adopts you into His family, and seals you by the Holy Spirit.

Now that you are positionally right with God, you maintain the relationship by knowing God's will and doing God's will. You choose to practice instant obedience, confess sin, and continue the ministry of Jesus on the earth. Maintaining a right relationship with God includes having a right relationship with others. Love others, serve others, and forgive others. Share the gift of eternal life with others so that they can have a personal love relationship with Jesus.

- *"He himself bore our sins in his body on the tree, that we might die to sin and live to righteousness. By his wounds you have been healed." 1 Pet. 2:24 (ESV)*

God gave Moses further instructions to develop the sacrificial system so that the people of Israel could have a right relationship with God and with others. They were to participate in the process by bringing their offerings to the tent of meeting. God was very specific about how to deal with sin and how to be made right with Him.

~ *Stephen*

February 15

Distinguish the Sacred

Chronological Bible Reading Plan: (Day 46: Leviticus 8-10)

"And the Lord spoke to Aaron, saying, 'Drink no wine or strong drink, you or your sons with you, when you go into the tent of meeting, lest you die. It shall be a statute forever throughout your generations. You are to distinguish between the holy and the common, and between the unclean and the clean, and you are to teach the people of Israel all the statutes that the Lord has spoken to them by Moses.'" Leviticus 10:8-11 (ESV)

You are made to worship. God has placed within you the desire to worship. If you are not careful and attentive, you can drift into worshiping creation rather than worshiping the Creator. You determine the focus of your worship. It is vital that you not only worship God, but that you worship God His way.

- *"Now Nadab and Abihu, the sons of Aaron, each took his censer and put fire in it and laid incense on it and offered unauthorized fire before the Lord, which he had not commanded them. And fire came out from before the Lord and consumed them, and they died before the Lord." Lev. 10:1-2 (ESV)*

Aaron's sons made a decision to forfeit worshiping God His way. Instead, they offered unauthorized fire before the Lord and God removed them from their priestly service by instant death. As you read this encounter, it appears to be abrupt and extreme. God is demonstrating the value He places on His holiness and the way we worship.

God has given us His Holy Spirit to help us distinguish between that which is holy and common, between the clean and unclean. Guard against becoming too casual in your worship of the One true living God. Revere God and esteem God as you worship Him privately and corporately. Affirm the holiness of God. He alone is worthy!

~ *Stephen*

February 16

Be Holy

Chronological Bible Reading Plan: (Day 47: Leviticus 11-13)

"'For I am the Lord who brought you up out of the land of Egypt to be your God. You shall therefore be holy, for I am holy.'" Leviticus 11:45 (ESV)

Is it possible to stay clean while living in a dirty world? Every possibility for contaminating our lives is available to us. Sin is rampant. We face trials from without and temptation from within. The cultural current is moving in the opposite direction of the Christ honoring flow. We must make a conscious and continuous decision to walk in purity.

- *"Since we have these promises, beloved, let us cleanse ourselves from every defilement of body and spirit, bringing holiness to completion in the fear of God." 2 Cor 7:1 (ESV)*
- *"Let no one despise you for your youth, but set the believers an example in speech, in conduct, in love, in faith, in purity." 1 Tim 4:12 (ESV)*

Purify yourself and perfect holiness. Purify your heart and set an example for the believers in purity. In Christ, you are positionally pure. In Christ, you are a new creation. Live out practically what you are presently and positionally in Christ. The only way to reign in this life is to allow Christ to reign in your life.

Staying clean while living in a dirty world is only possible in the strength Christ provides. Jesus has already set the example. Jesus has demonstrated the life of purity in a sin-polluted culture. Jesus lived a sinless life and died a sacrificial death so that you can walk in victory.

Embrace moral purity by yielding to the Lordship of Christ. Make Jesus the Lord of your life. God called you to live a holy life. Now give Jesus His rightful place in your life and allow Him to live His life through you.

~ *Stephen*

February 17

Separate Yourself

Chronological Bible Reading Plan: (Day 48: Leviticus 14-15)

"'Thus you shall keep the people of Israel separate from their uncleanness, lest they die in their uncleanness by defiling my tabernacle that is in their midst.'" Leviticus 15:31 (ESV)

Sin is an intruder. Sin disrupts fellowship with God, sin erodes peace with God, and sin inhibits the will of God. God is holy, righteous, and pure. We are selfish, sinful, and separated from God until we have a life changing experiencing by placing our trust in the completed work of Jesus on the cross. Once we come to faith in Jesus Christ, we are to embrace a lifestyle of moral purity and be set apart unto the Lord's work. In Christ, our life is reoriented to the will of God and to the ways of God.

- *"Who shall ascend the hill of the Lord? And who shall stand in his holy place? He who has clean hands and a pure heart, who does not lift up his soul to what is false and does not swear deceitfully." Ps. 24:3-4 (ESV)*
- *"But put on the Lord Jesus Christ, and make no provision for the flesh, to gratify its desires." Rom. 13:14 (ESV)*

God instructed Moses and Aaron to prevent defiling the tabernacle in their midst. God gave them specific instructions related to how to deal with uncleanness within the camp. God values purity and order. He required that His people abide by the rules and regulations He established in order to enjoy His abiding presence. God gave detailed instructions on how to deal with leprosy, mildew, and intimate marital relations. Cleanliness, purification, and holiness are features that God demands.

Is there anything in your life that disrupts your fellowship with God? Confess known sin and embrace a lifestyle of moral purity that reflects the purity of Christ. Separate yourself from sin. Live a life that brings honor to God.

~ *Stephen*

February 18

Scapegoat

Chronological Bible Reading Plan: (Day 49: Leviticus 16-18)

"And Aaron shall cast lots over the two goats, one lot for the Lord and the other lot for Azazel. And Aaron shall present the goat on which the lot fell for the Lord and use it as a sin offering, but the goat on which the lot fell for Azazel shall be presented alive before the Lord to make atonement over it, that it may be sent away into the wilderness to Azazel." Leviticus 16:8-10 (ESV)

In the Old Testament sacrificial system, the high priest would enter the holy of holies once a year on the Day of Atonement to offer sacrifices for the sins of his family and for all the people. One goat would be chosen to be sacrificed for the Lord and one goat would become the scapegoat (Lev. 16:10). The blood from the goat sacrificed as a sin offering would be sprinkled throughout the altar, sanctuary, and tent of meeting to remove defilement of the past year. The high priest would then place his hands on the head of the scapegoat and symbolically transfer the sins of the people to it. The scapegoat, also known as the goat of removal, would be led away from the people into the desert to picture the removal of sins.

Jesus bore our sins on the cross to pay the penalty for our sin. Jesus took our punishment for sin to satisfy God's justice. In His mercy, Christ was sacrificed to remove our sins. Our sin debt has been paid in full and our salvation purchased through the atoning work of Jesus on the cross. Jesus became our scapegoat to take away our sins.

Have you confessed your sins? Have your received God's provision for the forgiveness of your sins? Spend some time thanking Jesus for the removal of your sins.

~ *Stephen*

February 19

Love Others

Chronological Bible Reading Plan: (Day 50: Leviticus 19-21)

"'When you reap the harvest of your land, you shall not reap your field right up to its edge, neither shall you gather the gleanings after your harvest. And you shall not strip your vineyard bare, neither shall you gather the fallen grapes of your vineyard. You shall leave them for the poor and for the sojourner: I am the Lord your God.'" Leviticus 19:9-10 (ESV)

We are by nature self-absorbed, self-centered, and self-focused. When anything happens around us our first question is: How will this affect me? In many ways, we act as though the earth really does rotate around us. The reality of our fallen nature pops up from time to time like a ground hog trying to catch a glimpse of daylight.

Jesus acknowledges the presence of our self-love. We truly love ourselves. As one of my colleagues would often say, "Sometimes you just have to be good to yourself!" We have no problem being good to ourselves do we? We value comfort. We value pleasure. We value looking good and feeling good and sleeping good.

As we begin viewing others from God's perspective, we will begin to value others the way God values them. The resulting choice will be to love others as we love ourselves. In other words, we will begin to treat others the way we want to be treated. We will love others with the same kind of love that we desire to receive.

- *"If you really keep the royal law found in Scripture, 'Love your neighbor as yourself,' you are doing right." Jas. 2:8 (NIV)*

James identifies that we are doing right when we love others as we love ourselves. Longing to do right is not enough. Putting our faith in action by loving others brings honor to God.

~ Stephen

February 20

Practice the Sabbath

Chronological Bible Reading Plan: (Day 51: Leviticus 22-23)

"'Six days shall work be done, but on the seventh day is a Sabbath of solemn rest, a holy convocation. You shall do no work. It is a Sabbath to the Lord in all your dwelling places.'" Leviticus 23:3 (ESV)

God instructed Moses to speak to the people of Israel about the appointed feasts that were to be proclaimed as holy convocations. The appointed feasts included: the Sabbath, the Passover, the Feast of First Fruits, the Feast of Weeks, the Feast of Trumpets, the Day of Atonement, and the Feast of Booths. These holy convocations were intentional ways to express devotion, thanksgiving, gratitude, and worship unto the Lord.

The Sabbath is the seventh day, which is Saturday. As Christians, we gather for corporate worship on Sunday of each week in honor of the resurrection of Jesus Christ. Jesus died on the cross on a Friday and rose from the dead on Sunday. We come together on the first day of the week to worship God with our fellow believers.

How do we practice the Sabbath now that we operate under the new covenant of grace? God established the Sabbath and modeled Sabbath rest. "For in six days the Lord made heaven and earth, the sea, and all that is in them, and rested on the seventh day. Therefore the Lord blessed the Sabbath day and made it holy" (Exod. 20:11 ESV).

Practice a weekly Sabbath by setting aside one day each week to allow God to put you back together. Rest. Reflect. Refrain from producing and racing toward a deadline. Un-string your bow and cultivate a day of personal renewal. Choose a day each week to get off of the race track and pull onto pit road in order to make a pit stop. Allow God to restore you and to refill your tank.

~ *Stephen*

February 21

Go the Extra Mile

Chronological Bible Reading Plan: (Day 52: Leviticus 24-25)

"'If your brother becomes poor and cannot maintain himself with you, you shall support him as though he were a stranger and a sojourner, and he shall live with you.'" Leviticus 25:35 (ESV)

Are you compelled to go the extra mile for others even when it hurts? Do you have that kind of heart for people? Going the extra mile to portray the love of Christ may invade your plans or even delay your personal agenda. "'And if anyone forces you to go one mile, go with him two miles'" Matt. 5:41 (ESV). Consider the impact you can make by simply living to add value to others. Ready to go the extra mile?

The Roman law in Jesus' day gave a soldier the right to force a civilian to carry his equipment for a mile. It did not matter if the civilian had other plans or was going in the opposite direction. By law, the civilian had to carry the heavy load for a mile if selected by the soldier. That was the law as well as the clear expectation.

Jesus illuminated the path for the believer to go beyond the expectation and to be willing to go the extra mile. Can you imagine the expression on the face of a Roman soldier when the mile was almost complete and the civilian announced that he would be glad to carry the equipment another mile? That makes me wonder how many Roman soldiers will be in heaven because of the civilians who portrayed the servitude of Christ by going the extra mile. I can picture a soldier asking the believer what would motivate him to go the extra mile. The believer would then share how Jesus had transformed his life personally and transformed his perception of others.

Be willing to go the extra mile for a stranger or a close relative this week!

~ *Stephen*

February 22

Avoid Idoloatry

Chronological Bible Reading Plan: (Day 53: Leviticus 26-27)

"'You shall not make idols for yourselves or erect an image or pillar, and you shall not set up a figured stone in your land to bow down to it, for I am the Lord your God.'" Leviticus 26:1 (ESV)

What is an idol? Whatever you value more than God is an idol. We are made to worship. There is a tendency to bypass worshiping our Creator and choose instead to worship creation. God's uniqueness requires unique devotion. The desire to fashion God in our own image produces a distorted view of God and confuses our created purpose.

Moses was instructed to engage in conflict resolution as a result of Israel's rebellion: Then the LORD said to Moses, "Go down, for your people, whom you brought up out of the land of Egypt, have corrupted themselves. They have turned aside quickly out of the way that I commanded them. They have made for themselves a golden calf and have worshiped it and sacrificed to it and said, 'These are your gods, O Israel, who brought you up out of the land of Egypt!'" (Exod. 32:7-8 ESV).

Avoid idolatry! Remove those things you love more than God. God demands and deserves your loyalty. You demonstrate loyalty through Lordship. Who occupies the throne of your life? Be attentive to those things that are seeking to be enthroned in your life. Don't allow anything to usurp your affection and your devotion. Keep your focus on Jesus, the author and finisher of your faith. If you have drifted, return to your first love and make Jesus your top priority.

Practice moment-by-moment surrender to the Lordship of Christ. Allow Jesus to be the Lord of every area of your life. Give Him full access to your thoughts, your desires, your fears, and your future. Pray, "Lord, I'm Yours! Use me!"

~ *Stephen*

February 23

ORDER YOUR LIFE

Chronological Bible Reading Plan: (Day 54: Numbers 1-2)

"Thus did the people of Israel. According to all that the Lord commanded Moses, so they camped by their standards, and so they set out, each one in his clan, according to his fathers' house." Numbers 2:35 (ESV)

When Moses set out to deliver the people of Israel from Egyptian bondage, he discovered the challenge of moving a large mass of people through the wilderness. The assignment was overwhelming and the task was too large for him to pull off on his own. God commissioned Moses and God equipped Moses to fulfill the assignment.

The people of Israel were in the second month in the second year after they had come out of the land of Egypt. God instructed Moses to take a census of the people and to arrange them by clans based on the twelve tribes of Israel. The process was thorough and meticulous. God gave detailed instructions to Moses for the task.

We see demonstrated in the Old Testament and we learn in the New Testament, that God values order. "For God is not a God of confusion but of peace" (1 Cor. 14:33 ESV). God has infused His creation with order. The enemy attempts to bring disorder by inserting sin into the equation. Sin corrupts order in relationships, in families, in government, and in churches. Disorder brings confusion, inefficiency, and ineffectiveness. Disorder does not reflect the nature and character of God.

Bring honor to God by ordering your life. Take time to assess the current condition of your life, your routine, and your priorities. Is your life out of order? Is your life out of balance? Make intentional adjustments in your life to come into alignment with God's purposes and plan. What do you need to stop doing? What do you need to start doing? What do you need to continue doing?

~ Stephen

February 24

Focus Your Life

Chronological Bible Reading Plan: (Day 55: Numbers 3-4)

"The Lord spoke to Moses and Aaron, saying, 'The people of Israel shall camp each by his own standard, with the banners of their fathers' houses. They shall camp facing the tent of meeting on every side.'" Numbers 2:1-2 (ESV)

What is your preoccupation? What do you think about most? What consumes a majority of your energy and attention? Your answers to these questions will help unveil your focus. One healthy discipline is to intentionally assess the trajectory of your life. You need to know where you are heading and what you are giving your life to.

God gave specific instructions related to the massive encampment of the twelve tribes of Israel. God wanted the people to camp facing the tent of meeting. Making His presence known within the center of the camp via the tent of meeting, God wanted the people of Israel to focus their attention and their lives on Him.

- *"I will meditate on your precepts and fix my eyes on your ways." Ps. 119:15 (ESV)*
- *"Let us fix our eyes on Jesus, the author and perfecter of our faith, who for the joy set before him endured the cross, scorning its shame, and sat down at the right hand of the throne of God." Heb. 12:2 (NIV)*

Are you living the Christ-centered life? Is your life oriented around God's agenda? Regain your focus and ask God to restore your spiritual sight to be able to see what God wants you to do and where God wants you to go. Obey what God reveals to you. Maintain an unyielding devotion to bring pleasure to the Lord by continuing His ministry on the earth. Make an eternal difference by focusing your life today.

~ *Stephen*

February 25

Be Blessed

Chronological Bible Reading Plan: (Day 56: Numbers 5-6)

"Speak to Aaron and his sons, saying, Thus you shall bless the people of Israel: you shall say to them, 'The Lord bless you and keep you; the Lord make his face to shine upon you and be gracious to you; the Lord lift up his countenance upon you and give you peace.'" Numbers 6:23-26 (ESV)

God has blessed you to be a blessing. Your words have the power to build others up or to tear them down. Your words can inspire or discourage. Your words can motivate or devastate. Speak words that bless those whom God places in your path. Be a blessing to others by blessing others.

Aaron and his sons were instructed to bless the people of Israel. They were to deliver a word of blessing from the Lord. God imparts life and God inspires hope and bestows blessings upon His people. God affirmed His blessing, His protection, His favor, and His grace upon His people. God projected His affirmation of His enabling and His abiding peace.

Think about what you need to be on mission with God. Consider the resources necessary to do God's work God's way in this fallen world. You cannot live the Christian life in your own strength. God never intended for you to fulfill His plan in your own power. Receive God's blessing. Receive God's supernatural enabling to fulfill His mission on the earth.

May the Lord bless you. May the Lord keep you. May the Lord make His face shine upon you. May the Lord be gracious to you in your time of need. May the Lord lift up His countenance upon you and give you His sustaining peace. You are not on your own. You are not operating in isolation. God is blessing you so that you can be a blessing. You are blessed to bless!

~ *Stephen*

February 26

Hearing God's Voice

Chronological Bible Reading Plan: (Day 57: Numbers 7)

"And when Moses went into the tent of meeting to speak with the Lord, he heard the voice speaking to him from above the mercy seat that was on the ark of the testimony, from between the two cherubim; and it spoke to him."
Numbers 7:89 (ESV)

After twelve days of consecrating the tabernacle by the chiefs of Israel, Moses entered the tent of meeting. This was a divine moment in that Moses chose to draw near to God. In this holy encounter, God spoke to Moses from above the mercy seat that was on the ark of the testimony. The Creator of the universe communicated with Moses. God spoke!

As you read chapter seven of Numbers, you will detect the immense preparation that went into consecrating the tabernacle. Each of the twelve chiefs of Israel participated in the process of consecration. Each of the twelve chiefs invested personally and sacrificially in the process.

Compare the twelve days of preparation to how most people in our modern context approach God. So often, people in our society approach God as though He was just another individual we pass along the way. Even in our Christianity, we can become so casual with God that we lose sight of His holiness, His sovereignty, and His majesty.

- *"Let us then with confidence draw near to the throne of grace, that we may receive mercy and find grace to help in time of need."*
  Heb. 4:16 (ESV)

Our confidence in approaching God is not based on our arrogance or our sufficiency. We have the privilege of approaching God because of the matchless grace He dispensed through the atoning work of Jesus on the cross.

~ *Stephen*

February 27

Moving with God

Chronological Bible Reading Plan: (Day 58: Numbers 8-10)

"Whether it was two days, or a month, or a longer time, that the cloud continued over the tabernacle, abiding there, the people of Israel remained in camp and did not set out, but when it lifted they set out." Numbers 9:22 (ESV)

The tabernacle was constructed in such as way as to maximize flexibility and mobility. Instead of constructing a permanent structure, God instructed Moses to construct a mobile tabernacle. The tent of meeting was fashioned for ease of mobility. Why was this an important feature? God wanted the people of Israel to be able to worship Him and to move with Him. A permanent structure would not suffice.

Whenever the glory cloud lifted, the people would set out based on the orderly procedure Moses had established for taking down the tabernacle and transporting it to the next location. This process enabled them to move with God. When God moved, the people had the capability to move with God.

Are you flexible, teachable, and stretchable? Are you available for God to expand you and to invite you into His story? Choose to make yourself available for God's use. Live in ready-mode to join God in His activity and to move with God. It may mean a physical relocation or it may mean a change of attitude about your usefulness to God.

God wants to reveal Himself to you and to do a new work in your life so that He can do a new work through your life. Position yourself in such as way as to be able to move with God. Practice His Presence and join God in His activity. Be sensitive to what God is doing around you and be ready to be used of God to touch the lives of those in your sphere of influence.

~ *Stephen*

February 28

Focus on Giants or God

Chronological Bible Reading Plan: (Day 59: Numbers 11-13)

"But Caleb quieted the people before Moses and said, 'Let us go up at once and occupy it, for we are well able to overcome it.' Then the men who had gone up with him said, 'We are not able to go up against the people, for they are stronger than we are.'" Numbers 13:30-31 (ESV)

Are you facing something beyond your reach? Have you been agonizing over anything lately? Your situation may be relational, familial, financial, or physical. Whatever you view as your greatest obstacle just might be the greatest opportunity for God to reveal His glory.

After twelve of the Israelites returned from spying out the land of Canaan, they returned with a mixed report. Ten of the twelve indicated that the land was filled with giants and could not be conquered. Yet, Joshua and Caleb had a much different report. Instead of focusing on the giants, they focused on God and His ability to bring them into the land flowing with milk and honey.

Are you listening to the voices of doubt and fear or to the voice of God? God knows where you are and the specifics of what you are facing. Remember, nothing is hidden from God. Nothing catches God by surprise. Our limited perspective does not limit God.

God has a plan for you that factors in your circumstances. God will remove the obstacle or He will help you overcome the obstacle. God will eliminate the giant before you or elevate your faith to persevere in light of the giant you face. Take possession of the land God is giving you.

Will you focus on the giant or focus on God? Will you view your circumstances from your perspective or from God's perspective? If God has allowed this situation, He will use it for your good and His glory.

~ *Stephen*

March 1

Follow Fully

Chronological Bible Reading Plan: (Day 60: Numbers 14-15; Psalm 90)

"'But truly, as I live, and as all the earth shall be filled with the glory of the Lord, none of the men who have seen my glory and my signs that I did in Egypt and in the wilderness, and yet have put me to the test these ten times and have not obeyed my voice, shall see the land that I swore to give to their fathers. And none of those who despised me shall see it. But my servant Caleb, because he has a different spirit and has followed me fully, I will bring into the land into which he went, and his descendants shall possess it.'" Numbers 14:21-24 (ESV)

Tension mounted as the people of Israel grumbled against God and against Moses. God declared that none of those who despised God would see the land flowing with milk and honey. That would have been devastating news after all those years of wandering in the wilderness. God demonstrated that He does not bless disobedience.

Refreshingly, God affirmed His servant, Caleb. God affirmed that Caleb had a different spirit and that Caleb followed God fully. As a result, God promised to bring Caleb and His descendants into the land he had explored with Joshua. The Promised Land was Caleb's inheritance.

Would God identify you as a fully devoted follower of Christ? Would your devotion to the Lord set you apart as a person with a different spirit? Take some time to take personal inventory of your life and your commitment to the Lord. Measure your motives and calculate your commitment to God's Word and to God's will. Are you fully devoted to the Lord?

In order to exhibit a different spirit, you must allow the Holy Spirit to have full control of your life. Yield to His prompting and allow Him to empower you to follow Jesus fully!

~ *Stephen*

March 2

Discern God's Will

Chronological Bible Reading Plan: (Day 61: Numbers 16-17)

"On the next day Moses went into the tent of the testimony, and behold, the staff of Aaron for the house of Levi had sprouted and put forth buds and produced blossoms, and it bore ripe almonds. Then Moses brought out all the staffs from before the Lord to all the people of Israel. And they looked, and each man took his staff." Numbers 17:8-9 (ESV)

God reveals His will. Even when you are not clear about a direction you should take, God will bring you into the decision making process to reveal His plan. God created you and God has a specific plan for your life. Will you pursue Him daily and trust Him completely? Will you obey what God shows you?

Moses obeyed God's directive by securing the staffs of the twelve chiefs of Israel. Moses wrote their name on their staff and wrote Aaron's name on the staff of Levi. The morning after Moses placed the twelve staffs in the tent of meeting, he retrieved each staff and noticed that Aaron's staff had sprouted. Through this very interesting process, God revealed His will.

Perhaps you are going through a season of life in which you would love for God to reveal His will to you in a tangible way. You would be willing to secure a staff or any item that God would use to indicate His will. The reality is that God reveals His will through His Word.

Are you reading your Bible? Are you spending time in prayer and spending time diligently seeking God's will? As you obey what God has already revealed to you, He will illuminate the path He wants you to take. As you obey, God will show you the way.

~ *Stephen*

March 3

God's Way

Chronological Bible Reading Plan: (Day 62: Numbers 18-20)

"Then Moses and Aaron went from the presence of the assembly to the entrance of the tent of meeting and fell on their faces. And the glory of the Lord appeared to them, and the Lord spoke to Moses, saying, 'Take the staff, and assemble the congregation, you and Aaron your brother, and tell the rock before their eyes to yield its water. So you shall bring water out of the rock for them and give drink to the congregation and their cattle.'" Numbers 20:6-8 (ESV)

God's way is always the best way. When you are contemplating a direction you should take or a decision you should make, remember that God has a specific plan for you. God's will is to be done God's way.

Moses and Aaron learned a painful lesson about doing God's work God's way. Instead of speaking to the rock to provide water for the people of Israel, Moses struck the rock with his staff twice. Water came out abundantly and the congregation and the livestock drank. Everything appeared to go as planned until God spoke. "And the Lord said to Moses and Aaron, 'Because you did not believe in me, to uphold me as holy in the eyes of the people of Israel, therefore you shall not bring this assembly into the land that I have given them'" (Num. 20:12 ESV).

Disobedience brings discipline. "Besides this, we have had earthly fathers who disciplined us and we respected them. Shall we not much more be subject to the Father of spirits and live? For they disciplined us for a short time as it seemed best to them, but he disciplines us for our good, that we may share his holiness" (Heb. 12:9-10 ESV). God's way is always the best way. God blesses obedience.

~ *Stephen*

March 4

LOOK TO THE HEALER

Chronological Bible Reading Plan: (Day 63: Numbers 21-22)

"And the Lord said to Moses, 'Make a fiery serpent and set it on a pole, and everyone who is bitten, when he sees it, shall live.' So Moses made a bronze serpent and set it on a pole. And if a serpent bit anyone, he would look at the bronze serpent and live." Numbers 21:8-9 (ESV)

Have you ever seen the medical profession logo that features a snake wrapped around a pole? That image serves as the icon for the medical arena. You can trace the origin of that image to the instruction God gave Moses.

The people of Israel spoke against God and Moses in their frustration generated by their wandering in the wilderness. They longed to return to Egypt where they had served as slaves. God judged them for their grumbling by sending fiery serpents among the people to bite them. Many of the people died. The survivors came to Moses to plead for intercession and intervention. Moses prayed for the people.

God instructed Moses to make a fiery serpent and to set it on a pole. God gave further instructions that anyone bitten could look at the bronze serpent and live. God's grace was clearly evident by His response to their willful disobedience.

Jesus made reference to this experience during his conversation with Nicodemus. "And as Moses lifted up the serpent in the wilderness, so must the Son of Man be lifted up, that whoever believes in him may have eternal life" (John 3:14-15 ESV). Just as the people of Israel were healed by looking to the bronze serpent lifted up on the pole, so all believers today can be delivered from the sickness of sin by looking to the completed work of Jesus on the cross. Jesus has been lifted up on the cross to bring forth our ultimate healing!

~ *Stephen*

March 5

The Real Zeal

Chronological Bible Reading Plan: (Day 64: Numbers 23-25)

"When Phinehas the son of Eleazar, son of Aaron the priest, saw it, he rose and left the congregation and took a spear in his hand and went after the man of Israel into the chamber and pierced both of them, the man of Israel and the woman through her belly. Thus the plague on the people of Israel was stopped. Nevertheless, those who died by the plague were twenty-four thousand." Numbers 25:7-9 (ESV)

Instead of influencing the culture, the people of Israel were influenced by the culture. Instead of being a thermostat and setting the environment, the people of Israel became like a thermometer and reflected the environment. They drifted into Baal worship and forfeited their loyalty and devotion to the Lord their God.

Aaron's grandson, Phinehas, took the initiative to end the descent into pagan worship by piercing the Israelite and the Midianite woman he brought to his family in the sight of Moses and the congregation of the people of Israel. In response to this courageous move by Phinehas, God stopped the plague on the people of Israel.

This was a dark day for the people of Israel in that twenty-four thousand had died by the plague. God credited Phinehas with turning back His wrath on the people of Israel. God affirmed Phinehas for being jealous with God's jealousy among the people of Israel.

What is the life lesson from such a traumatic encounter? Value what God values! Place the same value on people that God does. Place the same value on God's will and God's way that God does. Be zealous for the things of God and be diligent to be an irresistible influence for the Lord. Don't allow the culture to shape you. Choose to shape culture by valuing what God values.

~ *Stephen*

March 6

Prepare for Transitions

Chronological Bible Reading Plan: (Day 65: Numbers 26-27)

"So the Lord said to Moses, 'Take Joshua the son of Nun, a man in whom is the Spirit, and lay your hand on him. Make him stand before Eleazar the priest and all the congregation, and you shall commission him in their sight. You shall invest him with some of your authority, that all the congregation of the people of Israel may obey.'" Numbers 27:18-20 (ESV)

Transitions are constant in this life. From the cradle to the grave, you experience countless transitions. Some of the transitions are more pronounced than others. Every transition is an opportunity to experience God's grace and to obey God's voice.

Moses had just received the difficult news of those who would die in the wilderness and not see the Promised Land. The list was long and included Moses. God had judged Moses for previously striking the rock with his staff twice instead of speaking to the rock in order to produce the flow of water for the people of Israel. These are the waters of Meribah of Kadesh in the wilderness of Zin. Moses and the people of Israel failed to uphold God as holy at the waters before their eyes (Num. 27:14).

Moses faced another major transition. It was now time to commission Joshua to succeed him as leader of the people of Israel. Moses was preparing for his own death and for the succession of his leadership.

Are you currently facing a transition? How are you responding to this particular season of your life? What do you sense God is up to? God will always develop your character to match His assignment. Be sensitive to God's activity and be open to God's leadership. You may be prompted to go in a new direction or you may be prompted to renew your commitment to your current assignment. God will give you the grace to match every transition you face.

~ *Stephen*

March 7

Keep Your Word

Chronological Bible Reading Plan: (Day 66: Numbers 28-30)

"Moses spoke to the heads of the tribes of the people of Israel, saying, "This is what the Lord has commanded. If a man vows a vow to the Lord, or swears an oath to bind himself by a pledge, he shall not break his word. He shall do according to all that proceeds out of his mouth." Numbers 30:1-2 (ESV)

How refreshing to spend time with a person of integrity! The guard comes down and pretense evaporates because you are in the presence of someone who keeps his or her word. You can count on them. You can trust them because they are trustworthy. You can rely on them because they are reliable. You can depend on them because they are dependable.

Moses spoke to the heads of the tribes of the people of Israel to affirm the value of a vow. Moses reminded them of the utter importance and vitality of keeping their word. Their conversation was to be consistently supported by their conduct. Their beliefs were to be authenticated by their behavior.

Do you keep your word? Are you a person of integrity? Does your conversation line up with your conduct? Take personal inventory of your life to assess the health of your integrity.

- *"But the Lord said to Samuel, 'Do not look on his appearance or on the height of his stature, because I have rejected him. For the Lord sees not as man sees: man looks on the outward appearance, but the Lord looks on the heart.'" 1 Sam 16:7 (ESV)*

Invite God to search your heart and to unveil anything in your heart that does not bring Him honor. Ask God to reveal any fraction of compromise or deception resident in your life. Be a person of integrity. Keep your word!

~ Stephen

March 8

Yes Lord

Chronological Bible Reading Plan: (Day 67: Numbers 31-32)

"And the people of Gad and the people of Reuben answered, 'What the Lord has said to your servants, we will do. We will pass over armed before the Lord into the land of Canaan, and the possession of our inheritance shall remain with us beyond the Jordan.'" Numbers 32:31-32 (ESV)

When you surrender to the Lordship of Christ, you are placing His agenda before your own. Lordship is a decision of stewardship. Stewardship is caring for what God has entrusted to you. Your devotion and commitment to Christ is demonstrated through the way you steward what God has entrusted to your care. Surrendering your life to the Lordship of Christ places Him in charge of your life and your decisions.

The people of Gad and the people of Reuben were willing to submit to what the Lord had said. They acknowledged that they were servants and their lives were marked by instant obedience. They were willing to do what the Lord said. Obedience to the Lord was not only valued, but also demonstrated by their actions.

- *"'Everyone then who hears these words of mine and does them will be like a wise man who built his house on the rock. And the rain fell, and the floods came, and the winds blew and beat on that house, but it did not fall, because it had been founded on the rock.'" Matt 7:24-25 (ESV)*
- *"But be doers of the word, and not hearers only, deceiving yourselves." James 1:22 (ESV)*

Start demonstrating the Lordship of Christ by being a hearer of God's Word. Consistently read and feed on God's Word. Grow in your understanding of the Bible. Move into becoming a doer of God's Word by putting God's Word into practice. Apply God's Word by practicing instant obedience. Live your life by perpetually saying, "Yes, Lord!"

~ Stephen

March 9

Journal Your Journey

Chronological Bible Reading Plan: (Day 68: Numbers 33-34)

"These are the stages of the people of Israel, when they went out of the land of Egypt by their companies under the leadership of Moses and Aaron. Moses wrote down their starting places, stage by stage, by command of the Lord, and these are their stages according to their starting places." Numbers 33:1-2 (ESV)

What if you begin to journal your journey with God? Whether you have been walking with God for a few months, a few years, or several decades, consider journaling your journey with God. There are two components to include. Write down the major spiritual markers in your life such as your conversion, baptism, and other major decisions the Lord guided you to make. Describe some of the moments in your walk with God when you encountered His Presence in a special way.

Another component to journaling your journey with God is the daily discipline of writing about the overflow of your time alone with God. For example, as you have your daily quiet time, write down a verse from your Bible that God used to speak to you that particular morning. Make some general observations about that verse and then write down a specific application that you sense God wants you to incorporate into your life. You may choose to even write down your prayer. This daily discipline will help you focus and it will give you a permanent record of your journey with God.

Moses wrote down the specific stages of the journey he was on with the people of Israel. He specifically identified their starting places. The consistent theme was, "They set out from..." Moses was intentional about recording their journey with God and we are benefiting now from what Moses wrote down then. Who may benefit from your journaled journey one day?

~ *Stephen*

March 10

Finding Refuge

Chronological Bible Reading Plan: (Day 69: Numbers 35-36)

"And the Lord spoke to Moses, saying, 'Speak to the people of Israel and say to them, When you cross the Jordan into the land of Canaan, then you shall select cities to be cities of refuge for you, that the manslayer who kills any person without intent may flee there. The cities shall be for you a refuge from the avenger, that the manslayer may not die until he stands before the congregation for judgment.'" Numbers 35:9-12 (ESV)

God featured His mercy and grace as He established the cities of refuge for the person who accidentally killed another person. God was providing protection from the avenger. When you consider the large number of people Moses was leading and when you consider the challenges of mobilizing around two-million people, the probability of conflict is rather high. Doing life together as a covenant community generated some major challenges and opportunities.

The cities of refuge were strategically placed and graciously established. God was demonstrating His nature and character through His tangible redemptive activity. Moses was charged with carrying out the plan of God and ensuring the protection of the person who accidentally killed another.

As followers of Jesus Christ, we look to God as our refuge and strength. He is the Creator of life and He is the sustainer of life. We look to Him because He is our faithful Shepherd and our consistent provider. As God's children adopted into His family, we have the privilege of casting all of our cares on Him and receiving mercy and grace to help us daily as we serve Him.

Are you in need of refuge? Instead of running from God, choose to run to God. God already knows your condition and He already has everything you need to live the abundant life He has for you in Christ. Find refuge in Him!

~ *Stephen*

March 11

Trace Your Tracks

Chronological Bible Reading Plan: (Day 70: Deuteronomy 1-2)

"These are the words that Moses spoke to all Israel beyond the Jordan in the wilderness, in the Arabah opposite Suph, between Paran and Tophel, Laban, Hazeroth, and Dizahab." Deuteronomy 1:1 (ESV)

Moses presents a series of strong sermons to a wandering people. Impressing God's Word on their hearts, Moses preaches the Law to the people of Israel. Moses reiterates the covenant community expectations as prescribed by God and reminds the people of Israel of God's faithfulness.

In the New Testament account of Stephen's speech to the Sanhedrin, we find a bold reference to the disobedience of the people of Israel. "Our fathers refused to obey him, but thrust him aside, and in their hearts they turned to Egypt, saying to Aaron, 'Make for us gods who will go before us. As for this Moses who led us out from the land of Egypt, we do not know what has become of him'" (Acts 7:39-40 ESV). Waves of obedience were followed by waves of disobedience.

In Deuteronomy, Moses traces the tracks of the wilderness wanderings and the inconsistency of the people of Israel. As Moses speaks forth the series of messages to the people, strong themes of obedience, disobedience, brokenness, and repentance arise. Through the ebb and flow of the people of Israel's response to God's activity, God remained faithful.

Trace your tracks. Where have you been and where are you going? Has God been true to His Word? Can you trace the faithfulness of God throughout your life? God invites you into His story. You are His masterpiece and His instrument of reconciling the world to Himself through Christ. Will you rest in God's faithfulness and trust in God's abundant provision?

~ *Stephen*

March 12

No Other God

Chronological Bible Reading Plan: (Day 71: Deuteronomy 3-4)

"Know therefore today, and lay it to your heart, that the Lord is God in heaven above and on the earth beneath; there is no other. Therefore you shall keep his statutes and his commandments, which I command you today, that it may go well with you and with your children after you, and that you may prolong your days in the land that the Lord your God is giving you for all time."
Deuteronomy 4:39-40 (ESV)

As I am writing this devotional, my team and I are about to board our plane to return to America after spending a week serving the people of East Asia. If you have ever had the opportunity to fly on a commercial jet, you will recall the unique perspective you gain by looking through the widow of the plane down to the earth below. You begin to realize how small you are and how big the earth is. Your daily pressures and the basic anxieties of life are suspended for the duration of your flight.

You don't have to board a plane and ascend to an altitude of 37,000 feet in order to gain a new perspective on life. Simply acknowledge and take to heart that the Lord is God. He is God of heaven and He is God of earth. He created the entire universe and He created you. There is no other God. He is the One true living God who rules and reigns. All other gods are simply gods. We serve the God of all creation.

One way to demonstrate your acknowledgement of God is by obeying His commands. God reveals Himself to you so that you can know Him personally and intimately. God reveals His Word to you so that you can obey Him immediately and consistently. Your obedience to God's Word is a true mark of spiritual maturity and an indication of your new identity in Christ.

~ *Stephen*

March 13

Love Your God

Chronological Bible Reading Plan: (Day 72: Deuteronomy 5-7)

"'Hear, O Israel: The Lord our God, the Lord is one. You shall love the Lord your God with all your heart and with all your soul and with all your might.'" Deuteronomy 6:4-5 (ESV)

What's love got to do with it? Everything! Your love will be directed to the object of your affection and to that which you treasure. Who or what are you loving? Does anyone or anything have prominence in your life? The Lord is your God. The Lord is one. He thought of you before you could think of Him. God designed you to be uniquely you and to fulfill a unique purpose in this life that only you can fill.

Will you love the Lord your God with all your heart? God deserves your utmost devotion. God is worthy of your affection and full attention. When you allow your loyalty to God and your love for God to erode, you experience mission drift. When you dilute your passion for the Lord, you misappropriate the relationship you are privileged to have with the Lord your God. Give God your very best and demonstrate His value in your life. Recognize where you would be without Him and enthrone Him through moment-by-moment surrender.

- *"Know therefore that the Lord your God is God, the faithful God who keeps covenant and steadfast love with those who love him and keep his commandments, to a thousand generations." Deuteronomy 7:9 (ESV)*

The safest place for you to be is in the center of God's will. It is clearly God's will for you to love Him with all your heart and with all your soul and with all your might. What adjustments do you need to make in order to love your God that way?

~ Stephen

March 14

WALK IN HIS WAYS

Chronological Bible Reading Plan: (Day 73: Deuteronomy 8-10)

"Know then in your heart that, as a man disciplines his son, the Lord your God disciplines you. So you shall keep the commandments of the Lord your God by walking in his ways and by fearing him." Deuteronomy 8:5-6 (ESV)

God has already established your value by sacrificing His only Son on the cross for you. His redemptive act made salvation available to you and the removal of your sin possible. Now that you are a recipient of God's unconditional love, you are a new creation and filled with the Holy Spirit. God has demonstrated His love for you through the atoning work of Christ on the cross.

God continues to demonstrate His love for you through dispensing discipline. God disciplines you because He loves you and is committed to conforming you into the image of Christ. As you learn to walk in His ways and to fear Him, God's discipline will be featured less and less in your life.

- *"For they disciplined us for a short time as it seemed best to them, but he disciplines us for our good, that we may share his holiness. For the moment all discipline seems painful rather than pleasant, but later it yields the peaceful fruit of righteousness to those who have been trained by it." Hebrews 12:10-11 (ESV)*

What area of your life is in need of God's disciplinary activity? Knowing that God disciplines you for your good so that you may share in His holiness, consider the peaceful fruit of righteousness that has become evident in your life. Continue to keep His commandments by walking in His ways and by fearing Him. You are in the process of becoming who you are in Christ. God is building you into the person He has created you to be for His glory.

~ *Stephen*

March 15

Obedience and Blessing

Chronological Bible Reading Plan: (Day 74: Deuteronomy 11-13)

"'See, I am setting before you today a blessing and a curse: the blessing, if you obey the commandments of the Lord your God, which I command you today, and the curse, if you do not obey the commandments of the Lord your God, but turn aside from the way that I am commanding you today, to go after other gods that you have not known.'" Deuteronomy 11:26-28 (ESV)

Life generates endless choices to make and countless paths to take. Some choices bring forth blessing while some choices bring forth curse and negative consequences. Some paths lead to blessing while some paths lead to devastation. You can become overwhelmed with the number of opportunities placed before you in this life. Your decisions determine your direction and ultimately your destination.

God set before the people of Israel a blessing and a curse. Obedience generated the blessing whereas disobedience generated the curse. God warned the people of turning aside from His way in order to go after other gods. Idolatry would produce devastating consequences.

Walking with God and making wise decisions is an act of worship and a mark of spiritual maturity. Your obedience to God is a tangible demonstration of your love for Him.

- *"Jesus answered him, 'If anyone loves me, he will keep my word, and my Father will love him, and we will come to him and make our home with him.'" John 14:23 (ESV)*

Choose the blessing. Surrender to the Lordship of Christ and take paths that are firm. Allow Jesus to guard your heart and to guide your steps. He will illuminate the path that brings blessing. Obey His voice and you will be making the right choice.

~ *Stephen*

March 16

Blessed to Bless

Chronological Bible Reading Plan: (Day 75: Deuteronomy 14-16)

"'If among you, one of your brothers should become poor, in any of your towns within your land that the Lord your God is giving you, you shall not harden your heart or shut your hand against your poor brother, but you shall open your hand to him and lend him sufficient for his need, whatever it may be.'" Deuteronomy 15:7-8 (ESV)

God has blessed you to be a blessing. God has lavished you with His love so that you can lavish His love on others. You have been given spiritual treasures to share with those in need. You have been endowed by God to become a conduit of His compassion.

Be generous. Diligently seek to meet needs as God places people in your path. Turn interruptions into opportunities to be a blessing to others. As you give, God's love will be dispensed. As you give, God's grace will be extended.

- *"Whoever oppresses a poor man insults his Maker, but he who is generous to the needy honors him." Prov. 14:31 (ESV)*

Honor God by being generous to the needy. Place the needs of others before your own. Of course, that is not a natural response; it is a supernatural response made possible by the Holy Spirit living in you. You have been enriched by God so that you can be generous in every way. As you generously bless others, you will be producing thanksgiving to God. In other words, by being generous toward others, you will be giving thanks to God who has blessed you with the ability to be a blessing.

Jesus is the gateway of generosity. He gave His live to you so that you can give your life to others.

~ *Stephen*

March 17

God Fights For You

Chronological Bible Reading Plan: (Day 76: Deuteronomy 17-20)

"And when you draw near to the battle, the priest shall come forward and speak to the people and shall say to them, 'Hear, O Israel, today you are drawing near for battle against your enemies: let not your heart faint. Do not fear or panic or be in dread of them, for the Lord your God is he who goes with you to fight for you against your enemies, to give you the victory.'" Deuteronomy 20:2-4 (ESV)

God gave the people of Israel tremendous favor as they obeyed His commands. He promised them victory as they drew near in battle against their enemies. There was no need to be in fear or to panic or to be in dread because God would go with them and fight for them against their enemies to ensure victory.

The battles we face as followers of Jesus Christ are spiritual in nature. We combat the devil, the world, and the flesh. The devil has an agenda that opposes God's will. The world has a current that flows counter to God's way. The flesh has an appetite that seeks to divert our devotion to God and to pollute our passion for the things of God.

- *"For we do not wrestle against flesh and blood, but against the rulers, against the authorities, against the cosmic powers over this present darkness, against the spiritual forces of evil in the heavenly places." Ephesians 6:12 (ESV)*
- *"But thanks be to God, who gives us the victory through our Lord Jesus Christ." 1 Corinthians 15:57 (ESV)*

As you draw near to battle today, put on the full armor of God. Live in the power of the Holy Spirit and claim the victory that Jesus won when He died sacrificially and rose from the dead supernaturally.

~ Stephen

March 18

Reverse the Curse

Chronological Bible Reading Plan: (Day 77: Deuteronomy 21-23)

"'And if a man has committed a crime punishable by death and he is put to death, and you hang him on a tree, his body shall not remain all night on the tree, but you shall bury him the same day, for a hanged man is cursed by God. You shall not defile your land that the Lord your God is giving you for an inheritance.'" Deuteronomy 21:22-23 (ESV)

God values holiness. His laws were established for the people of Israel to keep them from defiling their lives and to keep them from defiling the land He was giving them for an inheritance. God was protecting their covenant community and preserving their future. Consequences for sinful actions were enforced to ensure unity and solidarity.

- *"Christ redeemed us from the curse of the law by becoming a curse for us—for it is written, 'Cursed is everyone who is hanged on a tree'— so that in Christ Jesus the blessing of Abraham might come to the Gentiles, so that we might receive the promised Spirit through faith." Galatians 3:13-14 (ESV)*

In our own effort, we do not have the capacity to generate the holiness that God demands and that God deserves. We fall short and do not measure up to God's standard of righteousness. The Good News is that Jesus was willing to reverse the curse that our sin caused. Jesus was willing to become a curse for us by taking on our sin and by receiving the full wrath of God for our sin. Jesus paid our sin debt in full and enabled us to receive His imputed righteousness.

In Christ, you have a new identity. Your past has been forgiven. Your eternal security has been established. Now you can join God in His redemptive activity so that others can benefit from the reverse of the curse.

~ *Stephen*

March 19

Don't Forget

Chronological Bible Reading Plan: (Day 78: Deuteronomy 24-27)

"When you gather the grapes of your vineyard, you shall not strip it afterward. It shall be for the sojourner, the fatherless, and the widow. You shall remember that you were a slave in the land of Egypt; therefore I command you to do this." Deuteronomy 24:21-22 (ESV)

Take pride for a ride by spending some time reflecting on your condition before your conversion. Do you remember what it was like being lost? Can you recall the darkness that enveloped your soul as an unbeliever? You were hell bound and in bondage to the clutches of the enemy. You were alienated from God and separated from the favor of God.

- *"And you were dead in the trespasses and sins in which you once walked, following the course of this world, following the prince of the power of the air, the spirit that is now at work in the sons of disobedience—among whom we all once lived in the passions of our flesh, carrying out the desires of the body and the mind, and were by nature children of wrath, like the rest of mankind." Eph. 2:1-3 (ESV)*

In His mercy, God came to rescue you from your sin. Putting His compassion into action, God redeemed you from your sin and delivered you from the kingdom of darkness and placed you in the kingdom of light. The divine transaction was initiated by God and demonstrated His unconditional love for you.

Be generous to others just as God has been generous to you. Humble yourself by remembering your former condition and recognizing where you would be without God's gracious intervention. Place the needs of others before your own. Seize opportunities to show Christ's love to those He places in your path today.

~ Stephen

March 20

God's Favor

Chronological Bible Reading Plan: (Day 79: Deuteronomy 28-29)

"And the Lord will make you the head and not the tail, and you shall only go up and not down, if you obey the commandments of the Lord your God, which I command you today, being careful to do them, and if you do not turn aside from any of the words that I command you today, to the right hand or to the left, to go after other gods to serve them." Deuteronomy 28:13-14 (ESV)

Moses reminded the people of Israel of God's blessings and favor related to their obedience to God's commandments and laws. God blesses obedience and punishes disobedience. God's favor is unleashed when God's people obey. The demonstration of God's blessing was personally experienced as the people of Israel wandered in the wilderness. God provided them with manna from heaven in the morning, quail in the evening, and allowed them to drink water from the rock. God had delivered them from the threat of the Egyptian army and miraculously allowed them to cross through the Red Sea on dry ground. God's favor was upon them.

God's favor is upon you as you walk in His ways. Caring for the needs of others and living a life of generosity brings forth God's favor. Keeping yourself from being polluted by the world is another act of obedience that God blesses.

- *"Religion that is pure and undefiled before God, the Father, is this: to visit orphans and widows in their affliction, and to keep oneself unstained from the world." Jas. 1:27 (ESV)*

Eliminating idolatry and living a life of moral purity paves the way for God's favor to be evidenced in your life. God blesses you as you obey Him.

~ *Stephen*

March 21

No Need to Fear

Chronological Bible Reading Plan: (Day 80: Deuteronomy 30-31)

"Then Moses summoned Joshua and said to him in the sight of all Israel, 'Be strong and courageous, for you shall go with this people into the land that the Lord has sworn to their fathers to give them, and you shall put them in possession of it. It is the Lord who goes before you. He will be with you; he will not leave you or forsake you. Do not fear or be dismayed.'" Deuteronomy 31:7-8 (ESV)

Have you ever felt inadequate or insufficient for a task? Joshua experienced a defining moment as his mentor, Moses, handed off the mantle of leadership and transferred the baton of responsibility. In the sight of all Israel, Moses commissioned Joshua as the one who would lead the people of Israel into the land of Promise. Joshua would lead the charge to possess the land flowing with milk and honey.

Moses imparted words of comfort to his protégé, Joshua. Not only did Moses affirm possession of the land, but he also affirmed God's provision. Moses clarified to Joshua that the Lord would go before him. He assured Joshua that the Lord would be with him and would not leave him or forsake him. There was no need to fear. There was no need to be dismayed.

God always provides you with everything you need to accomplish His will. If you are facing a God-sized assignment, you can rest in God's sufficiency to equip you with everything you need to fulfill His assignment. If you are walking in the unknown and the uncertain, you can know God's provision and you can be certain of God's abundant supply. Wherever God guides, He always provides.

~ *Stephen*

March 22

Twelve Decades

Chronological Bible Reading Plan: (Day 81: Deuteronomy 32-34)

"And there has not arisen a prophet since in Israel like Moses, whom the Lord knew face to face, none like him for all the signs and the wonders that the Lord sent him to do in the land of Egypt, to Pharaoh and to all his servants and to all his land, and for all the mighty power and all the great deeds of terror that Moses did in the sight of all Israel." Deuteronomy 34:10-12 (ESV)

Moses spent twelve decades on the earth. He experienced forty years in the palace, forty years in the desert, and forty years in the wilderness. "By faith Moses, when he was grown up, refused to be called the son of Pharaoh's daughter, choosing rather to be mistreated with the people of God than to enjoy the fleeting pleasures of sin" (Heb. 11:24-25 ESV). There was none like him.

The miracles God did through Moses are extraordinary. Recall the burning bush, Moses' staff turning into a snake and then into a staff again, and Moses' hand becoming leprous and back to normal. Recount the ten plagues of Egypt, the passover, and the magnificent crossing of the Red Sea on dry ground. Consider the manna from heaven, the quail in the evening, water from the rock, and the Ten Commandments. Moses was sent by God to do all these signs and wonders to deliver the people of Israel out of Egyptian bondage.

The message of Moses' life is the faithfulness of God. Moses knew the Lord face to face. Moses even got a glimpse of the glory of God. Let Moses' life be a reminder to you that you can trust God. God keeps His Word. God loves you and God is for you. God will use you for His glory to accomplish His will on the earth.

~ *Stephen*

March 23

Cross This Jordan

Chronological Bible Reading Plan: (Day 82: Joshua 1-4)

"And when the priests bearing the ark of the covenant of the Lord came up from the midst of the Jordan, and the soles of the priests' feet were lifted up on dry ground, the waters of the Jordan returned to their place and overflowed all its banks, as before." Joshua 4:18 (ESV)

Crossing the Jordan River on dry ground was a tremendous experience of faith for the priests carrying the ark. They remained in the middle of the river while the children of Israel passed through on dry ground. Once the priests came up out of the river carrying the ark of the covenant, the waters of the Jordan returned to their place. God had worked a miracle and involved the people in the process!

The Christian life is a life of faith. To be a fully devoted follower of Christ, your life will be marked by a journey of faith. Faith is taking God at His Word and entrusting your life to His care. As you walk in daily dependency upon the Lord, you will discover the joy of seeing God at work and seizing opportunities to join God in His activity.

Continue to walk in faith. Sometimes your journey will be as clear as crystal, but at other times the way may appear foggy. You will experience seasons of high spiritual energy and focus and at other times, you will experience seasons of uncertainty. That's part of the faith journey! The scenery changes and the pace shifts from time to time.

Don't get so fixated on the destination that you miss the God-moments along the way. Enjoy the process of knowing and obeying God. Enjoy the journey. God has some Jordan Rivers for you to cross. He will turn your obstacles into opportunities for you to see His glory and for your faith to be exercised. Obey what you know!

~ *Stephen*

March 24
Remove Devoted Things

Chronological Bible Reading Plan: (Day 83: Joshua 5-8)

"The Lord said to Joshua, 'Get up! Why have you fallen on your face? Israel has sinned; they have transgressed my covenant that I commanded them; they have taken some of the devoted things; they have stolen and lied and put them among their own belongings. Therefore the people of Israel cannot stand before their enemies. They turn their backs before their enemies, because they have become devoted for destruction. I will be with you no more, unless you destroy the devoted things from among you.'" Joshua 7:10-12 (ESV)

Idolatry is a word we seldom use. Whenever you allow someone or something to take the place of God in your life, you commit the sin of idolatry. The first and second of the Ten Commandments speak to this concept directly (Exod. 20:3-4). Whatever or whomever becomes the object of your worship becomes your idol.

Jesus infuses this earthly tendency of ours into His teaching on becoming a disciple. To become a follower of Jesus Christ, you must be willing to remove the idols in your life. Your loyalty to Christ is to be unmatched and undivided. Jesus becomes your focus and the object of your worship, devotion, and loyalty.

Your love, loyalty, and devotion to Jesus is to be your top priority and the expressed passion of your life. Don't allow anything or anyone to compete for that place in your life. Don't allow anything or anyone to rob your allegiance to the One who gave His life for you. Jesus has already demonstrated His selfless and sacrificial love. Now, it's your turn to demonstrate your selfless and sacrificial love for Jesus. Remove devoted things. Remove anything that seeks to be enthroned in your life.

~ *Stephen*

March 25

AND THE LORD THREW

Chronological Bible Reading Plan: (Day 84: Joshua 9-11)

"And the Lord threw them into a panic before Israel, who struck them with a great blow at Gibeon and chased them by the way of the ascent of Beth-horon and struck them as far as Azekah and Makkedah. And as they fled before Israel, while they were going down the ascent of Beth-horon, the Lord threw down large stones from heaven on them as far as Azekah, and they died. There were more who died because of the hailstones than the sons of Israel killed with the sword." Joshua 10:10-11 (ESV)

Joshua's life was marked by conquest and depending on God's provision. Joshua courageously pursued his enemies as prompted by God and learned the value of taking God at His Word. In his battle at Gibeon, Joshua mobilized the men of war and engaged in strategic warfare. As Joshua obeyed God, the Lord threw his enemies into a panic. As they fled before Israel, the Lord threw large stones from heaven on them and they died. More died because of the hailstones than from the sword.

Living in a fallen world mandates preparation for spiritual warfare. We are to anticipate opposition to God's will and prepare for spiritual attack. We are in a battle to fulfill the Great Commission as we live out the Great Commandment.

- *"Finally, be strong in the Lord and in the strength of his might. Put on the whole armor of God, that you may be able to stand against the schemes of the devil." Eph. 6:10-11 (ESV)*

Find your strength in the Lord. Put on the full armor of God and prepare for battle. You are covered by God's sufficiency and He will fight your battles for you as you obey His prompting. God will enable you to stand against the schemes of the devil.

~ Stephen

March 26

WHOLLY FOLLOWED THE LORD

Chronological Bible Reading Plan: (Day 85: Joshua 12-15)

"Therefore Hebron became the inheritance of Caleb the son of Jephunneh the Kenizzite to this day, because he wholly followed the Lord, the God of Israel." Joshua 14:14 (ESV)

If someone were to shadow you for forty days, what would that person experience firsthand? Would that person be drawn to Christ or repelled? Would that person be encouraged in their faith or discouraged?

Joshua and Caleb had shadowed each other for forty-five years? They both had the privilege of shadowing Moses. They both were selected to spy out the land that flowed with milk and honey. They both returned with a positive report in spite of the negative report given by the other ten spies.

In this immediate text, Caleb is eighty-five years old and reflecting on his journey. It is now time for him to receive his allotted portion of the Promised Land. He was given Hebron as an inheritance because he wholly followed the Lord.

Would someone shadowing you say that you wholly follow the Lord? Would your walk with God give evidence to full devotion and complete commitment? Take a few moments to examine your life both internally and externally. Take inventory of your journey with God and try to assess your level of commitment over the years. Be honest about your current reality. Are you wholly following the Lord?

Let Caleb's life inspire you to a greater level of commitment to the Lord. Make it obvious to others that you are growing in your love relationship with Jesus. Share about your intimacy with the Lord. Commit to take your prayer life to a new level of intimacy and intentionality. Share your faith with those who do not have a personal relationship with the Lord. Wholly follow the Lord!

~ *Stephen*

March 27

Made to Worship

Chronological Bible Reading Plan: (Day 86: Joshua 16-18)

"Then the whole congregation of the people of Israel assembled at Shiloh and set up the tent of meeting there. The land lay subdued before them."
Joshua 18:1 (ESV)

You were created to worship. God has given you the freedom to choose your object of worship. You can choose to worship creation or you can choose to worship the Creator. God's will is for you to worship Him as your Creator. The enemy will tempt you to worship yourself, other people, or other things to divert your devotion from God.

- *"Again, the devil took him to a very high mountain and showed him all the kingdoms of the world and their glory. And he said to him, 'All these I will give you, if you will fall down and worship me.' Then Jesus said to him, 'Be gone, Satan! For it is written, You shall worship the Lord your God and him only shall you serve.'" Matt. 4:8-10 (ESV)*

The people of Israel methodically received their allotment of land. As you can imagine, the process was lengthy and thorough. The entire congregation of the people of Israel gathered at Shiloh to set up the tent of meeting. The priority of worship was guarded and the activity of worship was perpetual. The land lay subdued before them as they worshiped the One True Living God!

How will you respond to the temptation to bypass God in worship? Will you do what Jesus did? Stand firm in your resolve to worship the Lord your God and serve Him with passion and diligence. Establish the priority of worship in your daily routine and surrender to the Lordship of Christ. Make Jesus your number one priority as you unleash your worship to revere the One who died to set you free.

~ Stephen

March 28

Promises of God

Chronological Bible Reading Plan: (Day 87: Joshua 19-21)

"Not one word of all the good promises that the Lord had made to the house of Israel had failed; all came to pass." Joshua 21:45 (ESV)

A promise is only as good as the character of the one making the promise. A person who keeps his or her promise is a person who is deemed trustworthy. Keeping your promise is equivalent to keeping your word. When a promise is not kept a person's character comes into question.

God's Word is rooted in God's nature and character. God is holy, righteous, and perfect. God cannot lie and God cannot do anything contrary to His nature and character. God keeps His Word because God is trustworthy. He keeps His promises!

The Lord demonstrated His faithfulness to the house of Israel. Everything God promised to them came to pass. God kept His Word! God delivered on His promises!

God has a plan for your life. He created you to include you in His story of redemption. God thought of you long before you could think of Him. God pursued you long before you had the capacity to respond to His pursuit. You are not an accident. You are God's idea and you are God's masterpiece. Your life matters to God and He established your worth by allowing His precious Son, Jesus, to die on the cross for you. He has paid your sin debt in full and purchased your salvation. In Christ, you have become a child of the King!

As a new creation, you have the wonderful privilege of being fathered by our Heaven Father who is the ultimate Promise Keeper. Your security is based on your new identity in Christ and rooted in the fertile soil of God's character. You can stand on the promises of God!

~ *Stephen*

March 29

Focused Passion

Chronological Bible Reading Plan: (Day 88: Joshua 22-24)

"'Now therefore fear the Lord and serve him in sincerity and in faithfulness. Put away the gods that your fathers served beyond the River and in Egypt, and serve the Lord. And if it is evil in your eyes to serve the Lord, choose this day whom you will serve, whether the gods your fathers served in the region beyond the River, or the gods of the Amorites in whose land you dwell. But as for me and my house, we will serve the Lord.'" Joshua 24:14-15 (ESV)

Joshua's passion for God was contagious. He was willing to take responsibility for the spiritual condition of his home. Joshua made a bold proclamation that as for he and his household, they would serve the Lord. He did not apologize for his passion to obey God. His loyalty to God was expressed through his passion for God. Joshua's passion to lead his family spiritually impacted the nation.

- *"He said, 'Then put away the foreign gods that are among you, and incline your heart to the Lord, the God of Israel.' And the people said to Joshua, 'The Lord our God we will serve, and his voice we will obey.'" Josh. 24:23-24 (ESV)*

It is interesting that Joshua did not ask the people to do anything he had not already done. Joshua put his passion in action by leading his family to revere and serve the Lord. Now the people could respond to his example and to his exhortation.

Are you putting your passion in action in such a way as to impact your family and those in your sphere of influence? Is your passion for God contagious or difficult to detect? Resolve to serve the Lord. Focus your passion on serving the Lord and continuing His ministry on the earth.

~ *Stephen*

March 30

YOUR FUNERAL

Chronological Bible Reading Plan: (Day 89: Judges 1-2)

"And Joshua the son of Nun, the servant of the Lord, died at the age of 110 years. And they buried him within the boundaries of his inheritance in Timnath-heres, in the hill country of Ephraim, north of the mountain of Gaash."
Judges 2:8-9 (ESV)

Some of the most meaning funerals I have ever preached have been those in which the children of the deceased person stand to speak about their parent's life. One day you will take your final breath on the earth and your funeral will be conducted. What should your children be able to say at your funeral?

Our parents taught us how to walk with God. If you want your children to walk with God, then model the value of intimacy with God. Let them see you having your daily quiet time. Share the overflow of what God is teaching you in your daily walk with Him. Place your children in environments that will help them develop their walk with God.

Our parents taught us how to love others. Validate the value God places on others. Show your children how to love others. Your children are watching you closely. They know if you genuinely love people. Another important step is to seize opportunities that will enable your children to serve others.

Our parents were still living by faith when they died. In order to leave a legacy you must live a legacy. Guard your priorities in order to finish strong. Keep your love relationship with Jesus your number one priority.

It's never too late to start leaving a legacy of faith for your children and grandchildren. What will they say at your funeral?

~ *Stephen*

March 31

DRIFTING FROM GOD

Chronological Bible Reading Plan: (Day 90: Judges 3-5)

"And the people of Israel did what was evil in the sight of the Lord. They forgot the Lord their God and served the Baals and the Asheroth." Judges 3:7 (ESV)

How quick they were to forget the Lord their God after all He had done to deliver them from Egyptian bondage! Sound familiar? The generation following Joshua's death was marked by disobedience. They drifted from the Lord.

- *"And all that generation also were gathered to their fathers. And there arose another generation after them who did not know the Lord or the work that he had done for Israel." Judg. 2:10 (ESV)*
- *"Therefore we must pay much closer attention to what we have heard, lest we drift away from it." Heb. 2:1 (ESV)*

We are made to worship. We will worship something or someone. Idolatry seeps in when devotion to the Lord shifts. An idol is anything that dilutes our passion for God or diverts our affection from God. Drifting from God is a perpetual reality for the child of God who neglects practicing instant obedience. We are to pay close attention to what we have received from the Lord and adhere to the principles of God's Word so that we can walk in alignment with God's purpose and plan.

Jesus left the glory of heaven to come to earth in order to provide the atoning sacrifice for our sin. Jesus was obedient to death on a cross. His passion was to fulfill God's will and to finish His work. The story of redemption is marked by the instant obedience that Jesus practiced throughout His life and ministry on earth.

Instead of drifting from God, decide to yield to the Lordship of Christ and be a follower of Christ who is wholly devoted to Him.

~ Stephen

April 1
GOD'S WAY TO VICTORY

Chronological Bible Reading Plan: (Day 91: Judges 6-7)

"The Lord said to Gideon, 'The people with you are too many for me to give the Midianites into their hand, lest Israel boast over me, saying, My own hand has saved me.'" Judges 7:2 (ESV)

Gideon considered his clan to be the weakest in Manasseh and himself the least of his father's house. He did not feel qualified to lead the charge to defeat the Midianites. God confirmed His will through a fire, a fleece, and a formula. Gideon prepared a sacrifice and God sent an angel of the Lord. "Then the angel of the Lord reached out the tip of the staff that was in his hand and touched the meat and the unleavened cakes. And fire sprang up from the rock and consumed the meat and the unleavened cakes" (Judg. 6:21 ESV).

Gideon asked for additional clarification by asking God to fill a wool fleece with dew while keeping all the ground dry. God performed the miracle and Gideon wrung enough dew from the fleece to fill a bowl with water. The fleece was used again to test the validity of God's will. This time, Gideon asked God to let the fleece remain dry while allowing there to be dew on all the ground. God performed that miracle.

The formula God chose for Gideon demonstrated God's power in the midst of Gideon's weaknesses. The formula involved reducing Gideon's army from 32,000 to 300. Gideon and his army of 300 won the victory!

God's way to victory does not always line up with our logical thought process. In our humanity, we tend to judge our circumstances from our limited point of view. God's ways are higher than our ways (Isa. 55:9).

The victory over our sin, our death, and our dilemma was won God's way through the death, burial, and resurrection of Jesus!

~ *Stephen*

April 2

TUG OF REBELLION

Chronological Bible Reading Plan: (Day 92: Judges 8-9)

"As soon as Gideon died, the people of Israel turned again and whored after the Baals and made Baal-berith their god. And the people of Israel did not remember the Lord their God, who had delivered them from the hand of all their enemies on every side, and they did not show steadfast love to the family of Jerubbaal (that is, Gideon) in return for all the good that he had done to Israel."
Judges 8:33-35 (ESV)

When you trace the journey of the people of Israel, you will notice a pattern of obedience, rebellion, discipline, and repentance. God blesses obedience and God disciplines disobedience. The people of Israel would obey God for a season and then allow the tug of rebellion to captivate their attention. Instead of worshiping the Lord their God, they would digress into idolatry.

As a follower of Jesus Christ, the Apostle Paul identified the tug of rebellion that originated in his sinful nature. Even though he was born again and filled with the Holy Spirit, Paul had to perpetually combat the cravings of the sin nature.

- *"For I know that nothing good dwells in me, that is, in my flesh. For I have the desire to do what is right, but not the ability to carry it out. For I do not do the good I want, but the evil I do not want is what I keep on doing. Now if I do what I do not want, it is no longer I who do it, but sin that dwells within me." Rom. 7:18-20 (ESV)*

How do you triumph over the tug of rebellion? Walk in full surrender to the Lordship of Christ. Acknowledge your total dependency upon the Lord to empower you to live in victory. Run from sin and run to Jesus as you practice instant obedience.

~ Stephen

April 3

Continual Realities

Chronological Bible Reading Plan: (Day 93: Judges 10-12)

"And the Lord said to the people of Israel, 'Did I not save you from the Egyptians and from the Amorites, from the Ammonites and from the Philistines? The Sidonians also, and the Amalekites and the Maonites oppressed you, and you cried out to me, and I saved you out of their hand. Yet you have forsaken me and served other gods; therefore I will save you no more. Go and cry out to the gods whom you have chosen; let them save you in the time of your distress.'"
Judges 10:11-14 (ESV)

God delivered some strong words to the people of Israel after their willful disobedience in spite of God's perpetual gracious treatment. God rescued them and delivered them from their oppressors. They still chose to forsake God and served other gods.

As a result of their incessant rebellion, God told the people of Israel to go and cry out to the gods whom they had chosen. God encouraged them to let their gods save them in their time of distress. Of course, their gods would not respond.

The propensity to sin is a common thread throughout human history. Living in a fallen world and combating the sinful nature are continual realities. To live in victory requires forsaking sin and following Christ.

- *"But put on the Lord Jesus Christ, and make no provision for the flesh, to gratify its desires." Rom. 13:14 (ESV)*
- *"So flee youthful passions and pursue righteousness, faith, love, and peace, along with those who call on the Lord from a pure heart." 2 Tim. 2:22 (ESV)*

Your flesh craves sin. Crucify the flesh by starving the flesh. Be robed in the righteousness of Christ and walk in the power of His resurrection. Make no provision for the flesh.

~ *Stephen*

April 4

Birth of a Blessing

Chronological Bible Reading Plan: (Day 94: Judges 13-15)

"And the angel of the Lord appeared to the woman and said to her, 'Behold, you are barren and have not borne children, but you shall conceive and bear a son. Therefore be careful and drink no wine or strong drink, and eat nothing unclean, for behold, you shall conceive and bear a son. No razor shall come upon his head, for the child shall be a Nazirite to God from the womb, and he shall begin to save Israel from the hand of the Philistines.'" Judges 13:3-5 (ESV)

God performed a miracle by enabling Manoah and his barren wife to have a son, Samson. To their amazement and delight, Samson grew and the Lord blessed him. He was set apart as a Nazirite to God and positioned by God to save Israel from the hand of the Philistines.

Eventually Samson married a daughter of the Philistines at Timnah. This was part of God's plan since the Philistines ruled over Israel. Samson was deceived by his father-in-law and sought revenge by setting fire to the stacked grain and standing grain as well as the olive orchards. In his rage, Samson struck down 1,000 men with the jawbone of a donkey.

- *"And he was very thirsty, and he called upon the Lord and said, 'You have granted this great salvation by the hand of your servant, and shall I now die of thirst and fall into the hands of the uncircumcised?' And God split open the hollow place that is at Lehi, and water came out from it. And when he drank, his spirit returned, and he revived. Therefore the name of it was called En-hakkore; it is at Lehi to this day. And he judged Israel in the days of the Philistines twenty years." Judg. 15:18-20 (ESV)*

God supernaturally provided for Samson throughout his life and He will provide for you. Entrust your life to His care.

~ Stephen

April 5
Energy Allocation

Chronological Bible Reading Plan: (Day 95: Judges 16-18)

"Then Samson called to the Lord and said, 'O Lord God, please remember me and please strengthen me only this once, O God, that I may be avenged on the Philistines for my two eyes.' And Samson grasped the two middle pillars on which the house rested, and he leaned his weight against them, his right hand on the one and his left hand on the other. And Samson said, 'Let me die with the Philistines.' Then he bowed with all his strength, and the house fell upon the lords and upon all the people who were in it. So the dead whom he killed at his death were more than those whom he had killed during his life." Judges 16:28-30 (ESV)

What are you doing with the life God has given you? Have you established your priorities and do they reflect God's priorities? You were created to make a difference in the world for God's glory. It is not about what you can do for God, but what God wants to do in you and through you to accomplish His purposes and His plan.

Priorities and stewardship go hand-in-hand. Your priorities will determine how you stewardship your energy and influence. You must determine how you will allocate the energy and influence God has given you. How will you invest your life to make an eternal difference?

Samson was blessed by God to be a blessing and to rescue his people from the Philistines. Samson drifted from God and was corrupted by lust and trapped by the seduction of Delilah. However, God granted Samson's final request to be strengthened so he could be avenged on the Philistines for his two eyes.

What would have been different about Samson's life had he wisely allocated his energy and influence for God's glory? What about your life? How are you allocating your energy and influence?

~ *Stephen*

April 6

Lordship and Leadership

Chronological Bible Reading Plan: (Day 96: Judges 19-21)

"In those days there was no king in Israel. Everyone did what was right in his own eyes." Judges 21:25 (ESV)

Chaos saturated the people of Israel as each chose to do what was right in his own eyes. The sense of covenant community was fragmented and the evidence of unity was shattered. Without a king in Israel, the cultural current of immorality intensified.

What is your moral compass? Where do you look to gain clarity on what brings honor to God? How do you know what you are supposed to be giving your life to?

- *"Your word is a lamp to my feet and a light to my path."*
  Ps. 119:105 (ESV)
- *"When the Spirit of truth comes, he will guide you into all the truth, for he will not speak on his own authority, but whatever he hears he will speak, and he will declare to you the things that are to come."*
  John 16:13 (ESV)

You are blessed with access to God's revelation through His Word. How may Bibles do you have? The Bible is the owner's manual for your life. As you read and feed on the Bible, God will illuminate the path He wants you to take.

The Holy Spirit lives in you to guide you into all truth. He lives in you to intercede for you and to empower you to decipher truth from falsehood. As you walk in the truth revealed to you by the Holy Spirit, you will learn to surrender to the Lordship of Christ and you will learn to submit to His leadership.

~ *Stephen*

April 7

Restorer of Life

Chronological Bible Reading Plan: (Day 97: Ruth)

"Then the women said to Naomi, 'Blessed be the Lord, who has not left you this day without a redeemer, and may his name be renowned in Israel! He shall be to you a restorer of life and a nourisher of your old age, for your daughter-in-law who loves you, who is more to you than seven sons, has given birth to him.'" Ruth 4:14-15 (ESV)

The story of Ruth is filled with God's grace. Ruth became a widow after her mother-in-law had already become a widow. Instead of leaving Naomi to start a new life, Ruth chose to stay with her. Her loyalty and devotion to Naomi were demonstrated consistently.

- *"But Ruth said, 'Do not urge me to leave you or to return from following you. For where you go I will go, and where you lodge I will lodge. Your people shall be my people, and your God my God.'" Ruth 1:16 (ESV)*
- *"So Boaz took Ruth, and she became his wife. And he went in to her, and the Lord gave her conception, and she bore a son." Ruth 4:13 (ESV)*

God provided a kinsmen redeemer. The portrait of God's grace continues in the first chapter of Matthew in the genealogy of Jesus where Ruth is named.

When you examine your story, you should be able to detect God's grace. Consider how Jesus redeemed you and delivered you from the kingdom of darkness and placed you in the kingdom of light. Measure the grace God lavished on you to adopt you into His family and to fill you with His Spirit. You are a child of the living God! You are the apple of His eye and the masterpiece of His marvelous ministry of grace.

~ *Stephen*

April 8
TRUST GOD

Chronological Bible Reading Plan: (Day 98: 1 Samuel 1-3)

"As she continued praying before the Lord, Eli observed her mouth. Hannah was speaking in her heart; only her lips moved, and her voice was not heard. Therefore Eli took her to be a drunken woman. And Eli said to her, 'How long will you go on being drunk? Put your wine away from you.'" 1 Samuel 1:12-14 (ESV)

When you are hurting, your emotions will be expressed through anger, suppression, depression, or grief. At some point, your hurt will manifest. For Hannah, her pain was being expressed through heartfelt prayer. She was unveiling her broken heart before the Lord. Hannah was barren. Eli misinterpreted her pain as that of being drunk. That was far from the truth of Hannah's condition. She wasn't drunk. She was devastated with the reality of her circumstances. Can you relate?

- *"But Hannah answered, 'No, my lord, I am a woman troubled in spirit. I have drunk neither wine nor strong drink, but I have been pouring out my soul before the Lord. Do not regard your servant as a worthless woman, for all along I have been speaking out of my great anxiety and vexation.'" 1 Sam. 1:15-16 (ESV)*

God knows what you are feeling right now. God knows where you are and where you are headed. Nothing catches God by surprise. Maybe you are experiencing a delay that just doesn't make sense to you. Know that God has a purpose for every delay we endure. God understands our feelings and our frustrations even when others may not understand. God is all-knowing. God has the final say!

For those who have misunderstood you, will you entrust them to God? For the delays you are experiencing, will you entrust them to God as well?

~ Stephen

April 9

Departed Glory

Chronological Bible Reading Plan: (Day 99: 1 Samuel 4-8)

"So the Philistines fought, and Israel was defeated, and they fled, every man to his home. And there was a very great slaughter, for thirty thousand foot soldiers of Israel fell. And the ark of God was captured, and the two sons of Eli, Hophni and Phinehas, died." 1 Samuel 4:10-11 (ESV)

Israel experienced a devastating blow as they were defeated in battle. When Eli heard about the ark of God being captured and his two sons being killed in war, he fell over backward from his seat by the side of the gate and died. Eli served as judge of Israel for forty years. The daughter-in-law of Eli and the wife of Phinehas gave birth to a son and then died.

- *"And she named the child Ichabod, saying, 'The glory has departed from Israel!' because the ark of God had been captured and because of her father-in-law and her husband. And she said, 'The glory has departed from Israel, for the ark of God has been captured.'" 1 Sam. 4:21-22 (ESV)*

The ark of God represented God's abiding Presence among the people of Israel. His favor rested upon them until they turned from Him in rebellion. God removed His glory from Israel.

When you became a follower of Jesus Christ, you became the walking tabernacle of God's Presence. Your body is the temple of the Holy Spirit. God's glory is revealed in your life through salvation and through your life as you continue the ministry of Jesus on the earth. Other people get a glimpse of God's glory as they examine your life fully yielded to the Lordship of Christ.

Is there anything in your life that inhibits the glory of God being revealed through your life? Live a life that brings honor to God and that benefits others.

~ Stephen

April 10

Saul and God's Sovereignty

Chronological Bible Reading Plan: (Day 100: 1 Samuel 9-12)

"Now Samuel called the people together to the Lord at Mizpah. And he said to the people of Israel, 'Thus says the Lord, the God of Israel, 'I brought up Israel out of Egypt, and I delivered you from the hand of the Egyptians and from the hand of all the kingdoms that were oppressing you.' But today you have rejected your God, who saves you from all your calamities and your distresses, and you have said to him, 'Set a king over us.' Now therefore present yourselves before the Lord by your tribes and by your thousands.'" 1 Samuel 10:17-19 (ESV)

Samuel gathered the people of Israel to confront their reality and to position them for their future. He had a word from the Lord to deliver directly to them. Samuel reminded the people of Israel of God's faithfulness and reminded them of God's provision of deliverance from the hand of the Egyptians. It was time for Samuel to go public on God's plan to raise up Saul to be their king and to deliver them from the Philistines.

God used Samuel in the process to prepare Saul for the new assignment God had for him. Saul was simply searching the countryside to recover some of his father's lost donkeys. God had an awesome adventure awaiting Saul that he would have never imagined for his own life.

The sovereignty of God is demonstrated through Israel's history and throughout your own personal life. Think of where you are right now and consider all that God has done to see you through the ages and stages of your life. God rules and reigns and nothing can thwart His will. God will accomplish His plan and He will develop you in the process. Submit to His prompting and trust His timing.

~ *Stephen*

April 11
Go Vertical

Chronological Bible Reading Plan: (Day 101: 1 Samuel 13-14)

"And Saul built an altar to the Lord; it was the first altar that he built to the Lord." 1 Samuel 14:35 (ESV)

Saul had been preoccupied with his mission of mobilizing his army against the Philistines. His warriors were weary and faint since they had not been allowed to eat. In desperation, they killed animals and ate them with the blood. When Saul heard about their conduct, he summoned everyone to bring his ox or sheep to where he was and to slaughter the animals there. Saul reminded the people to not sin against the Lord by eating with the blood. At this time, Saul built an altar to the Lord.

- *"And Saul inquired of God, 'Shall I go down after the Philistines? Will you give them into the hand of Israel?' But he did not answer him that day." 1 Sam. 14:37 (ESV)*

Saul chose to go vertical through worship and through prayer. He was seeking guidance from the Lord and wanted to know if he should pursue the Philistines and if God would give them into his hands. God did not answer him that day.

Have you experienced anything recently that caused you to go vertical through worship and prayer? Have you known desperation at the level of being compelled to seek God and wait upon His directive? Pursue God daily and persistently. Go vertical with your focus and with your energy. Keep your passion for God alive by consistently feeding on His Word and consistently communing with Him in prayer. Your love relationship with the Lord is the most important relationship in your life. Maintain intimacy with God.

What adjustments do you need to make in your life in order to align your life with God's priorities? What is keeping you from going vertical?

~ *Stephen*

April 12

Decipher the Voice

Chronological Bible Reading Plan: (Day 102: 1 Samuel 15-17)

"Saul said to Samuel, 'I have sinned, for I have transgressed the commandment of the Lord and your words, because I feared the people and obeyed their voice. Now therefore, please pardon my sin and return with me that I may bow before the Lord.'" 1 Samuel 15:24-25 (ESV)

In our culture we are bombarded with messages that appeal to our senses and seek our attention. Multifaceted voices come our way through technology, verbal interaction, written word, and our thoughts. Deciphering the messages can be a challenge at times. Learning to hear and respond to the voice of God is vital for us to live in victory and to live a life that brings honor to God.

Saul was torn between the tug of trying to please God and trying to appease people. Someone was going to feel cheated. Someone was going to be let down. Instead of fearing God and revering God, Saul chose to slide into the trap of trying to please people. He feared the people and obeyed their voice at the expense of disobeying the voice of God. God clearly instructed Saul through Samuel, "Now go and strike Amalek and devote to destruction all that they have. Do not spare them, but kill both man and woman, child and infant, ox and sheep, camel and donkey" (1 Sam. 15:3 ESV). In overt disobedience to God, Saul and the people spared Agag and the best of the sheep, oxen, fattened calves, and lambs.

Can you decipher the voice of God among all the voices that seek your attention? When you detect the voice of God you will be detecting the voice of Truth. It is not enough to hear God's voice; you must be willing to obey God's voice. Are you obeying what God has already said to you? Start there!

~ Stephen

April 13

My Fortress and my Refuge

Chronological Bible Reading Plan: (Day 103: 1 Samuel 18-20; Psalms 11,59)

"Saul sent messengers to David's house to watch him, that he might kill him in the morning. But Michal, David's wife, told him, 'If you do not escape with your life tonight, tomorrow you will be killed.' So Michal let David down through the window, and he fled away and escaped." 1 Samuel 19:11-12 (ESV)

God gave David tremendous favor as he stood before Goliath with his sling and smooth stone and defeated the giant in front of the army of Israel. God's favor was upon David as he went into battle and as he sought to soothe Saul by playing the lyre. Saul hurled a spear at David seeking to pin hm to the wall, but David evaded him twice. David was now on the run in response to Saul's evil pursuit and inflamed jealousy.

David had married Saul's daughter, Michal, and she found out that her father was scheming to take David's life. Wisely, she warned David and let him down through the window so that he could flee and escape Saul's wrath.

- *"But I will sing of your strength; I will sing aloud of your steadfast love in the morning. For you have been to me a fortress and a refuge in the day of my distress. O my Strength, I will sing praises to you, for you, O God, are my fortress, the God who shows me steadfast love."*
  Ps. 59:16-17 (ESV)

In one of David's darkest moments, he wrote this song to affirm his trust in God's steadfast love. He acknowledged that God was his fortress and refuge. David sang praise to God and affirmed his dependency upon the Lord.

How do you respond to unfair treatment? How do you respond to adversity? Rest in God's steadfast love. Find refuge in the Lord and affirm Him as your fortress. In your weakness, He is strong!

~ *Stephen*

April 14

MAKING THE WISE DECISION

Chronological Bible Reading Plan: (Day 104: 1 Samuel 21-24)

"And the men of David said to him, 'Here is the day of which the Lord said to you, 'Behold, I will give your enemy into your hand, and you shall do to him as it shall seem good to you.' Then David arose and stealthily cut off a corner of Saul's robe. And afterward David's heart struck him, because he had cut off a corner of Saul's robe. He said to his men, 'The Lord forbid that I should do this thing to my lord, the Lord's anointed, to put out my hand against him, seeing he is the Lord's anointed.'" 1 Samuel 24:4-6 (ESV)

The timing could not have been any better. David and his men where hiding in the inner portion of a cave and Saul came into the entrance of that exact cave to relieve himself. King Saul was in a most vulnerable situation and David could have easily killed him. Instead, David chose to simply cut off a corner of Saul's robe. David told his men that he would not dare put out his hand against the Lord's anointed.

After Saul left the cave unaware of David's presence, David arose and went out of the cave to reveal himself to Saul and to feature the corner of the robe that he had cut off. Saul was deeply moved by David's gracious act of mercy and reverence.

- *"He said to David, 'You are more righteous than I, for you have repaid me good, whereas I have repaid you evil. And you have declared this day how you have dealt well with me, in that you did not kill me when the Lord put me into your hands.'" 1 Sam. 24:17-18 (ESV)*

What life lesson do you draw from this powerful encounter? Perhaps we should learn to entrust ourselves and our future to the Lord's care.

~ *Stephen*

April 15

Delivered Out of Affliction

Chronological Bible Reading Plan: (Day 105: Psalms 7,27,31,34,52)

"The Lord is near to the brokenhearted and saves the crushed in spirit. Many are the afflictions of the righteous, but the Lord delivers him out of them all." Psalm 34:18-19 (ESV)

Being adopted into God's family is the result of God's gracious redemptive activity. He included you in His plan of redemption. Now that you are a child of God, you are considered an enemy to the devil and you stand in opposition to the devil's mission. Just as Jesus had to combat the devil by quoting Scripture, you will have to be armed for battle.

Claim God's promise that He is near the brokenhearted. Doing life on a broken planet is filled with obstacles to overcome and adversity to advance through. The Lord is near you. You will never walk alone. Even when you are crushed in spirit, the Lord will save you. Suffering is a part of the landscape for those who love the Lord and choose to live for His glory.

- *"For to this you have been called, because Christ also suffered for you, leaving you an example, so that you might follow in his steps." 1 Pet. 2:21 (ESV)*
- *"But I am like a green olive tree in the house of God. I trust in the steadfast love of God forever and ever." Ps. 52:8 (ESV)*

The Lord will deliver you out of your afflictions. Even if you let go of Him, Jesus will not let go of you. Follow in His steps and trust in the steadfast love of God. You are a child of the living God. You are like a green olive tree in the house of God. No weapon formed against you shall prosper. Trust the Lord with your present and your future.

~Stephen

April 16

Tears in His Bottle

Chronological Bible Reading Plan: (Day 106: Psalms 56,120,140-142)

"You have kept count of my tossings; put my tears in your bottle. Are they not in your book?" Psalm 56:8 (ESV)

God created you for a divine purpose to fulfill. You are not here by accident; you are here by divine appointment. God designed you so that you can know Him personally and fulfill His plan intentionally. Fulfilling God's agenda requires God's enabling. You cannot continue His ministry in your own strength.

Fatigue, exhaustion, and feeling depleted are normal features of living in a fallen world. God intimately knows your inmost feelings and He keeps count of all your wanderings. He puts your tears in His bottle. He records every step you take and every decision you make. Nothing escapes God's attention.

- *"I know that the Lord will maintain the cause of the afflicted, and will execute justice for the needy." Ps. 140:12 (ESV)*
- *"With my voice I cry out to the Lord; with my voice I plead for mercy to the Lord. I pour out my complaint before him; I tell my trouble before him." Ps. 142:1-2 (ESV)*

Prayer enables you to express your heart to God. You have the sacred privilege of communicating with God through the grace-paved avenue of prayer. Acknowledge your dependency upon Him. The Lord executes justice for the needy and maintains the cause of the afflicted. You can lift up your voice to plead for mercy.

In prayer, you have the invitation to pour out your complaints before the Lord. God can handle your frustrations and He can bring calm to your troubled waters. Run to the Lord and watch how His mercy floods back to you!

~ Stephen

April 17

Show Restraint

Chronological Bible Reading Plan: (Day 107: 1 Samuel 25-27)

"And David answered and said, 'Here is the spear, O king! Let one of the young men come over and take it. The Lord rewards every man for his righteousness and his faithfulness, for the Lord gave you into my hand today, and I would not put out my hand against the Lord's anointed. Behold, as your life was precious this day in my sight, so may my life be precious in the sight of the Lord, and may he deliver me out of all tribulation.'" 1 Samuel 26:22-24 (ESV)

David showed immense restraint a second time. He had the perfect opportunity to bring Saul's evil pursuit to an end by killing Saul while he slept among his soldiers within the encampment. Saul's spear was stuck in the ground at his head and could have easily been used by David to bring forth death.

- *"And David said, 'As the Lord lives, the Lord will strike him, or his day will come to die, or he will go down into battle and perish. The Lord forbid that I should put out my hand against the Lord's anointed. But take now the spear that is at his head and the jar of water, and let us go.'" 1 Sam. 26:10-11 (ESV)*

Instead of taking matters into his own hands, David entrusted Saul to God's care. Instead of inflicting the just vengeance on his enemy, David allowed God to have His rightful place in executing justice in His own time. David showed tremendous restraint. If he were to interpret the circumstances before him, David would have quickly concluded that God had given Saul into his hands. David wisely looked beyond his immediate circumstances and viewed his opportunity through the grid of God's sovereignty.

What do you need to entrust to God's sovereign care? Show restraint in your circumstances. Trust God!

~ *Stephen*

April 18

Earnestly Seeking God

Chronological Bible Reading Plan: (Day 108: Psalms 17,35,54,63)

"O God, you are my God; earnestly I seek you; my soul thirsts for you; my flesh faints for you, as in a dry and weary land where there is no water."
Psalm 63:1 (ESV)

How passionate is your pursuit of God? Is He your preoccupation? Our passion can easily divert to other things or other people. We can slip into being passionate about activities that have no eternal value. We can channel our passion in areas that diffuse our focus and keep us from keeping the main thing the main thing.

David demonstrated a vibrant walk with God. He would earnestly seek God and thirst for Him as in a dry and weary land. In his love relationship with God, David embodied a hunger and thirst for God that compelled him to pursue God daily and passionately.

- *"I call upon you, for you will answer me, O God; incline your ear to me; hear my words." Ps. 17:6 (ESV)*
- *"Let those who delight in my righteousness shout for joy and be glad and say evermore, 'Great is the Lord, who delights in the welfare of his servant!' Then my tongue shall tell of your righteousness and of your praise all the day long." Ps. 35:27-38 (ESV)*

If someone were to shadow you for seven days, what would they say about your passion? Would that person be able to detect your passion for the things of God? Would that person detect your devotion to the Lord and be inspired by your daily walk with the Lord?

Take some time to conduct a spiritual inventory of your life. Trace your walk with God and determine your level of intensity and try to measure your passion. Earnestly seek God. Thirst for Him. He is your God!

~ Stephen

April 19

THUS SAUL DIED

Chronological Bible Reading Plan: (Day 109: 1 Samuel 28-31; Psalm 18)

"Then Saul said to his armor-bearer, 'Draw your sword, and thrust me through with it, lest these uncircumcised come and thrust me through, and mistreat me.' But his armor-bearer would not, for he feared greatly. Therefore Saul took his own sword and fell upon it. And when his armor-bearer saw that Saul was dead, he also fell upon his sword and died with him. Thus Saul died, and his three sons, and his armor-bearer, and all his men, on the same day together."
1 Samuel 31:4-6 (ESV)

David successfully eluded Saul's constant threats and consistent attempts to eliminate him. Saul had hurled his javelin at David while David played the lyre to soothe the king. Saul marshaled his army to pursue David on several occasions. In the midst of it all, David faithfully submitted to the Lord's sovereignty, feared God, and honored the office of the king. David entrusted vengeance to the Lord.

- *"The Lord lives, and blessed be my rock, and exalted be the God of my salvation—the God who gave me vengeance and subdued peoples under me, who delivered me from my enemies; yes, you exalted me above those who rose against me; you rescued me from the man of violence."*
  Ps. 18:46-48 (ESV)

Let God be God in your life and in the midst of your circumstances. Trust God to handle the people He has created and to help you overcome trying circumstances. God will see you through. You can anchor your faith to the Rock of Ages. You can rest in the abundant provision of the God of your salvation. God will lavish you with His love and dispense His grace to match your need. Keep walking with God and trust Him to illuminate the path He wants you to take.

~ *Stephen*

April 20

Your Help

Chronological Bible Reading Plan: (Day 110: Psalms 121, 123-125, 128-130)

"I lift up my eyes to the hills. From where does my help come? My help comes from the Lord, who made heaven and earth." Psalm 121:1-2 (ESV)

Where do you look for help? Where do you turn when life takes a turn for the worse? Lift up your eyes to the hills. Your help comes from the Lord. He made you. He made heaven. He made earth. The Creator of the universe created you and He knows you better than anyone else on the planet. God knows where you have been, where you are, and where you are going. He knows your fears, your frustrations, and your frailty. Lift up your eyes and call out to the One who loves you, who gave His only Son for you, and who has included you in His story of redemption.

- *"Our help is in the name of the Lord, who made heaven and earth." Ps. 124:8 (ESV)*
- *"Out of the depths I cry to you, O Lord! O Lord, hear my voice! Let your ears be attentive to the voice of my pleas for mercy!" Ps. 130:1-2 (ESV)*

Cry out to the Lord for mercy in your time of need. Don't suppress your pain. Express your heart to the Lord through prayer and receive nourishment for your soul. Your help comes from the Healer. Your help comes from the Maker of heaven and earth. Your help comes from the Creator who designed you and develops you for His glory.

God allows you to experience adversity in this life to build your spiritual muscles and to demonstrate His faithfulness to you. When you are in need of help, your desperation becomes a canvas upon which God can apply His paint of mercy and grace.

~ Stephen

April 21

DAVID ANNOINTED KING

Chronological Bible Reading Plan: (Day 111: 2 Samuel 1-4)

"And the men of Judah came, and there they anointed David king over the house of Judah." 2 Samuel 2:4 (ESV)

God's will cannot be thwarted. God will accomplish His purposes and God will fulfill His plan. God's timing is not always easy for us to understand with our human limitations. God is infinite and we are finite. There is a tremendous gap that our intellect cannot fill. God is omniscient, omnipotent, and omnipresent. In His grace and mercy, God chooses to use us in His master plan.

From a human perspective, David seemed to be the least likely candidate to be anointed as king. In fact, his father Jesse did not even include him in the lineup when Samuel showed up. After Samuel examined the sons of Jesse, he inquired if Jesse had any other sons. Jesse revealed to Samuel that he had his youngest son out in the field tending sheep.

- *"And he sent and brought him in. Now he was ruddy and had beautiful eyes and was handsome. And the Lord said, 'Arise, anoint him, for this is he.' Then Samuel took the horn of oil and anointed him in the midst of his brothers. And the Spirit of the Lord rushed upon David from that day forward. And Samuel rose up and went to Ramah."*
  1 Sam. 16:12-13 (ESV)

God affirmed His selection by telling Samuel to anoint David. Many years passed from that moment of affirmation to the moment when the men of Judah came to anoint David king over the house of Judah. David had experienced major battles, heartbreak, and mourning the death of King Saul and Jonathan. Now it was time for David to reign as king.

Wait for God's timing. His timing is impeccable. God is working all things together for your good and His glory.

~ *Stephen*

April 22

My Rock and My Redeemer

Chronological Bible Reading Plan: (Day 112: Psalms 6, 8-10, 14, 16, 19, 21)

"I am weary with my moaning; every night I flood my bed with tears; I drench my couch with my weeping. My eye wastes away because of grief; it grows weak because of all my foes." Psalm 6:6-7 (ESV)

David was well acquainted with victory, despair, and grief. He had known the favor of God and the wrath of Saul. David combated his enemies while seeking to remain true to the Lord his God. Through seasons of adversity, he became weary with his moaning and flooded his bed with tears. Grief overwhelmed him as he drenched his couch with his weeping. He grew weak because of his foes. In the midst of his abiding pain, David revealed the solidarity of his faith in the Lord.

- *"You make known to me the path of life; in your presence there is fullness of joy; at your right hand are pleasures forevermore." Ps. 16:11 (ESV)*
- *"Let the words of my mouth and the meditation of my heart be acceptable in your sight, O Lord, my rock and my redeemer." Ps. 19:14 (ESV)*

Latch onto the Lord who will be a stronghold in times of trouble. Place your total confidence and trust in the Lord for He will not forsake those who seek Him. In God's presence, you will receive fullness of joy. God will make known unto you the path of life. Outside of Him, you will not find life. God places pleasures at your right hand.

Maintain integrity by practicing moment-by-moment surrender to the Lordship of Christ. Submit your tongue to the Lord and yield your heart to His prompting. May the words of your mouth and the meditation of your heart be acceptable in His sight. The Lord is your rock and your redeemer.

~ Stephen

April 23

Orchestrated by God

Chronological Bible Reading Plan: (Day 113: 1 Chronicles 1-2)

"Adam, Seth, Enosh; Kenan, Mahalalel, Jared; Enoch, Methuselah, Lamech; Noah, Shem, Ham, and Japheth." 1 Chronicles 1:1-4 (ESV)

People matter to God. As you read chapter one and chapter two of 1 Chronicles, you read a list of names. Some of them may be familiar to you while some of the names may seem foreign. The chronicler detailed the Davidic dynasty in Judah and traced the genealogies to demonstrate how David and Judah were chosen by God. Only one of Noah's three sons, Shem, would be the one through whom the redemptive blessing would come.

God's story of redemption is filled with people. God uses all kinds of people to accomplish His purposes and His plans. Nothing can thwart God's will. Remember, that life is not about your story that you invite God into. Life is about God's story that He invites you into. Will you allow God to have His way in your life?

What names do you have on your list? If you were to write down the name of every person God has used in your life to point you to Christ, to encourage you in the faith, or to model Christ before you, how many names would be on your list? God strategically places people in your life to help you become the fully devoted follower of Christ you were created to become. Throughout your journey, God sprinkles relationships along the path to draw you closer to Christ and to sensitize you to His abiding presence.

Don't rush past the people God places in your life. Slow down and enjoy the abundance of God's blessings. Just as people matter to God, you matter to God! Allow God to use you to be an irresistible influence for His glory. You are on His list.

~ *Stephen*

April 24

Exceeding Joy

Chronological Bible Reading Plan: (Day 114: Psalms 43-45, 49, 84-85, 87)

"Send out your light and your truth; let them lead me; let them bring me to your holy hill and to your dwelling! Then I will go to the altar of God, to God my exceeding joy, and I will praise you with the lyre, O God, my God."
Psalm 43:3-4 (ESV)

Have you ever used a GPS? The Global Positioning System specifically identifies your location and assists you to your desired destination. It is like having your own car concierge. If you make an improper turn, the GPS recalibrates to get you back onto the proper path.

The light of God's Word will lead you onto the path God has for you. To know God's will, you must know God's Word. God has revealed His plan in His Word. As you read and feed on God's Word, you will be led into God's presence and you will know His exceeding joy as you praise Him.

- *"Why are you cast down, O my soul, and why are you in turmoil within me? Hope in God; for I shall again praise him, my salvation and my God." Ps. 43:5 (ESV)*

As you travel down the lanes of living in a fallen world, you can easily get distracted and lose your focus. Your soul will go through seasons of being downcast and you will experience seasons of inner turmoil. Let God speak to you. Open your heart to His directive and obey His promptings. God will always point you back to His will and to His way.

Hope in God. Place your total confidence in the completed work of Jesus on the cross. Anchor your faith to the Rock of your salvation and praise God for His faithfulness. Express the exceeding joy of the Lord which is your strength!

~ Stephen

April 25
Prayer of Jabez and Jesus

Chronological Bible Reading Plan: (Day 115: 1 Chronicles 3-5)

"Jabez was more honorable than his brothers; and his mother called his name Jabez, saying, 'Because I bore him in pain.' Jabez called upon the God of Israel, saying, 'Oh that you would bless me and enlarge my border, and that your hand might be with me, and that you would keep me from harm so that it might not bring me pain!' And God granted what he asked." 1 Chronicles 4:9-10 (ESV)

You can discover what is important to people by listening to their prayers. Jabez prayed for God's blessing, for God's abundance, for God's provision, and for God's protection. As Jesus prayed to His Father in heaven, He requested to be blessed by God so that He in turn could bring glory to God.

There are 650 prayers in the Bible and the Gospels record nineteen occasions upon which Jesus prayed. The longest prayer we have of Jesus is found in the twenty-six verses of John 17. The Disciples had the privilege of overhearing this prayer of Jesus while they were in the Upper Room. Jesus prays for Himself, He prays for the Disciples, and then He prays for future followers, which includes us.

- *"When Jesus had spoken these words, he lifted up his eyes to heaven, and said, 'Father, the hour has come; glorify your Son that the Son may glorify you.'" John 17:1 (ESV)*

As you study the life of Christ in the Gospels, you will discover that Jesus oriented His life around the focus of bringing glory to God. His message, His miracles, and His personal touch ministry were featured to bring glory to God.

What do you value? What have you been praying? Your prayers indicate what you value. Do you value bringing glory to God? God deserves all of the glory for what He has rescued you from and saved you for.

~ *Stephen*

April 26

Heart and Hand

Chronological Bible Reading Plan: (Day 116: Psalms 73, 77-78)

"With upright heart he shepherded them and guided them with his skillful hand."
Psalm 78:72 (ESV)

Does the tongue in your mouth line up with the tongue in your shoe? Is your talk in alignment with your walk? If so, that's integrity! Honesty and truthfulness are garments that every child of God should feature. To be a person of integrity is to be honest about who you are and truthful in your conversation and your conduct.

Perhaps you know of people who are loaded with talent, but lack integrity. In many cases, their talent took them farther than their character could sustain them. We have watched countless talented men and women fall into grave immorality due to the lack of integrity.

In God's economy, talent and skill are insufficient without integrity. God wants us to use the gifts and abilities He has blessed us with through the avenue of integrity. The level of our integrity determines the veracity of our testimony. Purity, honesty, and authenticity are vital components for the person God uses.

King David was not perfect. He made some poor choices and leveraged his position to indulge his sinful appetite. Yet, in brokenness and humility, he confessed his sin and received God's forgiveness. David shepherded the people with integrity. He led the people with skillful hands. David learned to depend upon God and to trust in His daily provision.

If God can make someone like King David into a man after God's own heart, then there's hope for us. We can walk in integrity through our daily dependence upon God. Without His ample supply of grace, we have no chance of living a life of integrity. Let's surrender completely to the Lord's control and allow Him to live His life of integrity through us.

~ *Stephen*

April 27
Do Your Part

Chronological Bible Reading Plan: (Day 117: 1 Chronicles 6)

"These are the men whom David put in charge of the service of song in the house of the Lord after the ark rested there. They ministered with song before the tabernacle of the tent of meeting until Solomon built the house of the Lord in Jerusalem, and they performed their service according to their order."
1 Chronicles 6:31-32 (ESV)

God blesses order. As one of my mentors would often say, "Where there is order, there is fruitfulness." As you examine creation, you will quickly detect that God values order. God designed order in the family unit as well as in the establishment of government.

David positioned the worship leaders to minister with song before the tabernacle of the tent of meeting. They performed their service according to their order. In God's economy, everybody matters. Everyone has a contribution to make in God's order.

- *"I planted, Apollos watered, but God gave the growth. So neither he who plants nor he who waters is anything, but only God who gives the growth." 1 Cor. 3:6-7 (ESV)*

Who is more important, the one who plants or the one who waters? Who is more important, the one who builds a tabernacle or the one who ministers with song? Neither! It is all about God and all about what God wants to accomplish through His people. God gives the growth. God gets the glory.

We are created in God's image to fulfill God's plan. Your function in the body of Christ is vital. You are a crucial component to the redemptive activity of God. Do your part! Invest your time, energy, and resources in doing your part to advance God's work on the earth. Make an eternal difference right where you are. Bloom where God has planted you!

~ *Stephen*

April 28

Walk in His Ways

Chronological Bible Reading Plan: (Day 118: Psalms 81, 88, 92-93)

"'But my people did not listen to my voice; Israel would not submit to me. So I gave them over to their stubborn hearts, to follow their own counsels. Oh, that my people would listen to me, that Israel would walk in my ways!'"
Psalm 81:11-13 (ESV)

God miraculously delivered the people of Israel out of Egyptian bondage. They witnessed the ten plagues of Egypt as orchestrated by God. He enabled them to cross the Red Sea on dry ground and supernaturally provided them with manna from heaven in the morning and quail in the evening. God quenched their thirst with water from the rock and their clothes did not wear out. However, they did not listen to God's voice. They would not submit to Him, and they refused to walk in His ways.

- *"But I say, walk by the Spirit, and you will not gratify the desires of the flesh." Gal. 5:16 (ESV)*
- *"Therefore, as you received Christ Jesus the Lord, so walk in him, rooted and built up in him and established in the faith, just as you were taught, abounding in thanksgiving." Col. 2:6-7 (ESV)*

To walk in God's ways, you must know Him personally by transferring your trust from yourself to Jesus alone for salvation. Once you come into union with Christ, you are empowered by the Holy Spirit to walk in His ways. Walking by the Spirit is synonymous with walking in Christ. To walk in God's ways is to walk as Jesus walked and to do what Jesus did.

As you read and feed on God's Word, you will learn what God values and what God hates. You will discover God's will and you will detect God's agenda. Align your life with the heart of God and submit to His authority. Walk in His ways!

~ Stephen

April 29

Keep the Faith

Chronological Bible Reading Plan: (Day 119: 1 Chronicles 7-10)

"So Saul died for his breach of faith. He broke faith with the Lord in that he did not keep the command of the Lord, and also consulted a medium, seeking guidance. He did not seek guidance from the Lord. Therefore the Lord put him to death and turned the kingdom over to David the son of Jesse." 1 Chronicles 10:13-14 (ESV)

Where do you turn for guidance? What is your source for knowing God's will? Saul drifted from God and forfeited his faith through his willful disobedience. Instead of seeking God for guidance, he consulted a medium. Instead of keeping the command of the Lord, Saul went his own way. He did not keep the faith. As a result, the Lord allowed Saul to be put to death and gave the kingdom to David.

You have the capacity to choose how you will live your life. You can embrace the way of selfishness and choose the way that satisfies your personal ambition and fleshly cravings or you can choose the way of the Lord. You can bypass the faith and take paths that are contrary to the will of God or you can seek the Lord and obey His promptings. The Apostle Paul, in his final letter to Timothy, affirmed the heavenly reward of keeping the faith.

- *"I have fought the good fight, I have finished the race, I have kept the faith. Henceforth there is laid up for me the crown of righteousness, which the Lord, the righteous judge, will award to me on that Day, and not only to me but also to all who have loved his appearing."*
  2 Tim. 4:7-8 (ESV)

Fight the good fight. Finish the race. Keep the faith. The Lord will award you with the crown of righteousness.

~ *Stephen*

April 30

Father of Compassion

Chronological Bible Reading Plan: (Day 120: Psalms 102-104)

"For as high as the heavens are above the earth, so great is his steadfast love toward those who fear him; as far as the east is from the west, so far does he remove our transgressions from us. As a father shows compassion to his children, so the Lord shows compassion to those who fear him. For he knows our frame;he remembers that we are dust." Psalm 103:11-14 (ESV)

Three comparisons are made to demonstrate the vastness of God's love toward us. The immense gap between the heavens and the earth is one picture of how great God's steadfast love is toward us. God's love is grandiose.

Try to measure the distance between the east and west and you will be able to capture the distance between our sin and us. God places our sin as far as the east is from the west. Infinity is the immeasurable distance. You cannot place a measurement on the distance that God places between our sin and ourselves. When God removes our sin, He completely removes our sin.

Just as a compassionate father shows compassion to his children, our Heavenly Father shows compassion to us. The abundance of God's compassion cannot be depleted. God's compassion is endless. The ultimate portrait of His compassion is found in Romans 5:8, "But God shows his love for us in that while we were still sinners, Christ died for us."

God created us and knows our limitations and the frailty of our humanity. He knows our frame. He knows every fiber of our being. God has not forgotten that we are dust. As God's steadfast love is lavished on us and His compassion is dispensed, He knows the challenges we face in this fallen world. He is our Father of Compassion!

~ Stephen

May 1

Trust God's Timing

Chronological Bible Reading Plan: (Day 121: 2 Samuel 5; 1 Chronicles 11-12)

"All these, men of war, arrayed in battle order, came to Hebron with a whole heart to make David king over all Israel. Likewise, all the rest of Israel were of a single mind to make David king. And they were there with David for three days, eating and drinking, for their brothers had made preparation for them."
1 Chronicles 12:38-39 (ESV)

Before David became king, he genuinely served King Saul and waited patiently for God's timing. David endured severe persecution and unfair treatment by King Saul. David's own family doubted his suitability. By the world's standards, David did not fit the mold.

- *"When they came, he looked on Eliab and thought, 'Surely the Lord's anointed is before him.' But the Lord said to Samuel, 'Do not look on his appearance or on the height of his stature, because I have rejected him. For the Lord sees not as man sees: man looks on the outward appearance, but the Lord looks on the heart.'" 1 Sam. 16:6-7 (ESV)*

God continued to work and paved the way for David to become king. In God's perfect timing, David fulfilled the position God had established for him. Nothing can thwart God's will and nothing can dismantle God's impeccable timing. God will always accomplish His plan in His perfect timing.

Do you trust God's timing? Is there anything you are worrying about or fretting over? Release your fears and reaffirm your faith in the Living God. Pray specifically about those things that are weighing you down. Submit your uncertainties and your frustrations to the Lord in prayer. God looks at the heart and He know your heart. Before God formed you He knew you personally and before you were born God set you apart for Himself.

~ *Stephen*

May 2

Ensure Unity

Chronological Bible Reading Plan: (Day 122: Psalm 133)

"Behold, how good and pleasant it is when brothers dwell in unity! It is like the precious oil on the head, running down on the beard, on the beard of Aaron, running down on the collar of his robes! It is like the dew of Hermon, which falls on the mountains of Zion! For there the Lord has commanded the blessing, life forevermore." Psalm 133:1-3 (ESV)

Division breeds disunity. The absence of unity signals the presence of division. Where there is division, there are two visions. God's vision for us is that we will dwell together in unity. As His children, we are the body of Christ. Unity in the midst of diversity is a mark of spiritual maturity. God desires that we do life together in unity as fellow believers in His family.

- *"I therefore, a prisoner for the Lord, urge you to walk in a manner worthy of the calling to which you have been called, with all humility and gentleness, with patience, bearing with one another in love, eager to maintain the unity of the Spirit in the bond of peace." Eph. 4:1-3 (ESV)*
- *"Finally, all of you, have unity of mind, sympathy, brotherly love, a tender heart, and a humble mind." 1 Pet. 3:8 (ESV)*

Ensuring unity requires sympathy, sensitivity, and humility. Love compels you to place the needs of others before your own. Love inspires you to forfeit your own personal agenda in order to embrace God's agenda. In humility, you ensure unity by being considerate of others and being conscientious of God's will.

Think about the health of the relationships in your life at this time. Is there anyone sowing discord? Is there anything creating suspicion and eroding trust? Do your part to confront the disunity in order to ensure unity.

~ *Stephen*

May 3

Say So

Chronological Bible Reading Plan: (Day 123: Psalms 106-107)

"Oh give thanks to the Lord, for he is good, for his steadfast love endures forever! Let the redeemed of the Lord say so, whom he has redeemed from trouble and gathered in from the lands, from the east and from the west, from the north and from the south." Psalm 107:1-3 (ESV)

One of the features of a High School football game is the cheer squad. The cheerleaders seek to engage the fans in the stands in order to motivate them to cheer on the team. Regardless of the score, the cheerleaders seek to get the fans involved in the game in a positive manner. Often the cheerleaders utilize a megaphone to project their cheers and to amplify their message.

God has transformed your life by His grace so that you can become a megaphone to amplify the Good News of Jesus Christ. That's right! You are a megaphone for the Master! The message of Christ is to project from your life and from your lips. Are you encouraging people to get into the game? Are you sharing the Good News of Jesus Christ with those in your sphere of influence?

God did not transform your life so that you could keep your Christianity behind closed doors. God did not deliver you from the kingdom of darkness and place you in the kingdom of light so that you could become a silent saint. You have been saved by the grace of God to become a megaphone for the Maker of heaven and earth. Your faith in God is to be projected for others to encounter the redeeming love of Christ.

Go public with your faith. If you know so, then say so!

~ *Stephen*

May 4

Entrusted with the Gospel

Chronological Bible Reading Plan: (Day 124: 1 Chronicles 13-16)

"And the ark of God remained with the household of Obed-edom in his house three months. And the Lord blessed the household of Obed-edom and all that he had." 1 Chronicles 13:14 (ESV)

Obed-edom must have been a very special man to be chosen to bring the ark of God into his house. For three months, Obed-edom took care of the ark of God. He was entrusted with the sacred ark. The Lord's favor was upon Obed-edom's household and all that he had was blessed by God.

- *"Sing to the Lord, all the earth! Tell of his salvation from day to day. Declare his glory among the nations, his marvelous works among all the peoples!" 1 Chron. 16:23-24 (ESV)*
- *"For our appeal does not spring from error or impurity or any attempt to deceive, but just as we have been approved by God to be entrusted with the gospel, so we speak, not to please man, but to please God who tests our hearts." 1 Thess. 2:3-4 (ESV)*

As a follower of Jesus Christ, you have been entrusted with the gospel. You have been chosen by God to declare His glory among the nations. You have the privilege and the responsibility of making Jesus known. Now that you know Jesus personally, make Him known intentionally.

What are you doing with the gospel entrusted to you? How are you communicating the saving news of Jesus Christ? Think about the opportunities God has given you to make Jesus known. Seize the divine appointments God orchestrates for you to join Him in His redemptive activity. God wants to use you in spreading the fragrance of Christ.

Does your life draw people to Christ? Commit to point people to Jesus. You have been entrusted with the cure for the cancer of sin.

~ *Stephen*

May 5
My Shepherd

Chronological Bible Reading Plan: (Day 125: Psalms 1-2,15, 22-24, 47, 68)

"The Lord is my shepherd; I shall not want. He makes me lie down in green pastures. He leads me beside still waters. He restores my soul. He leads me in paths of righteousness for his name's sake. Even though I walk through the valley of the shadow of death, I will fear no evil, for you are with me; your rod and your staff, they comfort me. You prepare a table before me in the presence of my enemies; you anoint my head with oil; my cup overflows. Surely goodness and mercy shall follow me all the days of my life, and I shall dwell in the house of the Lord forever." Psalm 23:1-6 (ESV)

God never intended for you to walk through adversity alone. Maybe you have heard someone say that God will never put more on you than you can handle. That's not true. God will not put more on you than you can handle with His help. When you come to know Christ as your personal Savior and Lord, you find the Shepherd and Overseer of your soul (1 Pet. 2:25).

The Christian life is not a solo flight. God does not launch you into the world and expect you to live the Christian life on your own. God provides refuge when you need to retreat, strength when you need to endure, and help when you need relief. Your Heavenly Father knows exactly what you need and the exact moment you need it.

Are you in need of help? Are you hurting, lonely, or discouraged? Share your heart with God in prayer and anticipate His response. No need to count sheep, just talk to your Shepherd. He will lead you beside still waters. His goodness and mercy shall follow you all the days of your life.

~ Stephen

May 6

Serve with Gladness

Chronological Bible Reading Plan: (Day 126: Psalms 89, 96, 100 - 101, 105,132)

"Make a joyful noise to the Lord, all the earth! Serve the Lord with gladness! Come into his presence with singing! Know that the Lord, he is God! It is he who made us, and we are his;we are his people, and the sheep of his pasture." Psalm 100:1-3 (ESV)

Through the experience of surviving a Jet Ski accident at age sixteen, God called me to preach. My entire life was redirected. I had always dreamed of becoming an architect to design and build great buildings. God had a different plan for my life. He refocused my life on building lives for eternity. I had the joy of being an interim pastor the summer before I entered college. My first business card had a tag line which stated, "Serving the Lord with gladness."

My mother and mamaw modeled the value of serving the Lord through the local church my entire life. My mother played the piano and my mamaw played the organ. My junior year in college, I met Tonya and we got married a year and a half later. Tonya has faithfully modeled the value of serving the Lord with gladness through the local church. Our desire is to model that consistently before our children.

- *"Now there are varieties of gifts, but the same Spirit; and there are varieties of service, but the same Lord; and there are varieties of activities, but it is the same God who empowers them all in everyone. To each is given the manifestation of the Spirit for the common good." 1 Corinthians 12:4-7 (ESV)*

Where do you serve? How are you exercising the spiritual gifts God has given you? God has saved you so that you can serve Him with gladness. He made you and you are His.

~ Stephen

May 7
Cultivate Gratitude

Chronological Bible Reading Plan: (Day 127: 2 Samuel 6-7; I Chronicles 17)

"Then King David went in and sat before the Lord and said, 'Who am I, O Lord God, and what is my house, that you have brought me thus far? And this was a small thing in your eyes, O God. You have also spoken of your servant's house for a great while to come, and have shown me future generations, O Lord God!'" 1 Chronicles 17:16-17 (ESV)

King David expressed utmost gratitude for what God had done for him. Cultivate gratitude. Put gratitude in your attitude. Consider Jim Elliot's insight, "One of the greatest blessings of heaven is the appreciation of heaven on earth." Be thankful. Be appreciative. Be grateful.

As you cultivate gratitude, you will notice that your perspective on life will become healthier. Your interaction with others will be seasoned with grace. Instead of being critical of others, you will become compassionate towards others. Gratitude will enable you to enjoy what God has given you and will enable you to appreciate the blessings God has lavished on you.

- *"Oh give thanks to the Lord; call upon his name; make known his deeds among the peoples!" Ps. 105:1 (ESV)*
- *"And all the angels were standing around the throne and around the elders and the four living creatures, and they fell on their faces before the throne and worshiped God, saying, 'Amen! Blessing and glory and wisdom and thanksgiving and honor and power and might be to our God forever and ever! Amen.'" Rev. 7:11-12 (ESV)*

Cultivating gratitude will unleash God's love in you and through you. Be thankful for what God has done to reconcile you to Himself. Be appreciative of God's invitation for you to join Him in His activity. Be grateful for the opportunities God gives you to spread the love of Christ.

~ *Stephen*

May 8

Blessed Nation

Chronological Bible Reading Plan: (Day 128: Psalms 25, 29, 33, 36, 39)

"Blessed is the nation whose God is the Lord, the people whom he has chosen as his heritage!" Psalm 33:12 (ESV)

We acknowledge verbally in our Pledge of Allegiance that we are one nation under God. How accurate is that statement? Are we really one nation under God? The Psalmist affirms that a nation is blessed whose God is the Lord. God has chosen them as His heritage. Would the United States of America fall into that category?

We desire the blessing of God. Do we choose to bless God as a nation? We want God to open the floodgates of heaven and pour out his abundance upon us, but are we ready to open our hearts and surrender to the Lordship of Christ as a nation?

- *"Your steadfast love, O Lord, extends to the heavens, your faithfulness to the clouds. Your righteousness is like the mountains of God; your judgments are like the great deep; man and beast you save, O Lord." Ps. 36:5-6 (ESV)*
- *"'O Lord, make me know my end and what is the measure of my days; let me know how fleeting I am!'" Ps. 39:4 (ESV)*

Affirm the steadfast love of God. Acknowledge the faithfulness of God. Consider the righteousness of God and the soundness of His judgements. Rejoice in the redemptive activity of God.

God is sovereign. He rules and He reigns. The Lord God knows the measure of your days and how fleeting they are. Stay humble before the Lord and acknowledge your dependency upon Him. Set the example by honoring Him with your life and validating your faith by your love. Pray for national revival and let it begin in you.

~ Stephen

May 9

Unleash God's Love

Chronological Bible Reading Plan: (Day 129: 2 Samuel 8-9; 1 Chronicles 18)

"And Mephibosheth the son of Jonathan, son of Saul, came to David and fell on his face and paid homage. And David said, 'Mephibosheth!' And he answered, 'Behold, I am your servant.' And David said to him, 'Do not fear, for I will show you kindness for the sake of your father Jonathan, and I will restore to you all the land of Saul your father, and you shall eat at my table always.'"
2 Samuel 9:6-7 (ESV)

What does your love look like? Is your love reserved for those who can benefit you or do you lavish your love on those who can do nothing in return? Unleash God's love by living a life of love that benefits others.

King David unleashed God's love by blessing the most unlikely person. Mephibosheth was Saul's grandson and Jonathan's son. Mephibosheth was lame in both his feet. King David gave all that belonged to Saul to Mephibosheth and offered unlimited seating at the King's table. That's right! Mephibosheth would now eat at the King's table.

- *"'So whatever you wish that others would do to you, do also to them, for this is the Law and the Prophets.'" Matt. 7:12 (ESV)*
- *"'I was a stranger and you did not welcome me, naked and you did not clothe me, sick and in prison and you did not visit me.'" Matt. 25:43 (ESV)*

When you unleash God's love to benefit others, you are continuing the ministry of Jesus. Treat others the way you want to be treated. Value others the way you want to be valued. Serve the underprivileged. Go beyond yourself to bless and benefit those who can do nothing in return for you. As you love others you will be loving Jesus. As you honor others you will be honoring Jesus.

~ Stephen

May 10

From Atheist to Authentic Christian

Chronological Bible Reading Plan: (Day 130: Psalms 50, 53, 60, 75)

"The fool says in his heart, 'There is no God.' They are corrupt, doing abominable iniquity; there is none who does good. God looks down from heaven on the children of man to see if there are any who understand, who seek after God. They have all fallen away; together they have become corrupt; there is none who does good, not even one." Psalm 53:1-3 (ESV)

The atheist is a fool and believes there is no God. The agnostic believes that there may be a God, but that you cannot know Him. In both cases, the reality is that there is no one who seeks after God. God is the Seeker and pursues us with His redeeming love. Before we had the capacity to know God, in His mercy, God took the initiative to make Himself known. God took the initiative to demonstrate His love for us by allowing His only Son to pay the penalty of our sin in full. Jesus became the sacrificial lamb that was slain for the sins of the world.

- *"And this is the testimony, that God gave us eternal life, and this life is in his Son. Whoever has the Son has life; whoever does not have the Son of God does not have life." 1 John 5:11-12 (ESV)*

As Dr. David Fleming says, "You cannot be wrong about Jesus and right with God." It does matter what you believe about Jesus and it does matter whether you believe in Jesus. Eternal life is found in Jesus alone by grace alone through faith alone. Do you have the Son? Have you transferred your trust from yourself to Jesus alone for salvation?

The bad news is that Jesus is the only way. The good news is that Jesus is the only way. Jesus is our only hope. What will you do with Jesus? Even an atheist can become an authentic Christian by receiving the gift of eternal life found in Jesus alone.

~ Stephen

May 11

Where Is Your Trust

Chronological Bible Reading Plan:

(Day 131: 2 Samuel 10; 1 Chronicles 19; Psalm 20)

"Some trust in chariots and some in horses, but we trust in the name of the Lord our God." Psalm 20:7 (ESV)

Trust is a fragile item in the life of a believer. Trust is like the petal of a rose. Trust can beautify a difficult path and create an aroma pleasing to Christ. Trust can also wilt when betrayed. Like a gem in the hand of a jeweler, trust in God can lead to an irresistible life in which God's glory radiates.

Where is the trust? In our society draped with affluence, it is so easy to trust in materialism. If we can only acquire one more object of our affection or jump into one more activity that produces an adrenaline rush, then we will be fulfilled...so we think. The things of this world just don't deliver what they promise. The chariots of our culture and the horses of our entertainment are not trustworthy.

- *"I have been crucified with Christ. It is no longer I who live, but Christ who lives in me. And the life I now live in the flesh I live by faith in the Son of God, who loved me and gave himself for me." Gal. 2:20 (ESV)*

Only God can deliver on the magnitude of His promises. God always lives up to the level of His nature and character of perfection. There is no lack! There is no discrepancy! God is all sufficient and more than enough!

Place your trust in the Lord. Anchor your faith to the Rock of ages. He is the source of your strength and empowers you to fulfill God's agenda. As your faithful Shepherd, the Lord will help you overcome obstacles and live in victory.

~ *Stephen*

May 12

Unhindered Prayer

Chronological Bible Reading Plan: (Day 132: Psalms 65-67, 69-70)

"If I had cherished iniquity in my heart, the Lord would not have listened. But truly God has listened; he has attended to the voice of my prayer."
Psalm 66:18-19 (ESV)

Sin is an offense to God. Sin is absent in heaven and yet fully present on earth. Sin saturates the landscape of life on this broken planet. The curse of sin can only be reversed through the atoning work of Jesus on the cross. When a person comes to faith in Jesus Christ, sin is removed and the righteousness of Christ is imputed.

Without purity, there is no power in prayer. As a child of God, it is imperative to stay close and clean by confessing sin instantly and receiving God's forgiveness intentionally. You have to combat the impact of memory. "For I know my transgressions, and my sin is ever before me" (Ps. 51:3 ESV). David had to navigate the reality of his memory. Even after confessing his sin of adultery and murder, he had to acknowledge that his sin was ever before him via memory.

What hinders prayer? The most vicious impediment to prayer is sin. Sin violates the covenant relationship you have with God. Sin grieves the heart of God and quenches the Spirit of God living in you. Husband, when you do not live with your wife in an understanding way, your prayers are hindered.

- *"Likewise, husbands, live with your wives in an understanding way, showing honor to the woman as the weaker vessel, since they are heirs with you of the grace of life, so that your prayers may not be hindered."*
  1 Pet. 3:7 (ESV)

The purity of your relationship with God and the purity of your relationships with others has a direct impact on the effectiveness of your prayer life.

~ *Stephen*

May 13

Predictable Process

Chronological Bible Reading Plan: (Day 133: 2 Samuel 11-12; 1 Chronicles 20)

"It happened, late one afternoon, when David arose from his couch and was walking on the roof of the king's house, that he saw from the roof a woman bathing; and the woman was very beautiful. And David sent and inquired about the woman. And one said, 'Is not this Bathsheba, the daughter of Eliam, the wife of Uriah the Hittite?'" 2 Samuel 11:2-3 (ESV)

We have God-given desires that are natural and are vital to life. For example, we have the desire for food. Without that desire we would die. We also have the desire for rest. Without that desire we would die. Yet, both desires can become sin when we take them beyond God's intended purpose. If we take our desire for food too far, we commit the sin of gluttony. In like manner, if we take our desire for rest too far, we commit the sin of laziness.

King David experienced a fatal attraction. His lust lassoed him into a sinful spiral. Not only did he commit the sin of adultery, but he committed murder to cover up the affair. David could have won the victory over sin by avoiding the temptation from the start.

Arm yourself with the knowledge of the predictable process of temptation. We idolize something we desire. The next step is that we rationalize why we should have the desire fulfilled. In other words, we talked ourselves into compromising convictions. Then we strategize by coming up with a plan to obtain the object we are idolizing. Ultimately, we capitalize on the opportunity by seizing what we have desired. Remorse and guilt follow.

Look back over poor choices you have made in your lifetime. See if you can identify this predictable process. Here's the key to victory: The sooner in the process you avoid the sin, the more likely you will overcome the temptation.

~ *Stephen*

May 14

EVERYTHING YOU NEED

Chronological Bible Reading Plan: (Day 134: Psalms 32, 51, 86, 122)

"I acknowledged my sin to you, and I did not cover my iniquity; I said, 'I will confess my transgressions to the Lord,' and you forgave the iniquity of my sin."
Psalm 32:5 (ESV)

The prophet Nathan confronted King David about his sin by sharing a parable and announcing, "You are the man." King David could have had Nathan killed, but instead, the king got real about his own sin before God. David acknowledged his sin, uncovered his iniquity, and confessed his transgressions to the Lord.

- *"Have mercy on me, O God, according to your steadfast love; according to your abundant mercy blot out my transgressions. Wash me thoroughly from my iniquity, and cleanse me from my sin!"*
  Ps. 51:1-2 (ESV)
- *"For you, O Lord, are good and forgiving, abounding in steadfast love to all who call upon you." Ps. 86:5 (ESV)*

God forgave David for his sin of adultery and murder and enabled David to become a man after God's own heart. David became a portrait of God's grace and a mascot of God's mercy.

Spend some time reviewing your life and invite the Lord to search your heart and to reveal any unconfessed sin in your life. The convicting work of the Holy Spirit will illuminate the areas of your life that are out of alignment with the holiness of God. Confess sin instantly and specifically.

Satan seeks to discourage you and to defeat you. Don't give him a foothold. Keep walking in the light God gives you. Avoid sin. Take ways that are firm. Fear God and keep His commandments. Walk in the power of the Holy Spirit living in you.

~ Stephen

May 15

Desperation and Prayer

Chronological Bible Reading Plan: (Day 135: 2 Samuel 13-15)

"But David went up the ascent of the Mount of Olives, weeping as he went, barefoot and with his head covered. And all the people who were with him covered their heads, and they went up, weeping as they went. And it was told David, 'Ahithophel is among the conspirators with Absalom.' And David said, 'O Lord, please turn the counsel of Ahithophel into foolishness.'"
2 Samuel 15:31-32 (ESV)

What do you do when your world is falling apart? David had to combat discord within his family and within his kingdom. Absalom tried to usurp King David's authority and sought to generate a conspiracy to overtake the throne. David entered a season of brokenness and wept before the Lord in prayer.

The people with David emulated David's posture and covered their heads and wept as they went up the ascent of the Mount of Olives. In desperation, David prayed for God's divine intervention. David asked the Lord to turn the counsel of Ahithophel into foolishness before Absalom.

How do you respond to adversity? What do you do when you experience unfair treatment by another person? You can choose to become bitter and allow your circumstances to dictate your feelings or you can choose to turn to the Lord in prayer. In desperation and brokenness before the Lord, express your pain and your plight to the Lord in prayer. Unveil your feelings and your frustrations.

God invites you to come before him with the truth of your circumstances. If God allows adversity to come into your life, He will use it for your good and for His glory. Allow God to conform you into the image of Christ in the midst of the challenges you face. Trust God to work in you and through you to accomplish His plan.
~ *Stephen*

May 16

My Strength and Shield

Chronological Bible Reading Plan: (Day 136: Psalms 3-4, 12-13, 28, 55)

"The Lord is my strength and my shield; in him my heart trusts, and I am helped; my heart exults, and with my song I give thanks to him." Psalm 28:7 (ESV)

How many years have you been walking with God? Think through each year and decipher when your love relationship with God catapulted to a new level. Sometimes God will use a season of adversity in your life to bring your experience with Him to a deeper level. Sometimes God will bring someone into your life to spur you on in your daily walk with Him.

As you navigate the terrain of living in a fallen world, you come to know by experience that the Lord is your strength. He nourishes your soul and infuses you with power to be on mission with Him. You also come to learn that the Lord is your shield. He extinguishes the flaming arrows of the evil one. The Lord shields you from the onslaught of darkness, doubt, and defeat. Your help comes from the Lord.

- *"Cast your burden on the Lord, and he will sustain you; he will never permit the righteous to be moved." Ps. 55:22 (ESV)*

Exalt the Lord and give Him thanks for all that He has done to provide you with everything you need for life and godliness. Sing praise to His Name for He alone is worthy. Place your burdens before the Lord and rest in His sustaining power. Learn to praise Him when you are on the mountaintop and when you are in the valley. Learn to trust Him when the path is clear and when the fog refuses to lift. Keep your eyes on the prize. Keep your faith grounded in the reality of God's redeeming love.

~ *Stephen*

May 17

Dealing with Disappointment

Chronological Bible Reading Plan: (Day 137: 2 Samuel 16-18)

"And the king ordered Joab and Abishai and Ittai, 'Deal gently for my sake with the young man Absalom.' And all the people heard when the king gave orders to all the commanders about Absalom." 2 Samuel 18:5 (ESV)

While all the army marched out by hundreds and by thousands, King David stood at the side of the gate. His fatherly compassion was articulated as he instructed the commanders to deal gently with Absalom. David's own son had become an enemy. Absalom had orchestrated an ambush on David and his fighting men. David wanted Absalom brought to him unharmed.

In the midst of Absalom's pursuit of David, the mule he was riding went under some of the thick branches of a great oak. Absalom's head got wedged between the branches and the mule continued on leaving Absalom suspended. When Joab heard about Absalom's vulnerable status, he violated King David's request and took matters into his own hands by thrusting three javelins into the heart of Absalom while he was still alive in the oak (2 Sam. 18:14 ESV).

When the news of Absalom's death was personally delivered to David, he went up to the chamber over the gate and wept. "And as he went, he said, 'O my son Absalom, my son, my son Absalom! Would I had died instead of you, O Absalom, my son, my son!'" (2 Sam. 18:33 ESV).

How do you deal with disappointments? People are fallible and will let you down at times. Occasionally, your own family members will disappoint you. There are times when you may disappoint others. Seasons of disappointment arise related to unfortunate circumstances that you find yourself in. Find comfort in the fact that God is on His throne and nothing will thwart His will.

~ *Stephen*

May 18

New Song

Chronological Bible Reading Plan: (Day 138: Psalms 26, 40, 58, 61-62, 64)

"I waited patiently for the Lord; he inclined to me and heard my cry. He drew me up from the pit of destruction, out of the miry bog, and set my feet upon a rock, making my steps secure. He put a new song in my mouth, a song of praise to our God. Many will see and fear, and put their trust in the Lord."
Psalm 40:1-3 (ESV)

God answers prayer. As you wait patiently for the Lord He will incline His ear and He will hear your cry. When you express the agony of your soul, God will respond with His comfort and compassion. The Lord invites you to walk intimately with Him as you surrender to His Lordship.

God intervenes. The circumstances of life can sometimes generate seasons of heartache. God will draw you out of the pit of despair and He will make your steps secure by placing your feet upon a rock. God intervenes by rescuing you from your self-sufficiency and reminds you of your total dependence upon His daily provision.

God puts a new song in your mouth. When you became a fully devoted follower of Jesus Christ, your eternal destiny in heaven was secured. You have the privilege of having a song to sing that expresses your new identity in Christ. The new song in your mouth is filled with the grace and mercy of God.

Your life is a testimony of God's activity. As others view your life, you can affirm the promises of God and know that He places you in the display window of life to draw others to Jesus.

Praise God that you have a new song to sing. Your life has been transformed by the grace of God.

~ *Stephen*

May 19
KEEP YOUR WORD

Chronological Bible Reading Plan: (Day 139: 2 Samuel 19-21)

"Now there was a famine in the days of David for three years, year after year. And David sought the face of the Lord. And the Lord said, 'There is bloodguilt on Saul and on his house, because he put the Gibeonites to death.' So the king called the Gibeonites and spoke to them. Now the Gibeonites were not of the people of Israel but of the remnant of the Amorites. Although the people of Israel had sworn to spare them, Saul had sought to strike them down in his zeal for the people of Israel and Judah. And David said to the Gibeonites, 'What shall I do for you? And how shall I make atonement, that you may bless the heritage of the Lord?'" 2 Samuel 21:1-3 (ESV)

The Gibeonites requested that King David bring seven of Saul's sons to them so they could terminate their lives. David desired to position the Gibeonites to bless the heritage of the Lord. Their request would have a fatal impact on Mephibosheth. "But the king spared Mephibosheth, the son of Saul's son Jonathan, because of the oath of the Lord that was between them, between David and Jonathan the son of Saul" (2 Sam. 21:7 ESV).

David kept his word. He and Jonathan established an oath before the Lord and David demonstrated integrity by protecting Jonathan's son, Mephibosheth.

- *"But the wisdom from above is first pure, then peaceable, gentle, open to reason, full of mercy and good fruits, impartial and sincere. And a harvest of righteousness is sown in peace by those who make peace." Jas. 3:17-18 (ESV)*

Ask God to give you wisdom to make decisions that will honor Him and benefit others. May a harvest of righteousness be sown in peace as you seek to make peace.

~ *Stephen*

May 20

THIRSTING FOR GOD

Chronological Bible Reading Plan: (Day 140: Psalms 5, 38, 41-42)

"As a deer pants for flowing streams, so pants my soul for you, O God. My soul thirsts for God, for the living God. When shall I come and appear before God?" Psalm 42:1-2 (ESV)

What are you passionate about? What makes you come alive? Consider your relationship with God. Long before you thought of God, He thought of you. Long before you could pursue Him, God pursued you with His redeeming love.

Life in a fallen world has a confetti of allurements clasping for your attention. Your appetites crave being fulfilled. In temptation, Satan seeks to get you to meet a legitimate need in an illegitimate way. Don't allow the magnetic tug of this world to erode your passion for God.

Does your soul pant for God? Does your soul thirst for the living God? Focus your faith and allocate your affection. Nothing deserves your passionate pursuit more than the Creator of the universe. He has created you for His pleasure. You have been uniquely designed by God to fulfill His will. Pursue the Lord daily and eliminate idols. Remove anything that dilutes your passion for the Lord.

- *"By day the Lord commands his steadfast love, and at night his song is with me, a prayer to the God of my life."* Ps. 42:8 (ESV)

Start each day with God by having a daily quiet time. Spend time feeding on God's Word and communing with God in prayer. Thirst for God and pursue Him daily.

~ *Stephen*

May 21
Our Savior King

Chronological Bible Reading Plan: (Day 141: 2 Samuel 22-23; Psalm 57)

"'*The Lord is my rock and my fortress and my deliverer, my God, my rock, in whom I take refuge, my shield, and the horn of my salvation, my stronghold and my refuge, my savior; you save me from violence.*'" 2 Samuel 22:1-3 (ESV)

King David knew who saved him from all of his enemies. He acknowledged the Lord as his Savior and deliverer. Christ, our Lord and Savior, saved us from the enemy of our souls by paying the ultimate sacrifice for our reconciliation. Jesus died to provide for the forgiveness of our sins and to remove the barrier separating us from Holy God. As the sinless sacrifice, Jesus provided to us heaven and eternal life.

Now that you have been reconciled to God, extend the ministry of reconciliation to those disconnected from Christ. You are reconciled in order to reconcile. You have been given this life-changing ministry from God. God has empowered you to be a minister of reconciliation.

Build intentional relationships with those who are disconnected from Christ. Join God in reconciling the world to Him. Your reconciliation qualifies you to partner with God in reconciling others through Christ.

- *"All this is from God, who through Christ reconciled us to himself and gave us the ministry of reconciliation; that is, in Christ God was reconciling the world to himself, not counting their trespasses against them, and entrusting to us the message of reconciliation."* 2 Cor. 5:18-19 (ESV)
- *"For your steadfast love is great to the heavens, your faithfulness to the clouds."* Ps. 57:10 (ESV)

Because of God's faithfulness, you have been given a ministry to extend. Give praise to the Lord by sharing His steadfast love with those who don't know Christ.

~ *Stephen*

May 22
Express Your Praise

Chronological Bible Reading Plan: (Day 142: Psalms 95, 97-99)

"Oh come, let us sing to the Lord; let us make a joyful noise to the rock of our salvation! Let us come into his presence with thanksgiving; let us make a joyful noise to him with songs of praise! For the Lord is a great God, and a great King above all gods. In his hand are the depths of the earth; the heights of the mountains are his also. The sea is his, for he made it, and his hands formed the dry land." Psalm 95:1-5 (ESV)

We were made to worship. God placed within us the desire to worship. In the natural, we choose to worship created things instead of the Creator. When we worship things or other people, we commit the sin of idolatry. Idolatry is a perversion of God's intended purpose for our lives. We combat the gravitational pull of idolatry by surrendering to the Lordship of Christ and yielding our allegiance to Him.

Choose to sing to the Lord. Sing to the Lord when you are alone. Sing to the Lord when you are joining fellow believers in corporate worship. Sing to the Lord when you are sitting, walking, jogging, or driving. Sing to the Lord when you are in the valley and when you are on the mountaintop. Even if you are not a gifted vocalist, make a joyful noise to the rock of your salvation.

Express your praise to God for He is a great God. He is a great King above all other gods. The earth is His. The mountains are His. The sea is His. The dry land is His. You are His. There is no one else like you. God has uniquely created you so that you can uniquely worship Him and express your praise to Him.

~ *Stephen*

May 23

Mourning Into Dancing

Chronological Bible Reading Plan:
(Day 143: 2 Samuel 24; 1 Chronicles 21-22; Psalm 30)

"Then Satan stood against Israel and incited David to number Israel. So David said to Joab and the commanders of the army, 'Go, number Israel, from Beersheba to Dan, and bring me a report, that I may know their number.'"
1 Chronicles 21:1-2 (ESV)

When you see God at work you can rest assured that Satan is also at work. God loves you and has a plan for your life. Satan hates you and he also has a plan for your life. God's plan is for you to honor Him and benefit others. Satan's plan is for you to compromise your commitment to the Lord and for you to become casual in your Christianity.

David's decision to number Israel was in violation to God's will. "But God was displeased with this thing, and he struck Israel. And David said to God, 'I have sinned greatly in that I have done this thing. But now, please take away the iniquity of your servant, for I have acted very foolishly'" (1 Chron. 21:7-8 ESV).

David recognized his own iniquity and acknowledged his sin before God and asked God to remove the iniquity. Mourning over his sin, David confessed the foolishness of his actions. God gave David the opportunity to choose the consequences. David chose the pestilence of the land and 70,000 men of Israel fell. David personally experienced the mercy of God.

- *"You have turned for me my mourning into dancing; you have loosed my sackcloth and clothed me with gladness, that my glory may sing your praise and not be silent. O Lord my God, I will give thanks to you forever!" Ps. 30:11-12 (ESV)*

Have you mourned over your sin? Confess your sin and receive God's forgiveness and allow Him to turn your mourning into dancing.

~ *Stephen*

May 24

Global Thanksgiving and Praise

Chronological Bible Reading Plan: (Day 144: Psalms 108-110)

"I will give thanks to you, O Lord, among the peoples; I will sing praises to you among the nations. For your steadfast love is great above the heavens; your faithfulness reaches to the clouds." Psalm 108:3-4 (ESV)

Go global with your thanksgiving and praise. Go global with your gratitude for all that God has done to rescue you, to restore you, and to reconcile you to Himself. God has poured out His mercy and He has dispensed His grace so that you can know Him personally and intimately through a saving relationship with Jesus. God has lavished you with His love. You have a new identity in Christ and you have a message to declare. Your eternal destiny has been sealed by the Holy Spirit.

How will you respond to what God has done to transform your life? Will you give thanks to Him among the peoples? Will you sing praise to Him among the nations? Thank the Lord for His steadfast love. Praise Him for his faithfulness. Acknowledge where you would be without Him. Affirm your dependency upon the Lord.

- *"Continue steadfastly in prayer, being watchful in it with thanksgiving." Col. 4:2 (ESV)*

Infuse your prayer life with thanksgiving. Begin to specify before the Lord the people you are thankful for. Name them and express your gratitude for each person the Lord has brought into your life. Thank the Lord for their influence. Praise the Lord for His activity in their lives. Bless the Lord for the impact they have had on your life.

Thank the Lord for the circumstances He has brought you through. Praise Him for His divine intervention in the situations that He has shielded you from. Praise the Lord for revealing His peace, for distributing His provisions, and for healing your hurts. Testify of His faithfulness.

~ *Stephen*

May 25

PROGRESSIVE WORSHIP

Chronological Bible Reading Plan: (Day 145: 1 Chronicles 23-25)

"These were the sons of Levi by their fathers' houses, the heads of fathers' houses as they were listed according to the number of the names of the individuals from twenty years old and upward who were to do the work for the service of the house of the Lord. For David said, 'The Lord, the God of Israel, has given rest to his people, and he dwells in Jerusalem forever. And so the Levites no longer need to carry the tabernacle or any of the things for its service.'"
1 Chronicles 23:24-26 (ESV)

The Levites experienced a transition in their role before the Lord. They were assigned to carry the tabernacle which was a tent of mobility that allowed Israel to worship God as God led them through the wilderness with a pillar of cloud by day and a pillar of fire by night. Under King David's reign, the transition took place as God raised up Solomon to build the temple in Jerusalem. God had given rest to His people and had chosen to dwell in Jerusalem. The Levites embraced their new assignment of doing the work for the service of the house of the Lord.

Worship of the Lord God transitioned from the tabernacle in the wilderness to the temple in Jerusalem. God was preparing the way for Christ to become the sacrificial lamb for our sin. When a person becomes a child of God by placing their faith in Jesus alone for salvation, that person's body becomes the habitation of the Holy Spirit. "Do you not know that you are God's temple and that God's Spirit dwells in you?" (1 Cor. 3:16 ESV). In Christ, you become the walking tabernacle or temple of God's presence. You now have direct access to God's presence. You don't have to go into a tabernacle or a temple to encounter God's presence.

~ *Stephen*

May 26

God's Sovereignty

Chronological Bible Reading Plan: (Day 146: Psalms 131, 138-139, 143-145)

"O Lord, you have searched me and known me! You know when I sit down and when I rise up; you discern my thoughts from afar. You search out my path and my lying down and are acquainted with all my ways. Even before a word is on my tongue, behold, O Lord, you know it altogether." Psalm 139:1-4 (ESV)

Perspective is everything. When you view life from your own perspective, the view can be incomplete. In our humanity, we may only view ten yards at a time on the football field. God is in the press box. He sees the entire field of our lives. God is not limited by time or space.

God is eternal. God was never born and God will never die. God is not decaying nor growing old. God is immutable in that He is the same yesterday, today, and forever (Heb. 13:8). In other words, God is.

God is omnipresent. There is nowhere God is not. God is omniscient. There is nothing God does not know. Nothing ever occurs to God. Nothing catches God by surprise. Nothing happens without God's permission. God is sovereign. He rules and He reigns.

Aren't you thankful that God has searched your heart and God knows you? He knows you better than anyone else knows you. God knows every detail of your past, present, and future. The wonderful news is that God still loves you in spite of all that He knows.

Choose to live your life in light of eternity. Realize that there is more to this life than what you see. There is life beyond the grave. Every moment counts. Therefore, make every moment of your life count for God's glory. Live in such a way as to compel those outside of the family of faith to become followers of Jesus Christ.

~ *Stephen*

May 27

Heritage from the Lord

Chronological Bible Reading Plan: (Day 147: 1 Chronicles 26-29; Psalm 127)

"Behold, children are a heritage from the Lord, the fruit of the womb a reward. Like arrows in the hand of a warrior are the children of one's youth. Blessed is the man who fills his quiver with them! He shall not be put to shame when he speaks with his enemies in the gate." Psalm 127:3-5 (ESV)

Maybe you have heard parents remark that they want you to do as they say and not as they do. Of course, you would define that behavior as hypocrisy. God wants us to live in such a way that we encourage others to do as we say and as we do. We are to strive to live in such a way that the way we live lines up with what we say.

Did you know that you will multiply what you model? Now that is convicting! That means that it truly does matter how you live your life. It truly matters how you conduct your daily living. Your beliefs and your behavior both matter to God and impact others. So how do you live a life of love? Imitate God!

What kind of love does God want you to model? God wants you to model sincere love. God wants you to set an example for others to follow. In other words, be a model to follow. Model the kind of life that draws others to Christ. Live the kind of life that models the fruit of the Spirit: love, joy, peace, patience, kindness, goodness, faithfulness, gentleness, and self-control.

May your children and those in your sphere of influence become fully devoted followers of Christ as a result of the sincere faith and love that you are modeling before them. Children are a heritage from the Lord.

~ *Stephen*

May 28

When Death is Precious

Chronological Bible Reading Plan: (Day 148: Psalms 111-118)

"Precious in the sight of the Lord is the death of his saints." Psalm 116:15 (ESV)

Death is a normal part of life. For the entirety of our lives on earth, we combat the perpetual process of decay. Our bodies are susceptible to sickness, sorrow, and suffering. When we think of death we think of the end of life as we know it. When a loved one dies we enter the five stages of grief: denial, anger, bargaining, depression, and acceptance. Death is all around us and death is an inevitable part of life.

Why would God consider the death of his saints as precious in His sight? How can death be precious? We equate death with pain and loss and separation. God has a different view of death. From God's perspective, the death of a saint is not a wall to climb but a bridge to cross. Death is not the end of the journey. There is life beyond the grave. When a child of God dies, that person is immediately ushered into the presence of the Lord.

- *"So we are always of good courage. We know that while we are at home in the body we are away from the Lord, for we walk by faith, not by sight." 2 Cor. 5:6 (ESV)*
- *"For to me to live is Christ, and to die is gain." Phil. 1:21 (ESV)*

The death of a Christian is precious in the Lord's sight because that person was created not for time, but for eternity. To transition from life on our fallen sin-cursed planet to the glory of heaven is precious. To be delivered from the sin, suffering, and sorrow that saturates the earth is precious. Being in heaven for all eternity is precious. One day we will have the glorious opportunity to be reunited with our loved ones who have gone on home before us. We will see Jesus face to face!

~ *Stephen*

May 29

Trust in the Lord

Chronological Bible Reading Plan: (Day 149: 1 Kings 1-2; Psalms 37, 71, 94)

"Trust in the Lord, and do good; dwell in the land and befriend faithfulness. Delight yourself in the Lord, and he will give you the desires of your heart." Psalm 37:3-4 (ESV)

When you identify an area that you are gifted in or an activity that comes naturally to you, it is easy to place your confidence in that area or activity. Sometimes our competence becomes our confidence. We begin to trust the gifts and abilities that God has given us to the neglect of relying upon His strength. Sometimes we may even forget how we have become victorious. What do you trust in? Who are you relying upon to live the victorious Christian life.

God gives us the victory. The credit does not belong to us for weathering the storms of life. God gives us the grace we need to both live and die. God provides us with His ample supply of Manna and quail. God multiplies the loaves and fish to nourish us.

Spend a few moments thanking God for coming to your rescue. Be mindful of how needy you are and how generous God is. Weigh the privilege of trusting God and using the gifts and abilities He has given in order to live for His glory. Don't miscalculate the value God places on your life and on your obedience.

As you trust in the Lord and do good, you will dwell in the land and enjoy safe pasture. As you delight yourself in the Lord, He will give you the desires of your heart. Delighting in the Lord involves aligning your life with His agenda. His heart for people becomes your heart for people. Your passion becomes pleasing God!

~ *Stephen*

May 30

Store Up God's Word

Chronological Bible Reading Plan: (Day 150: Psalm 119)

"With my whole heart I seek you; let me not wander from your commandments! I have stored up your word in my heart, that I might not sin against you." Psalm 119:10-11 (ESV)

What guides your decision making process? What is your moral compass? How do you know if your decisions line up with God's will? As you seek the Lord with all your heart, He will make His will known to you. God is a God of revelation. His desire is for you to know Him personally and to obey Him instantly. Passionately pursue God's agenda. Focus your life on accomplishing His will. Practice moment-by-moment surrender to His Lordship and respond to His prompting.

God has given you His Word. As you read and feed on the Bible, God will unveil His will. You will discover what God loves and what God hates. You will begin to discern what God has for you to join Him in. God invites you to join Him where He is working so that you can experience His love and benefit His kingdom.

Choose to meditate upon God's Word. Read through a few chapters of the Bible and slow down on the verses that speak into your life. Ask God to illuminate His Word as you read. Meditate on what you sense God is saying to you and then apply that truth in practical living. Obey what God shows you.

Seek the Lord with all your heart and demonstrate obedience as you hide God's Word in your heart. Internalize God's Word so that you can live a life of instant obedience. Hide God's Word in your heart and embrace a lifestyle of moral purity. God's way is always the best way!

~ Stephen

May 31

Request Wisely

Chronological Bible Reading Plan: (Day 151: 1 Kings 3-4)

"And God said to him, 'Because you have asked this, and have not asked for yourself long life or riches or the life of your enemies, but have asked for yourself understanding to discern what is right, behold, I now do according to your word. Behold, I give you a wise and discerning mind, so that none like you has been before you and none like you shall arise after you.'" 1 Kings 3:11-12 (ESV)

The Lord appeared to Solomon and granted him the opportunity to request anything. Solomon acknowledged his own inadequacy and insufficiency for serving as king and chose to ask God for an understanding mind to govern the people and to discern between good and evil. God granted Solomon's request by infusing him with unusual wisdom. God also gave Solomon what he did not ask for, namely, both riches and honor. In addition, God promised to lengthen Solomon's days if he would walk in God's ways and keep His statutes and commandments.

- *"And God gave Solomon wisdom and understanding beyond measure, and breadth of mind like the sand on the seashore, so that Solomon's wisdom surpassed the wisdom of all the people of the east and all the wisdom of Egypt." 1 Kings 4:29-30 (ESV)*

Solomon was placed in a special category among men. God promoted Solomon and elevated him in the eyes of the people.

What is your request? What is your greatest need? Approach the throne of grace and present your requests to God. Pray in faith and claim the promises of God. God wants to lavish you with His love and He wants to empower you to do His will His way.

Request wisely. Ask God to open the eyes of your heart and to illuminate the path He has for you. Practice instant obedience as God reveals the next step He wants you to take.

~ *Stephen*

June 1

Wondrous Things

Chronological Bible Reading Plan: (Day 152: 2 Chronicles 1; Psalm 72)

"Blessed be the Lord, the God of Israel, who alone does wondrous things. Blessed be his glorious name forever; may the whole earth be filled with his glory! Amen and Amen!" Psalm 72:18-19 (ESV)

Are you living for the audience of one? God alone is worthy of your worship and adoration. He alone does wondrous things. God wants you to live a life worthy of the Lord. Consider all that Jesus did to purchase your salvation and to provide for your abiding peace. Think about what Jesus did to take care of your forever. You are saved for all eternity. Heaven is your home!

As you live to please God, He desires for you to bear fruit, grow in your knowledge of Him, be strengthened by His might, and perpetually and joyfully give thanks to Him. God has qualified you to participate in the inheritance of the saints. You are blessed and highly favored of the Lord. You are fruitful, you are growing, you are strengthened, and you are joyful in the Lord. As a child of the living God, you have been lavished with His unconditional love.

As you trust God daily to provide the strength for Christian living, you will bring pleasure to Him. God loves you and wants you to please Him in every way. Be conscious of His abiding presence. Be alert to opportunities to bear fruit, as you stay connected to Christ. Allow the life of Christ to be evidenced through your life as you do what Jesus did to love God and to serve others.

Bless His name forever. Be a conduit of filling the earth with the glory of God. Radiate the love of God!

~ *Stephen*

June 2

Communicating Value

Chronological Bible Reading Plan: (Day 153: Song of Solomon)

"Behold, you are beautiful, my love, behold, you are beautiful! Your eyes are doves behind your veil. Your hair is like a flock of goats leaping down the slopes of Gilead. Your teeth are like a flock of shorn ewes that have come up from the washing, all of which bear twins, and not one among them has lost its young. Your lips are like a scarlet thread, and your mouth is lovely. Your cheeks are like halves of a pomegranate behind your veil." Song of Solomon 4:1-3 (ESV)

Being selfish requires no effort. Selfishness comes naturally to us. If we aren't careful, we will operate our lives on the assumption that life revolves around us. Being self-centered and self-absorbed is the antithesis of marriage. In the marriage relationship, the husband and wife must release selfishness and embrace selflessness.

Our culture is not marriage-friendly. The pace of life and the demands on our time can strain a marriage relationship. As a partner, you have to make room for marriage. You have to conscientiously and intentionally make room for the one you love. In order to have a healthy, vibrant, and growing marriage, you have to create space for the relationship. It takes time to nurture a meaningful relationship with your spouse.

Busyness is the prominent enemy to intimacy. We divert our energy to parenting, to our career, to recreation, and to other things to the neglect of our marriage relationship. It is so easy to neglect the sacred union God calls us to with our spouse. We can give our best to others and give our spouse the crumbs. That's a recipe for an unhealthy marriage. Remember, you will make room for what you value!

~ *Stephen*

June 3

Wisdom for the Upright

Chronological Bible Reading Plan: (Day 154: Proverbs 1-3)

"For the Lord gives wisdom; from his mouth come knowledge and understanding; he stores up sound wisdom for the upright; he is a shield to those who walk in integrity, guarding the paths of justice and watching over the way of his saints." Proverbs 2:6-8 (ESV)

God's way is paved with wisdom. You have unlimited options available and countless decisions to make during your earthly existence. Each day of your life is filled with choices. You have the freedom to choose your own way or to choose God's way. You have the freedom to fulfill your personal agenda or to fulfill God's agenda.

Knowledge and understanding come from the Lord. He imparts wisdom so that you can know how to make decisions each day that honor God and benefit others. The Lord stores up sound wisdom for the upright. He is a shield to you as you walk in integrity. God guards the paths of justice for they are consistent with His nature and character. God watches over the way of His saints.

What do you do if you lack wisdom? Where do you turn when you do not know which direction to take or what decision to make? "If any of you lacks wisdom, let him ask God, who gives generously to all without reproach, and it will be given him. But let him ask in faith, with no doubting, for the one who doubts is like a wave of the sea that is driven and tossed by the wind" (Jas. 1:5-6 ESV).

Walk in the light God gives you. Stay broken before the Lord and dependent upon His daily provision. Remain teachable as the Lord imparts His wisdom and understanding. Use discretion as inspired by God to make wise decisions. Allow time for God to affirm the direction He wants you to take.

~ *Stephen*

June 4

Exercise Spiritual Discernment

Chronological Bible Reading Plan: (Day 155: Proverbs 4-6)

"Let your eyes look directly forward, and your gaze be straight before you. Ponder the path of your feet; then all your ways will be sure. Do not swerve to the right or to the left; turn your foot away from evil." Proverbs 4:25-27 (ESV)

Have you ever peeked into the rear view mirror of life and wondered, "Why did I choose that path?" Perhaps you made a decision to go in a certain direction at a critical time in your life that catapulted you onto a path that took you places you really did not want to go. You may be living with regret even now as you revisit your moment of decision that placed you on the unhealthy path.

Your daily decisions determine the direction of your life. If you don't pick your path, a path will pick you. God wants you to walk in wisdom and to exercise spiritual discernment as you seek to operate in His will. Use Spirit infused discretion in your decision making. Ask yourself, "What is the wise thing to do?" Knowing what you know about God and His ways, make level paths for your feet. Allowing the Holy Spirit to take full possession of your life, take only ways that are firm.

God has a path for you to discover and to experience personally. Sometimes the path God has for you includes delays. You may not understand why you are in a season of uncertainty, but you know that God is with you and that He will allow the fog to lift in His perfect timing. While you are waiting for God to show you the next step on this path, obey what you already know. If you are on the wrong path, make a wise decision to move in the new direction God shows you.

~ *Stephen*

June 5

Worth Treasuring

Chronological Bible Reading Plan: (Day 156: Proverbs 7-9)

"My son, keep my words and treasure up my commandments with you; keep my commandments and live; keep my teaching as the apple of your eye; bind them on your fingers; write them on the tablet of your heart." Proverbs 7:1-3 (ESV)

What do you treasure? What do you keep close to your heart? You cannot pursue worldliness and godliness simultaneously. While living in the world, you can bring honor to God by keeping His words and treasuring up His commandments. Value God's Word by keeping His commandments.

The life God blesses is the life fully surrendered to God's Word. Keep His teaching as the apple of your eye. Bind it on your fingers and write it on the tablet of your heart. Value God's Word by aligning your life with God's revelation.

- *"All Scripture is breathed out by God and profitable for teaching, for reproof, for correction, and for training in righteousness, that the man of God may be complete, equipped for every good work."*
  2 Tim. 3:16-17 (ESV)
- *"For the word of God is living and active, sharper than any two-edged sword, piercing to the division of soul and of spirit, of joints and of marrow, and discerning the thoughts and intentions of the heart."*
  Heb. 4:12 (ESV)

Become a student of God's Word. Read your Bible daily and seek to connect with a small group Bible study. Grow in your understanding and application of God's Word by sitting under anointed preaching each week. Commit to a consistent intake of God's Word and develop your spiritual muscles.

God's Word is worth treasuring and worth sharing.

~ *Stephen*

June 6

Worth Capturing

Chronological Bible Reading Plan: (Day 157: Proverbs 10-12)

"The fruit of the righteous is a tree of life, and whoever captures souls is wise." Proverbs 11:30 (ESV)

You were worth capturing. God intentionally pursued you with His redeeming love. God poured out His love on you and lavished you with His grace and covered you with His compassion. Before you were conceived, God thought of you and developed a master plan for your life. His plan included the plan of redemption that delivered you out of the kingdom of darkness and placed you in the kingdom of light.

God pursued you, redeemed you, adopted you into His family, and sealed you by His Holy Spirit so that He can produce the fruit of righteousness through your life to influence others. In Christ, you become a tree of life. You have the God-given capacity to point others to the One who gives eternal life. Your life is to branch out and to bear fruit that draws others to Christ. God has sanctified you so that you can join Him in His redemptive activity.

Be sensitive to the opportunities God gives you today to capture souls. Be an irresistible influence for the Lord today and allow Him to shine His light through your life to radiate His love, His compassion, and His story of redemption.

- *"In the same way, let your light shine before others, so that they may see your good works and give glory to your Father who is in heaven." Matt. 5:16 (ESV)*

You will not cross paths with any human being that Christ cannot redeem. His atoning work on the cross is sufficient to save anyone, anywhere, at any time, in any culture! The fruit of His righteousness through you is a tree of life. Be wise! Capture souls!

~ Stephen

June 7

Walk with the Wise

Chronological Bible Reading Plan: (Day 158: Proverbs 13-15)

"Whoever walks with the wise becomes wise, but the companion of fools will suffer harm." Proverbs 13:20 (ESV)

Who do you walk with? Who are the people influencing your life? God instructs you to walk with the wise and to guard against becoming the companion of fools. God has created you to continue the ministry of Jesus on the earth by shining His light and by sharing His love. You are to be light in this dark world and you are to be salt in our decaying culture.

Be intentional about growing in your love relationship with Christ by walking with the wise. Surround yourself with people who have a vibrant love relationship with the Lord and exemplify the wisdom of Christ. Learn from their successes and from their failures. Observe how they think and why they do what they do. Learn from their life lessons and glean from their treasure chest of wisdom.

- *"Without counsel plans fail, but with many advisers they succeed." Prov. 15:22 (ESV)*
- *"Whoever ignores instruction despises himself, but he who listens to reproof gains intelligence." Prov. 15:32 (ESV)*

God places people of wisdom in your life to help you develop into the person God created you to be. As you walk with the wise, you will become wise. You will have more to offer those in your sphere of influence.

List the names of a few of the wise people God has placed in your life. Spend a few moments calling out each name before the Lord and thanking Him for enriching your life through those relationships. Continue to walk with the wise. Commit to become a person of wisdom so that others can walk with you. As others walk with you, may they be drawn to the wisdom of the ages, the Lord Jesus Christ!

~ Stephen

June 8

God's Will & Your Steps

Chronological Bible Reading Plan: (Day 159: Proverbs 16-18)

"The heart of man plans his way, but the Lord establishes his steps."
Proverbs 16:9 (ESV)

You have a new day before you today. Wonderful opportunities to experience God await your arrival. This day is filled with many options for you to select and decisions for you to make. God has placed inside you a desire to live, a desire to grow, and a desire to know and do His will.

Obey what God has shown you. As you obey, He will show you the way. Be sensitive to His prompting as you navigate the day before you. Look to see where God is at work so that you can join Him.

- *"For I know the plans I have for you, declares the Lord, plans for welfare and not for evil, to give you a future and a hope."* *Jer. 29:11 (ESV)*
- *"Therefore, my beloved, as you have always obeyed, so now, not only as in my presence but much more in my absence, work out your own salvation with fear and trembling, for it is God who works in you, both to will and to work for his good pleasure."* Phil. 2:12-13 (ESV)

Remember that nothing can thwart God's will. God has the power to make all things work together in conformity with His divine will. God has a plan for your life that is unique to your life, your personality, your gift mix, and your DNA. God created you so that He can establish your steps and accomplish His will.

God included you in His story of redemption. Make yourself completely available for God's use today. He has blessed you so that you can be a blessing. Bloom where God plants you and make the most of every opportunity God gives you to spread the fragrance of Christ.

~ *Stephen*

June 9

UNLIMITED POTENTIAL

Chronological Bible Reading Plan: (Day 160: Proverbs 19-21)

"The purpose in a man's heart is like deep water, but a man of understanding will draw it out." Proverbs 20:5 (ESV)

How do you view other people? Do you settle for what they see in themselves or do you see what could be and what should be in their lives? God has saved you and sanctified you so that you can help others reach their God-given potential. God has placed eternity in their hearts and He has infused them with purpose. As God brings you alongside them, you are to be a person of understanding. As a person of understanding, you have the God-given capacity to draw out the best in them. You can help those God places in your sphere of influence to reach their unlimited potential.

- *"I hope in the Lord Jesus to send Timothy to you soon, so that I too may be cheered by news of you. For I have no one like him, who will be genuinely concerned for your welfare." Phil. 2:19-20 (ESV)*

Paul not only shared the Good News of Jesus with Timothy, he also invited Timothy to join him on his second missionary journey. Paul saw what Timothy could be and what Timothy should be and passionately drew out the best in Timothy. Paul invested in Timothy's spiritual development. Timothy eventually became the pastor of the church at Ephesus.

Think about someone in your life whom God used to draw out the best in you. Think about the person God used in your life to encourage you to become a fully devoted follower of Jesus Christ. As a person of understanding, he or she was willing to draw out the potential God has placed inside of you.

Will you be a person of understanding that the Lord can use to benefit others?

~ *Stephen*

June 10

Honor Your Dad

Chronological Bible Reading Plan: (Day 161: Proverbs 22-24)

"Listen to your father who gave you life, and do not despise your mother when she is old." Proverbs 23:22 (ESV)

As I was driving to the office earlier this week, I heard this powerful question on the Christian radio station I was listening to, "What did your dad do right?" That question captured my heart and gripped my soul. I turned the radio volume down and I began to pray a prayer of thanksgiving to God for the specific things my dad did right. Then, the Lord prompted me to call my dad and share with him what I felt that he did right. That phone conversation was one of the most meaningful interactions I have ever had with my dad since my parents' divorce thirty-six years ago.

Perhaps you had an engaging father who walked with God and led your family spiritually. You have so much to be thankful for. Maybe your dad did not have a vibrant relationship with the Lord and he was not a model father to you.

Take some time today to think about what your dad did right. You may want to consider writing down some specific things your dad did right and give God glory for each item. If your dad is still alive, give him a call or write him a letter to express what he did right. You will honor your father and you will bring him such joy and pleasure as you share your heart of gratitude with him.

Don't miss this wonderful opportunity to celebrate the faithfulness of God and the value of your earthly father. If you are a parent or a grandparent, live in such a way as to enable your children and grandchildren to generate an extensive list of what you did right!

~ *Stephen*

June 11

His Name

Chronological Bible Reading Plan: (Day 162: 1 Kings 5-6; 2 Chronicles 2-3)

"But now the Lord my God has given me rest on every side. There is neither adversary nor misfortune. And so I intend to build a house for the name of the Lord my God, as the Lord said to David my father, 'Your son, whom I will set on your throne in your place, shall build the house for my name.'"
1 Kings 5:4-5 (ESV)

God instructed Moses to build the tabernacle so that He could manifest His presence among the people of Israel. The tabernacle was mobile in order to allow for the children of Israel to follow the pillar of cloud by day and the pillar of fire by night. They would move when God moved.

God later communicated with David the plans for Solomon to build the temple. Solomon followed through with the instructions he had been given and made decisions based on the wisdom God had provided. The temple was ornate and every detail pointed to the majesty of God.

Through Christ, God has made your body to be the temple of the Holy Spirit. God has made you fit for His habitation. You are the walking tabernacle of God's presence. Your body is the temple that houses the Holy Spirit.

- *"Or do you not know that your body is a temple of the Holy Spirit within you, whom you have from God? You are not your own, for you were bought with a price. So glorify God in your body."*
  1 Cor. 6:19-20 (ESV)

What will be different about your outlook on life today knowing that you are the temple of the Holy Spirit? Ask the Lord to elevate your soul consciousness as you interact with others. Remember that the Holy Spirit goes with you everywhere you go and He knows everything you feel, think, and experience.

~ Stephen

June 12
Finish

Chronological Bible Reading Plan: (Day 163: 1 Kings 7; 2 Chronicles 4)

"Thus all the work that King Solomon did on the house of the Lord was finished. And Solomon brought in the things that David his father had dedicated, the silver, the gold, and the vessels, and stored them in the treasuries of the house of the Lord." 1 Kings 7:51 (ESV)

God created you to know Him personally and to do His will intentionally. You are designed by God to complete His assignment. God invites you into His redemptive story so that you can join Him in His redemptive activity.

Solomon joined God in His activity. He obeyed God's directives and finished the house of the Lord. As you read the description of the construction process, you will notice Solomon's careful attention to details.

- *"Jesus said to them, 'My food is to do the will of him who sent me and to accomplish his work.'" John 4:34 (ESV)*
- *"When Jesus had received the sour wine, he said, 'It is finished,' and he bowed his head and gave up his spirit." John 19:30 (ESV)*
- *"But I do not account my life of any value nor as precious to myself, if only I may finish my course and the ministry that I received from the Lord Jesus, to testify to the gospel of the grace of God." Acts 20:24 (ESV)*

Focus your life on the task the Lord has called you to complete. Do God's will with passion. If you don't know God's will, start obeying the last thing God said to you. As you obey, God will show you the way. Practice instant obedience and enjoy the journey God has for you. Trust Him to illuminate the path He wants you to take. Trust God to build the bridges He wants you to cross and to open the doors He wants you to walk through. Keep your "yes" on the altar!

~ *Stephen*

June 13

Joyful and Glad

Chronological Bible Reading Plan: (Day 164: 1 Kings 8; 2 Chronicles 5)

"On the eighth day he sent the people away, and they blessed the king and went to their homes joyful and glad of heart for all the goodness that the Lord had shown to David his servant and to Israel his people." 1 Kings 8:66 (ESV)

The elders of Israel and the priests brought up the ark to the Temple and positioned it in the Most Holy Place. Solomon obeyed God and honored his earthly father, David, by building the Temple and establishing the house of prayer. Solomon prayed a prayer of blessing over the people of Israel. This magnificent moment in the story of God's redemptive activity was filled with awe, wonder, sacrifice, and worship.

After the sacred seven day celebration, Solomon sent the people away and the people went to their homes filled with joy and gladness for all the goodness that the Lord had shown them. The faithfulness of God to His people had saturated their lives and filled their journey with joy and gladness.

- *"Restore to me the joy of your salvation, and uphold me with a willing spirit." Ps. 51:12 (ESV)*
- *"Rejoice in hope, be patient in tribulation, be constant in prayer." Rom. 12:12 (ESV)*

Contemplate the goodness of God in your life. Think about all that the Lord has done to see you through seasons of uncertainty and storms of adversity. Ponder the spiritual markers God has strategically placed in your journey with Him. Celebrate the faithfulness of God over each day of your life and each year of your existence. God has brought you out of Egypt and supernaturally enabled you to cross the Red Sea and the Jordan River on dry ground. God has delivered you from the bondage of Egypt and He has brought you safely into the land that flows with milk and honey.

~ *Stephen*

June 14

Hear, Forgive and Heal

Chronological Bible Reading Plan: (Day 165: 2 Chronicles 6-7; Psalm 136)

"When I shut up the heavens so that there is no rain, or command the locust to devour the land, or send pestilence among my people, if my people who are called by my name humble themselves, and pray and seek my face and turn from their wicked ways, then I will hear from heaven and will forgive their sin and heal their land." 2 Chronicles 7:13-14 (ESV)

How do you return to God after you have disobeyed Him? What do you do when you miss the mark of God's holiness and perfection? Is there hope for you after you have made a poor decision?

The wonderful news is that God is good and His steadfast love endures forever. You don't have to run from God, you can run to God. Even if you have drifted from God! You can run from your sin and you can run to the Lord.

Humble yourself before the Lord. Take pride for a ride and get real about your sin. Get real about your current condition. Embrace the reality of your humanity and the certainty of His divinity. Acknowledge your desperation for your gracious God.

Don't stay in your sin. Pray! Don't accept the detour as your intended path. Don't go numb and silent. Go verbal with God by engaging in meaningful communication with God. Pray and seek His face. You will seek Him and you will find Him when you seek Him with all of your heart (Jer. 29:13).

Turn from your sin and turn to the Lord. Repent! Change your mind about your sin and see your sin as God sees it. Run to God and confess your sin!

How will God respond? He will hear from heaven and forgive your sin. Be restored to a right relationship with God. Experience His healing. God loves you too much to leave you in your sin.

~ *Stephen*

June 15

Worship, Our Joy Expressed

Chronological Bible Reading Plan: (Day 166: Psalms 134, 146-150)

"I will praise the LORD as long as I live; I will sing praises to my God while I have my being." Psalm 146:1 (ESV)

We were created to worship God, and everywhere you or I look we can find another reason to worship Him.

Look at creation. What a creative and generous God we serve! Mountains, oceans, the animals on the African plain, and a host of other examples all communicate the beautiful ingenuity of our glorious God. He is worthy to be praised for His creation. Look at His creation today, be filled with joy, and respond in worship to the Lord of heaven and earth.

Look at God's provision for you. Do you have a home? Do you have a family? Do you have a church family? Do you have food for today? Do you have a job? Do you have a car or some other means of transportation? Do you have a Savior who has rescued you from eternal wrath through His sacrificial work on the cross when you were without hope? Do you have the revealed Word of God to help mold and shape you into the image of Christ by the empowerment of the Holy Spirit? Think about the many ways God has provided for you, be filled with joy, and respond in worship to our great and generous God.

I could go on and on with innumerable reasons to stand and worship our God, but I could never describe how He interacts with you personally on a daily basis. I challenge you to look today for the many ways God is active in your life and respond with a heart of gratitude and praise for His presence. Will you join with creation today in praising our God, who is worthy?

~Jared

June 16

Faithfulness to God's Calling

Chronological Bible Reading Plan: (Day 167: 1 Kings 9; 2 Chronicles 8)

"Thus was accomplished all the work of Solomon from the day the foundation of the house of the LORD was laid until it was finished. So the house of the LORD was completed." 2 Chronicles 8:16 (ESV)

The most important calling on Solomon's life had finally been completed. The temple of the Lord had been constructed and the Lord promised to keep His "eyes and (His) heart ... there for all time" (1 Kings 9:3 ESV). The temple allowed for the indwelling presence of God among His people, and Solomon's faithfulness to accomplish this work secured that reality.

Imagine, though, if Solomon had gotten distracted. Imagine if he decided that catching up on his latest TV show was more important than securing every detail as God declared for His holy house. Imagine if he had allowed his job as king to distract from his responsibility to build the house of the Lord. Imagine if he was just too lazy to follow the command of God. Imagine what blessings Solomon would have cost his people if he had not faithfully brought his calling to completion.

What is the Lord calling you to build with your life? What are you doing to insure that you faithfully see it through to completion? What could your faithfulness in seeing this calling through bring about in the lives of the people around you, both in your physical family and your church family?

The calling of God upon our lives carries purpose. He doesn't randomly assign vain tasks in order for you to feel valuable. No, His calling has greater purpose, so that every one of us who have been called to join His spiritual family must carefully consider the consequence of our unfaithfulness and the blessing of our perseverance.

What do you need to build today?

~ Jared

June 17

The Danger of a Flattering Tongue

Chronological Bible Reading Plan: (Day 168: Proverbs 25-26)

"A lying tongue hates its victims, and a flattering mouth works ruin." Proverbs 26:28 (ESV)

Jesus proclaims to us in John's gospel that "if you abide in my word, you are truly my disciples, and you will know the truth, and the truth will set you free" (John 8:31-32 ESV). Truth is liberating, even if initially it doesn't feel that way. Isn't it better to know that you have a piece of lettuce stuck in your teeth than walking around naively smiling largely for the whole world to see your shame?

The problem for many of us in today's culture is that we err on the side of self-esteem. We don't want to hurt anyone's feelings or cause them to doubt their self-worth by telling them the truth, even if it means that they build up a false reality in their own mind that will ultimately only lead to disappointment.

We must heed the advice of the wise author of Proverbs and Jesus Himself; we must be truthful for the good of those we love.

Be mindful, however, that how we speak truth is also important. Certainly, truth is good, but we must also speak it in grace so that it can be received. The truth isn't always easy to hear and our defense-mechanisms as sinful men and women tend to explain away criticism that is spoken without love. If, however, a hard truth is spoken with grace and compassion, you can take that information and hopefully become a better follower of Christ as a result.

The reality is that flattery is not reflective of the heart of Christ, because ultimately it encourages people to think of themselves as more than they are. Truth reminds us that we are all works in progress seeking to emulate the perfect work of Christ.

~ Jared

June 18

Sharpened into the Image of Christ

Chronological Bible Reading Plan: (Day 169: Proverbs 27-29)

"Iron sharpens iron, and one man sharpens another." Proverbs 27:17 (ESV)

We were created to do life together, not apart. Part of the reason God has knitted us into a particular people following His saving work in our lives is to help each other become increasingly more like Christ. As a Christian, our desire should be to put on display the character and nature of God that is at work within us. We want people, when they see us, to see Jesus.

The problem for us in accomplishing that goal is sometimes we fall back into bad habits or allow the fleeting pleasures of this world to once again take the rightful place of the Lord in our life as the sole object of our worship. Because of this tendency to regress instead of progress in our image formation, we need fellow brothers and sisters in Christ around us to remind us of our ultimate goal of displaying the image of Christ in us and reject those things that have prohibited us from doing so.

All of us need people who speak truth to us in grace and love, hoping to encourage redemption and restoration in our pursuit of Christ-likeness.

As you begin your day today, I ask you to consider two things: First, can you think of someone in your walk with Christ to this point who has sharpened you in your pursuit of Him? Take a moment and thank the Lord for their presence in your life and how He has used them to encourage you. Second, do you have anyone in your life now that you are allowing full access to your life so that they can help you see how to better display the image of Christ? If not, why not?

~ *Jared*

June 19

The Enduring Hope of Christ

Chronological Bible Reading Plan: (Day 170: Ecclesiastes 1-6)

"Again I saw all the oppressions that are done under the sun. And behold, the tears of the oppressed, and they had no one to comfort them! On the side of their oppressors there was power, and there was no one to comfort them."
Ecclesiastes 4:1 (ESV)

In the middle of The Preacher of Ecclesiastes' musings about the emptiness of this world, he directs his attention briefly to the reality of those who are oppressed and without any comfort. He wonders why the Lord allowed them to ever be born at all, suggesting that non-existence would have been better than this existence. Certainly, many of us in our time on this earth have seen oppression like that described here and likely thought the same thing. All the hunger, disease, abuse, and abandonment in the world can be overwhelming and lead to questions like: Why would God allow such a thing as this? Has He forgotten these people?

You and I know, however, that God has not forgotten these people. In fact, setting free those who are oppressed is one of the expressed reasons the Son of God stepped out of heaven and into our seemingly hopeless world:

- *"The Spirit of the Lord is upon me, because he has anointed me to proclaim good news to the poor. He has sent me to proclaim liberty to the captives and recovering of sight to the blind, to set at liberty those who are oppressed, to proclaim the year of the Lord's favor."*
  Luke 4:18-19 (ESV)

Because of the work of Christ, we no longer have to look upon the sad reality of this world as hopeless. Because of the gospel, these people who are oppressed, poor, captive, and sick have a future of hope! Our responsibility is to tell them about the work of Christ, so that they can be saved spiritually and, then, continue the work of Christ by taking care of them in their hour of need.

~Jared

June 20

The Whole Duty of Man

Chronological Bible Reading Plan: (Day 171: Ecclesiastes 7-12)

"The end of the matter; all has been heard. Fear God and keep his commandments, for this is the whole duty of man." Ecclesiastes 12:13 (ESV)

After a very long discussion of how this world can offer nothing that truly satisfies a man, the Preacher of Ecclesiastes comes to this very wise and final conclusion: our responsibility to the Lord as His creation is to honor Him by being fully satisfied by Him.

God created in order to share with a people the fullness of His Being, meaning all His characteristics and attributes. He wanted to show them His perfect love, peace, creativity, and provision so that in turn these people would respond in worship to Him, recognizing Him as the glorious God that He is.

Truly, this is why we exist: to glorify God and worship Him as we recognize our inability to be satisfied apart from Him.

Along the way, though, you and I have the tendency to get distracted and turn to created things to satisfy us in ways that only God can. This distraction is the essence of sin: looking at our God, who is the perfection of everything we need, and saying to Him, "I would rather have this thing you created than you." We give the glory reserved for God to something He created, and we do it all the time. Why would we rob our God, who alone is worthy of our praise, of the glory He deserves?

The Preacher says you can search this whole world and try everything under the sun to find satisfaction, but none of it will truly satisfy. So, quit looking down here for satisfaction that can only be found up there! Turn your attention to the Lord. Fear Him and keep His commandments, knowing that when you do, you will discover your ultimate purpose and be joyously satisfied in our infinite God.

~ *Jared*

June 21

Guard Your Affection for the Lord

Chronological Bible Reading Plan: (Day 172: 1 Kings 10-11; 2 Chronicles 9)

"And so he did for all his foreign wives, who made offerings and sacrificed to their gods." 1 Kings 11:8 (ESV)

Every one of us has something in our lives that competes for our worship and affection. For some, our job has the ability to steal our devotion and cheat the Lord of the worship He deserves. For others, our children have become our priority and our happiness is dependent upon their happiness rather than obedience to the command of God. For Solomon, his weakness was his women. He allowed his love for his foreign wives to take precedence over his love of the Lord. The man who built the temple of God Almighty began building temples for false foreign deities in order to appease women he had no business marrying in the first place.

When you and I begin to value the approval of men or satisfaction in this life over the approval of God and ultimate satisfaction in Him, we will begin to cheat Him of the worship He deserves and give our devotion to another. This is idolatry and we must be careful to avoid it. Solomon did not and all of Israel suffered for it. As long as he proved devoted to the commands of God, Israel was guaranteed favor and peace, but as soon as Solomon kindled the anger of the Lord, adversaries were raised to remind Solomon and his people of their great need for the Lord.

What are some sensitive areas in your life that compete for your affections? Is it an addiction? Is it a relationship? Is it an occupation? Be careful to guard your affections for the Lord. Otherwise, He may send a reminder of your great need for Him. Repent and return to a God who is alone worthy of our praise.

~ *Jared*

June 22

Value What God Values

Chronological Bible Reading Plan: (Day 173: Proverbs 30-31)

"Charm is deceitful, and beauty is vain, but a woman who fears the LORD is to be praised." Proverbs 31:30 (ESV)

At our church, we have a saying: behavior that is praised is multiplied. The core of this adage communicates that if we want to encourage hearts of service in our people, then we should applaud those who serve, thereby suggesting to our people that this is the kind of behavior that we desire to see in everyone who attends Champion Forest Baptist Church.

While this nugget of wisdom proves true in the interaction of a church body, it also proves true in the relationships between men and women. Women, who desire to be desired by men, will follow the example of women who are praised to earn that for themselves. For instance, if a young girl dreams of dating another young boy in her class at school, she will watch the kind of girls that boy is attracted to and seek to replicate that behavior in an effort to win him over.

The question for men today is, "What kind of behavior are we encouraging?" Are we implicitly suggesting to women that in order to be valuable they must look and act like some magazine cover? Or are we affirming in them the values established by God? Do we love women who display strength and dignity? Do we affirm women whose children rise up and call her blessed? Do we applaud a woman who dresses herself with strength, reflecting the purity that God has called her to? We must value what God values.

We need men who desire godliness in a woman; not godlessness. We also must encourage our women to seek the approval of God above the approval of man, knowing that any man who makes her call into question her devotion to the Lord is not worth her time or effort.

~ Jared

June 23

Be Careful of the Counsel You Keep

Chronological Bible Reading Plan: (Day 174: 1 Kings 12-14)

"And he said to him, 'I also am a prophet as you are, and an angel spoke to me by the word of the LORD, saying, "Bring him back with you into your house that he may eat bread and drink water." But he lied to him.'" 1 Kings 13:18 (ESV)

The Kingdom had been divided, and one of the new kings, Jeroboam, had transformed from a figure like Moses, who delivered the people of God from oppression, to one like Aaron, who fashioned golden calves and led the people of God into idolatry. As Jeroboam was preparing to sacrifice to his golden calves, a prophet of the Lord came to speak over him the Lord's judgment. The man of God had specific instructions from the Lord: speak your peace and leave immediately without taking food or drink from anyone. The man of God, of course, did this in the presence of the king, but was persuaded by an older prophet on his return home to eat with him. The older prophet lied about receiving a vision from the Lord that made the younger prophet's partaking of food and drink in his home acceptable to the Lord. The younger prophet, who just called Jeroboam to repentance by speaking the truth of God, lost his life because he allowed a false prophet to alter his course before the Lord.

Beware of false prophets. If the word of someone who claims to know the word of God does not line up with the Lord's already revealed word, do not listen to them. Trust what God has already spoken, for the Lord does not contradict Himself. Trust in His words and His provision; otherwise, you may encounter a lion on the road who takes your life and guards over you as a reminder. Pray for a discerning heart and a mind filled with God's truth.

~Jared

June 24

Set Your Heart to Seek the Lord

Chronological Bible Reading Plan: (Day 175: 2 Chronicles 10-12)

"And he did evil, for he did not set his heart to seek the LORD."
2 Chronicles 12:14 (ESV)

What an unfortunate legacy left by Solomon, who taught his children to seek their own good rather than the glory of God. As a result, his father's kingdom was divided and his son turned his heart from the Lord, resulting in turmoil for Israel as God not so gently called them back to Himself.

Let us be warned by Rehoboam's actions, though, for when you and I don't set our hearts and affections toward the Lord, we have the tendency to fall back into actions that do not honor the Lord. Even one day in which we don't place our heart on the altar of the Lord can allow in us a rebellious spirit that turns to old masters and old sins for fulfillment instead of turning to the Lord Almighty.

Paul writes in Colossians 3 that "if then you have been raised with Christ, seek the things that are above, where Christ is, seated at the right hand of God. Set your minds on things that are above, not on things on the earth" (Col. 3:1-2 ESV). When we set our hearts to seek the Lord, we allow our joy to be fulfilled by Him alone, thereby enabling us to "put to death therefore what is earthly in (us)" (Col. 3:5 ESV).

Rehoboam didn't focus on heavenly things; rather, he focused on earthly gain. As a result, a nation was divided and people plundered by Egypt. He allowed his heart to turn to evil things because he lost his first love. What about you? What are you focusing on? Set your heart to seek the Lord. Taste and see that He is good!

~ *Jared*

June 25

The Pervasive Effects of Sin

Chronological Bible Reading Plan: (Day 176: 1 Kings 15; 2 Chronicles 13-16)

"And as soon as he was king, he killed all the house of Jeroboam. He left to the house of Jeroboam not one that breathed, until he had destroyed it, according to the word of the LORD that he spoke by his servant Ahijah the Shilonite."
1 Kings 15:29 (ESV)

Jeroboam's sin and unfaithfulness before the Lord as King of Israel was met with the Lord's wrath upon all of his household, as the Lord promised He would do:

- *"Therefore behold, I will bring harm upon the house of Jeroboam and will cut off from Jeroboam every male, both bond and free in Israel, and will burn up the house of Jeroboam, as a man burns up dung until it is all gone" 1 Kings 14:10 (ESV).*

Bashaa, the newly throned ruler of Israel, carried out the decree of the Lord in prophetic power, bringing Jeroboam's household to ruin, so that no male was left to carry his lineage forward.

In the middle of rebellion before the Lord in our sinfulness, we rarely consider the consequences of our sin. Usually, we excuse our sin by suggesting to ourselves that we are the only ones truly affected by our decisions, when in reality that is generally not the case. Sin always has greater effects than you think, and it always incites the wrath of God!

The beauty of the gospel, though, for us on this side of Christ's atoning work is that while certainly we all deserved the same fate as Jeroboam for rejecting the Lord, Jesus took our punishment as His own and allowed us to be restored in right relationship with our worthy God.

~Jared

June 26

Courageous Heart

Chronological Bible Reading Plan: (Day 177: 1 Kings 16; 2 Chronicles 17)

"The Lord was with Jehoshaphat, because he walked in the earlier ways of his father David. He did not seek the Baals, but sought the God of his father and walked in his commandments, and not according to the practices of Israel. Therefore the Lord established the kingdom in his hand. And all Judah brought tribute to Jehoshaphat, and he had great riches and honor. His heart was courageous in the ways of the Lord. And furthermore, he took the high places and the Asherim out of Judah." 2 Chronicles 17:3-6 (ESV)

How many decisions do you anticipate making today? Life is filled with paths to take and decisions to make. Every decision determines a direction that leads to a destination. You can decide to walk with God or you can decide to stray from God. You can decide to bring honor to God or you can decide to bring dishonor to God. You can decide to live in the center of God's will or you can decide to live contrary to God's will.

Jehoshaphat made deliberate decisions to seek God and to walk in His ways. Jehoshaphat intentionally did not seek the Baals and did not follow the practices of Israel. He boldly took the high places and the Asherim out of Judah. God rewarded the faithfulness and obedience of Jehoshaphat by establishing the kingdom in his hand.

Is your heart courageous in the ways of the Lord? Do you boldly and intentionally pursue God's way? There is no better choice for you to make than aligning your life with God's will. Don't compromise your integrity. Don't dilute your devotion to the Lord. Passionately pursue God and walk in His ways.

~ *Stephen*

June 27

Recapture God's Perspective

Chronological Bible Reading Plan: (Day 178: 1 Kings 17-19)

"But he himself went a day's journey into the wilderness and came and sat down under a broom tree. And he asked that he might die, saying, 'It is enough; now, O Lord, take away my life, for I am no better than my fathers.'" 1 Kings 19:4 (ESV)

Elijah experienced the miracle working, idol defeating, prayer answering display of God's splendor. A major spiritual victory had been won on Mount Carmel. The 450 prophets of Baal and the 400 prophets of Asherah were slaughtered. The people of Israel responded to the demonstration of God's power by kneeling and proclaiming, "The Lord, He is God! The Lord, He is God!"

Once Elijah received a threat from Jezebel, he descended from the mountain of public victory to the valley of personal defeat. He ran for his life and entered the wilderness. As he sat under a broom tree, he hit a personal all-time low and wanted God to take away his life. Elijah spiraled down into the depths of depression.

Fear causes you to lose perspective. Fear blurs your focus and exaggerates your circumstances. Recapture God's perspective on your life and on your circumstances. Remember that you are designed by God and for God's glory. If God allows you to go through a difficult situation, He will use it for your good and for His glory.

God has the final say. Rest in His sovereignty. God has the power to change both you and your circumstances. Sometimes God removes your obstacles and sometimes God gives you the grace to navigate life in the midst of the obstacles you face.

God provided Elijah with rest, refreshment, revelation, and relationship. Elijah recaptured God's perspective on life.

~ *Stephen*

June 28

Seed of Greed

Chronological Bible Reading Plan: (Day 179: 1 Kings 20-21)

"But Jezebel his wife came to him and said to him, 'Why is your spirit so vexed that you eat no food?' And he said to her, 'Because I spoke to Naboth the Jezreelite and said to him, 'Give me your vineyard for money, or else, if it please you, I will give you another vineyard for it.' And he answered, 'I will not give you my vineyard.' And Jezebel his wife said to him, 'Do you now govern Israel? Arise and eat bread and let your heart be cheerful; I will give you the vineyard of Naboth the Jezreelite.'" 1 Kings 21:5-7 (ESV)

Have you ever wanted something you could not have? You can easily become obsessed with doing whatever it takes to feed the desire to acquire. Ahab coveted Naboth's vineyard and watered the seed of greed. When he did not get his way, Ahab pouted and refused to eat. When Ahab's wife, Jezebel, noticed his dejected state, she took matters into her own hands.

Jezebel watered the seed of greed through deception. She wrote letters in Ahab's name and used Ahab's seal and then sent them to the elders and leaders of Naboth's city. She devised a plan to have a fast proclaimed and to secure two worthless men to sit across from Naboth to bring a false charge against him resulting in punishment by death. The seed of greed became a fatal weed.

Ahab got the vineyard he wanted and Jezebel was willing to take a man's life for it. That's what the seed of greed can do! Greed has the power to lead you into making irrational decisions. Greed poisons the fertile ground of God's will.

Keep the seed of greed from taking root in your life. Practice generosity. Live to bless and benefit others.

~ *Stephen*

June 29
What the Lord Says

Chronological Bible Reading Plan: (Day 180: 1 Kings 22; 2 Chronicles 18)

"And the messenger who went to summon Micaiah said to him, 'Behold, the words of the prophets with one accord are favorable to the king. Let your word be like the word of one of them, and speak favorably.' But Micaiah said, 'As the Lord lives, what the Lord says to me, that I will speak.'" 1 Kings 22:13-14 (ESV)

Micaiah exhibited integrity, accuracy, and loyalty to God's Word. He had to decide whether he would align with what the other prophets had prophesied or to align with what God said to him. Wisely, Micaiah consistently spoke what the Lord had said to him. He simply made known to others what the Lord had said to him.

How many words do you speak each day? How many conversations do you have in a single day? God has saved you and filled you with His Holy Spirit so that you can continue His ministry on the earth. One vital component to doing God's will on the earth is to know what God says and to make His Word known to others.

- *"As each has received a gift, use it to serve one another, as good stewards of God's varied grace: whoever speaks, as one who speaks oracles of God; whoever serves, as one who serves by the strength that God supplies—in order that in everything God may be glorified through Jesus Christ. To him belong glory and dominion forever and ever. Amen."* 1 Pet. 4:10-11 (ESV)

When you speak, choose to speak as one who speaks the Word of God. Allow God's Word to saturate your life in such a way that when you speak His Word comes forth. Say what the Lord says and do what the Lord demonstrated during His earthly ministry.
~ *Stephen*

June 30

Divine Intervention

Chronological Bible Reading Plan: (Day 181: 2 Chronicles 19-23)

"'You will not need to fight in this battle. Stand firm, hold your position, and see the salvation of the Lord on your behalf, O Judah and Jerusalem.' Do not be afraid and do not be dismayed. Tomorrow go out against them, and the Lord will be with you." 2 Chronicles 20:17 (ESV)

Jehoshaphat proclaimed a fast throughout Judah in order to seek the Lord and to seek help from the Lord. A great multitude was coming against them in battle and they needed to hear from God. The Spirit of the Lord came upon Jahaziel and he communicated the will of God. He affirmed that the battle belonged to the Lord and that they were to stand firm and hold their position. Jahaziel exhorted the people to not be afraid and to not be dismayed because the Lord was with them.

- *"When Judah came to the watchtower of the wilderness, they looked toward the horde, and behold, there were dead bodies lying on the ground; none had escaped. When Jehoshaphat and his people came to take their spoil, they found among them, in great numbers, goods, clothing, and precious things, which they took for themselves until they could carry no more. They were three days in taking the spoil, it was so much."* 2 Chron. 20:24-25 (ESV)

What kind of battle are you facing? Seek the Lord and trust in Him to fight your battles. Don't worry. Don't fret. Entrust your life and your circumstances to the Lord's care. Obey what God has shown you and stay close to His Word. Write down promises from God's Word and claim them through prayer.

Perhaps you are in need of divine intervention. Cry out to God in prayer and express your desperation. Acknowledge your dependency upon God and walk in the light God gives you.

~ *Stephen*

July 1

I'm Not Ashamed

Chronological Bible Reading Plan: (Day 182: Obadiah; Psalms 82-83)

"Give justice to the weak and the fatherless; maintain the right of the afflicted and the destitute. Rescue the weak and the needy; deliver them from the hand of the wicked." Psalm 82:3-4 (ESV)

Imagine being transferred instantly before the throne of God. You are standing before God right now and you fall on your face before God and He asks you to give an account for your treatment of others. Where would that place you in the area of God's approval and affirmation? How would you measure up to God's standard of perfection?

God is a God of justice. And yes, God is a God of mercy. Without God's justice, mercy would not exist. Without God's mercy, justice would not exist. God declared His justice on your sin when Jesus took upon God's wrath for your sin on the cross. God demonstrated His mercy by providing for the forgiveness of your sin. How will you treat others in light of what God has done for you?

- *"'Blessed are the merciful, for they shall receive mercy.'" Matt 5:7 (ESV)*
- *"'Judge not, that you be not judged. For with the judgment you pronounce you will be judged, and with the measure you use it will be measured to you.'" Matt 7:1-2 (ESV)*

Our tendency is to use binoculars when judging our lives and using a microscope when judging the lives of others. Thank God for His mercy. God wants our conversation and our conduct to reflect the mercy we have received from Him. Treat others with the same mercy you have received from God. Rescue the weak and the needy.

~ *Stephen*

July 2
Empty Jars

Chronological Bible Reading Plan: (Day 183: 2 Kings 1-4)

"And Elisha said to her, 'What shall I do for you? Tell me; what have you in the house?' And she said, 'Your servant has nothing in the house except a jar of oil.'" 2 Kings 4:2 (ESV)

I want you to think about how far you have come during your life on the earth. Think about all that God has done to see you through each moment of each day of each month of each year of your life. Perhaps you have come close to death. Maybe you have experienced God coming through for you financially at just the right moment. As you look over your life, you may be able to remember specific encounters of God's divine intervention. You know that you would not be where you are today without God's abundant supply of grace. God has provided for you every step of the way.

The widow only had one jar of oil left in her house. The creditor had come to take her two sons and make them slaves. She and her sons were desperate for a move of God and for a miracle of God. Can you relate? She cried out to Elisha and he responded by instructing her to go to her neighbors in order to borrow empty vessels. Elisha told the widow and her sons to pour into all the vessels. Miraculously, as one jar became full, she would pour into another jar until it became full, and the process continued until all the jars were full. The oil stopped flowing. She sold the oil to pay her debts and then she and her sons lived on the rest.

God will make a way when there seems to be no way. Entrust your life to His care!

~ *Stephen*

July 3

Axe Head Floats

Chronological Bible Reading Plan: (Day 184: 2 Kings 5-8)

"So he went with them. And when they came to the Jordan, they cut down trees. But as one was felling a log, his axe head fell into the water, and he cried out, 'Alas, my master! It was borrowed.' Then the man of God said, 'Where did it fall?' When he showed him the place, he cut off a stick and threw it in there and made the iron float. And he said, 'Take it up.' So he reached out his hand and took it." 2 Kings 6:4-7 (ESV)

How can an axe head float? The company of the prophet Elisha witnessed a miracle as one of them encountered an unfortunate circumstance. The borrowed axe head detached and fell into the water. Elisha cut off a stick and threw it near and made the iron float. The axe head was recovered and the miracle happened.

Perhaps you have a situation in your life that is saturated with impossibilities. Maybe you have received heartbreaking news such as a bad report on your health. You could be facing a challenging situation that perplexes you and seems unfavorable in its potential outcome. Whatever you are going through, remember that God can make an axe head float.

- *"Jesus looked at them and said, 'With man it is impossible, but not with God. For all things are possible with God.'" Mark 10:27 (ESV)*
- *"And without faith it is impossible to please him, for whoever would draw near to God must believe that he exists and that he rewards those who seek him." Heb. 11:6 (ESV)*

Keep your eyes on the Lord and trust in His daily provision. Rest in His sovereignty. God always has the final say. Seek Him with all your heart.

~ Stephen

July 4
Walk Carefully

Chronological Bible Reading Plan: (Day 185: 2 Kings 9-11)

"But Jehu was not careful to walk in the law of the Lord, the God of Israel, with all his heart. He did not turn from the sins of Jeroboam, which he made Israel to sin." 2 Kings 10:31 (ESV)

Are you a fully devoted follower of Christ? Have you completely surrendered to the Lordship of Christ? Make Jesus the Lord of your life. Enthrone Him. Yield to His prompting. Obey His voice. Walk in His steps. Know God's Word so that you can obey God's will. Forsake sin. Remove anything that would hinder your love relationship with the Lord. Walk carefully.

- *"Blessed is the man who walks not in the counsel of the wicked nor stands in the way of sinners, nor sits in the seat of scoffers; but his delight is in the law of the Lord, and on his law he meditates day and night." Ps. 1:1-2 (ESV)*
- *"Look carefully then how you walk, not as unwise but as wise, making the best use of the time, because the days are evil." Eph. 5:15-16 (ESV)*

Jehu did not follow the Lord with all of his heart. He drifted into the same pattern of Jeroboam which made Israel to sin. Jehu's life was not marked by obedience to the Lord, but rather rebellion and neglect.

Delight in God's Word. Meditate on God's Word day and night. Allow God's Word to illuminate the path He wants you to take and to inform the decisions He wants you to make. Walk wisely. Take steps that are firm and make the most of the opportunities God places before you. Acknowledge the reality of the evil which is so prevalent in our society. Choose to walk carefully and employ the wisdom God gives you to walk in His ways.

~ *Stephen*

July 5

The Poison of Pluralism

Chronological Bible Reading Plan: (Day 186: 2 Kings 12-13; 2 Chronicles 24)

"And Jehoash did what was right in the eyes of the Lord all his days, because Jehoiada the priest instructed him. Nevertheless, the high places were not taken away; the people continued to sacrifice and make offerings on the high places." 2 Kings 12:2-3 (ESV)

Is Jesus your life or just a part of your life? When you add Jesus to your life in the midst of an array of other loyalties and devotions, then you embrace pluralism. The danger of pluralism is that you give weight and allegiance to other things that become idols in your life.

Jehoash was instructed by Jehoiada to do what was right in the eyes of the Lord. Jehoash was effective at some level of leading himself in the ways of God, but failed to influence his culture to do the same. Idolatry was rampant during his reign.

- *"I appeal to you therefore, brothers, by the mercies of God, to present your bodies as a living sacrifice, holy and acceptable to God, which is your spiritual worship. Do not be conformed to this world, but be transformed by the renewal of your mind, that by testing you may discern what is the will of God, what is good and acceptable and perfect." Rom. 12:1-2 (ESV)*
- *"But put on the Lord Jesus Christ, and make no provision for the flesh, to gratify its desires." Rom. 13:14 (ESV)*

Allow the Lord to transform your life. You have been saved by His grace and adopted into His family and sealed by His Spirit. In Christ, you are a child of God. Invest the rest of your life pursuing God and transforming the culture. Be a change agent. Shine God's light and share God's love. Be an irresistible influence for the Lord.

~ Stephen

July 6
COMBAT MEDIOCRITY

Chronological Bible Reading Plan: (Day 187: 2 Kings 14; 2 Chronicles 25)

"Amaziah was twenty-five years old when he began to reign, and he reigned twenty-nine years in Jerusalem. His mother's name was Jehoaddan of Jerusalem. And he did what was right in the eyes of the Lord, yet not with a whole heart." 2 Chronicles 25:1-2 (ESV)

Mediocrity is a symptom of hypocrisy. Whenever you coast in your Christianity, you drift from the posture of passionate devotion to being at ease in Zion (Amos 6:1). Casual Christianity is displayed when you forsake your first love and allow other things to dilute your devotion and pollute your passion for the Lord.

Amaziah did what was right in the eyes of the Lord up to a certain level. His commitment was compromised and his character was corroded as he infiltrated his life with idols.

- *"After Amaziah came from striking down the Edomites, he brought the gods of the men of Seir and set them up as his gods and worshiped them, making offerings to them. Therefore the Lord was angry with Amaziah and sent to him a prophet, who said to him, 'Why have you sought the gods of a people who did not deliver their own people from your hand?'" 2 Chron. 25:14-15 (ESV)*

Combat mediocrity by surrendering fully and completely to the Lordship of Christ. Live with a heightened sensitivity to God's activity and with a keen awareness of the corrosive consequences of sin. Guard your daily intimacy with the One who delivered you from the kingdom of darkness and brought you into the kingdom of light.

Ask the Lord to search your heart (Ps. 139:23). Confess known sin instantly and receive God's forgiveness completely. Remove idols and take paths that are firm. Make no room for mediocrity.

~ *Stephen*

July7

Second Chances

Chronological Bible Reading Plan: (Day 188: Jonah)

"And the Lord spoke to the fish, and it vomited Jonah out upon the dry land." Jonah 2:10 (ESV)

Where would you be if God were not the God of second chances? You would be without hope and without a future. God will not only pursue you with His redeeming love, but He also gives you a second chance to obey His will.

The fish obeyed God in the midst of Jonah's rebellion. God commanded the fish to vomit Jonah onto dry ground. Then the word of the Lord came to Jonah a second time (Jon. 3:1). After a three day aquatic experience of prayer in the belly of the fish, Jonah was now hurled onto the beach for a second chance to obey God's way. The wonderful news is that Jonah obeyed the word of the Lord and went to Nineveh (Jon. 3:3).

Jonah responded to God the first time by saying, "Lord, here I am, send someone else!" The second time, Jonah responded by saying, "Lord, here I am, send me!" On the ship Jonah was singing, "I did it my way!" Inside the fish Jonah was singing, "Have Thine Own Way, Lord!" Jonah came to know God as the God of second chances. Jonah learned a valuable lesson about obeying God.

Ponder the grace of God in your own life. Think through the decisions you have made over your lifetime to choose to go your own way. Do you remember how God pursued you with His redeeming love? God is so patient, so tender, and so persistent. He wants you to come to know Him by experience as the God of second chances.

Don't give up. God has not given up on you. What God has begun in your life, He will bring to completion (Phil. 1:6). God always finishes what He starts.

~ *Stephen*

July 8

The Pride Slide

Chronological Bible Reading Plan: (Day 189: 2 Kings 15; 2 Chronicles 26)

"But when he was strong, he grew proud, to his destruction. For he was unfaithful to the Lord his God and entered the temple of the Lord to burn incense on the altar of incense. But Azariah the priest went in after him, with eighty priests of the Lord who were men of valor, and they withstood King Uzziah and said to him, 'It is not for you, Uzziah, to burn incense to the Lord, but for the priests, the sons of Aaron, who are consecrated to burn incense. Go out of the sanctuary, for you have done wrong, and it will bring you no honor from the Lord God.'"
2 Chronicles 26:16-18 (ESV)

Uzziah did right in the eyes of the Lord and as he sought the Lord, God made him prosper. Over a period of time, pride began to seep into Uzziah's life resulting in a slide that had devastating consequences.

- *"Everyone who is arrogant in heart is an abomination to the Lord; be assured, he will not go unpunished." Prov. 16:5 (ESV)*
- *"Pride goes before destruction, and a haughty spirit before a fall." Prov. 16:18 (ESV)*

Uncover the poison of pride. You will never reach your full redemptive potential while fertilizing pride in your life. Pride has no place in the Christian life fully yielded to the Lordship of Christ. The poison of pride will inhibit the fruit of the Spirit and stifle your effectiveness in the kingdom.

Avoid the pride slide. Instead of an ego trip, we need to go on an integrity trip. Get honest about your destitution and your spiritual poverty before God. Identify and eliminate any fraction of pride in your life. Embrace the way of humility and recognize your dependency upon God and His abundant grace.

~ *Stephen*

July 9

Judgement and Restoration

Chronological Bible Reading Plan: (Day 190: Isaiah 1-4)

"Come now, let us reason together, says the LORD: though your sins are like scarlet, they shall be as white as snow; though they are red like crimson, they shall become like wool. If you are willing and obedient, you shall eat the good of the land; but if you refuse and rebel, you shall be eaten by the sword; for the mouth of the LORD has spoken." Isaiah 1:18-20 (ESV)

The covenant people of God had one primary responsibility to their God: reflect His glory to the nations! They of all people were to communicate the greatness of the God of Israel, or in this case Judah, and how He was truly the only God worthy of praise. They were to show how devotion to Him brought about blessing and favor, inviting other nations to join in adoration of the one, true God.

Instead of reflecting the glory of God, though, the people of God detracted from it, choosing to worship created things and false gods rather than the Creator. As a result, God reminded them of their great need for Him by allowing them to be taken into captivity. He had to break them of their idolatry in holy judgment.

The beauty of Isaiah, though, is that judgment is not the end of this process. The ultimate goal of the Lord in bringing judgement upon His people was restoration. He desired this time of discipline to bring them back to a place of devotion. Sometimes you and I need to be reminded of our great need for the Lord through a time of discipline. While certainly we have already been washed clean by the blood of Christ if we have submitted our lives to the Lordship of Christ and turned to Him alone for salvation, there are times where we get distracted and become idolaters. Remember these times of discipline are not meant to harm you, but rather quite the opposite. The Lord brings discipline for our good for us to remember our great need for Him.

~ Jared

July 10

A Holy Encounter and A Humble Response

Chronological Bible Reading Plan: (Day 191: Isaiah 5-8)

"And I said: "Woe is me! For I am lost; for I am a man of unclean lips, and I dwell in the midst of a people of unclean lips; for my eyes have seen the King, the LORD of hosts!" Isaiah 6:5 (ESV)

God is holy, and when you and I encounter the holiness of God in all of its splendor, we are reminded of how truly unholy we are. Isaiah saw the Lord sitting upon His throne, high and lifted up, and was forever changed. He knew his helplessness and yet because of God's infinite mercy, Isaiah was proclaimed clean. As a result of this gracious act, when the Lord asks for someone to go to His people and call them to repentance, Isaiah responds with one of the most famous lines in scripture, "Here am I! Send me" (Isa. 6:8 ESV).

Isaiah's humble response should be our response, having witnessed the glory of God displayed on the cross of Christ and the grace of God in our salvation. If we who were hopeless and lost, certain of a future of wrath, have been declared clean in spite of our unholiness by Christ's holiness, how could we not go and proclaim in humility our devotion to this God who has loved us so? The reality is that judgment is coming upon all of creation for its sinful rejection of its Creator, who is to be praised forever, and we are to be the messenger of God to these people, declaring His infinite goodness and desire for all to return back to Him in repentance.

The call is there for us who have been reconciled to call others to reconciliation. The question is, "Will you go?"

~ Jared

July 11

Pure and Undefiled Religion

Chronological Bible Reading Plan: (Day 192: Amos 1-5)

"For I know how many are your transgressions and how great are your sins-- you who afflict the righteous, who take a bribe, and turn aside the needy in the gate. Therefore he who is prudent will keep silent in such a time, for it is an evil time. Seek good, and not evil, that you may live; and so the LORD, the God of hosts, will be with you, as you have said. Hate evil, and love good, and establish justice in the gate; it may be that the LORD, the God of hosts, will be gracious to the remnant of Joseph." Amos 5:12-15 (ESV)

Mankind, in their rebellion of God's sovereign authority in their lives, generally seek to oppress others around them to gain more power for themselves. The tendency is to elevate oneself by whatever means possible in order to rule as many people as possible, becoming a "god" in his or her own mind. The people of God, however, are called to live differently. Instead of taking advantage of others for our own good, we are called to sacrifice ourselves for the good of others, reflecting the heart of God for all people.

The people of Israel forgot this and began to oppress other members of their holy nation for their own benefit. Yes, there was success in the land, but at what expense? The Lord sends Amos to remind the elite of Israel that He did not release them from bondage from another power in order for them to treat each other with so much disdain.

We must be careful as the new covenant people of God to not miss the heart of God. God's heartbeat is for the broken. Jesus Himself stated His purpose in coming was to set those who are oppressed free, not create a new system by which man can continue to oppress other men (Luke 4:18-19). Are you concerned with those who are less fortunate? Or do you use them for your own good? The heart of God in us as His children should demand that we love all people the way He loves them.

~ Jared

July 12

The Wrath of God

Chronological Bible Reading Plan: (Day 193: Amos 6-9)

"'For behold, I will raise up against you a nation, O house of Israel,' declares the LORD, the God of hosts; 'and they shall oppress you from Lebo-hamath to the Brook of the Arabah.'" Amos 6:14 (ESV)

Throughout the prophets of the Old Testament, we see this overwhelming truth: the wrath of God is real, and it is also just. We don't like to talk about God's wrath, because it's a scary thing. If we fail to acknowledge this aspect of God's character, though, we present an incomplete picture of who God is and we miss the full beauty of the gospel.

In this particular passage, God is bringing wrath upon the nation of Israel for how those with power and means have transgressed their covenant with Him by forsaking the poor in their community. They have failed to represent God faithfully. As a result, His holiness and justice demand that their transgression be accounted for in judgment, which in this case will come from the Assyrian army, and He has every right to display His wrath against the faithlessness of man.

The story of Israel in Amos is our story as well. We too have offended the core of God by worshiping created things and neglecting the poor among us for selfish gain, whether directly or indirectly. We are, as Paul writes it in Eph. 2:3, "children of wrath" and worthy of the coming destruction and judgment over all creation. The beauty of the gospel, though, is that while we deserved wrath, Jesus took that wrath upon Himself. He became our propitiation, or wrath-bearer. Now we who are in Christ are free from condemnation and are able to experience fully the joy of being satisfied in Christ. Without acknowledging the wrath of God, we miss much of the beauty of Christ's work in how He has so graciously taken our place.

Be mindful today for the wrath of God and thankful for how Jesus rescued you from it.

~ *Jared*

July 13

There is Hope

Chronological Bible Reading Plan: (Day 194: 2 Chronicles 27; Isaiah 9-12)

"For to us a child is born, to us a son is given; and the government shall be upon his shoulder, and his name shall be called Wonderful Counselor, Mighty God, Everlasting Father, Prince of Peace. Of the increase of his government and of peace there will be no end, on the throne of David and over his kingdom, to establish it and to uphold it with justice and with righteousness from this time forth and forevermore. The zeal of the LORD of hosts will do this."
Isaiah 9:6-7 (ESV)

At the end of chapter 8 of the book of Isaiah, things look pretty grim for the people of Judah. Isaiah proclaims that "they will look to the earth, but behold, distress and darkness, the gloom of anguish. And they will be thrust into darkness" (Isa. 8:22 ESV). As terrible as that may seem, though, the Lord offers a glimmer of hope for their future, proclaiming that while judgment is coming presently, in a latter time a Messiah will be born to bring about a new Kingdom and everlasting peace.

The message of the Messiah centrally is that in the midst of darkness, disease, and despair, just when all hope seems lost, God will redeem His people through the anointed work of Christ! Sin and its affects will not have victory over those who see the work of this "Prince of Peace" and turn to Him alone for salvation; rather, they shall be victorious and reign with Him in an eternal Kingdom defined by justice and holiness.

When you feel discouraged or without hope, remember the promise of Isaiah 9: Joy has come in Jesus. Our obligation now is to spread that joy to those who are still without hope.

~Jared

July 14

The True Heart of a Worshiper

Chronological Bible Reading Plan: (Day 195: Micah)

"'With what shall I come before the LORD, and bow myself before God on high? Shall I come before him with burnt offerings, with calves a year old? Will the LORD be pleased with thousands of rams, with ten thousands of rivers of oil? Shall I give my firstborn for my transgression, the fruit of my body for the sin of my soul?' He has told you, O man, what is good; and what does the LORD require of you but to do justice, and to love kindness, and to walk humbly with your God?" Micah 6:6-8 (ESV)

Religious activity can be a dangerous thing. If we are not careful, we will begin to think that our acts of devotion to the Lord are really bargaining chips, obligating the Lord to bless us because of our obedience to Him. Acts of service and worship, though, were never meant to earn the favor of God; rather they were meant to express our joy in having already found favor in Him. As Micah so eloquently writes in the above passage, the Lord could care less about the number of rams and calves we sacrifice. His concern is not the action itself but rather the heart motivating the action.

In the Lord's eyes, doing justice, loving kindness, and walking humbly are more appropriate reflections of the Lord's transformative work in our lives than sacrificing our firstborn or our best livestock, because when we do those things we aren't trying to earn anything from the Lord. We are simply reacting to what the Lord is already working in us.

Why do you serve the Lord? Do you serve Him in order to earn His favor? Or are you so overwhelmed by the love shown to you in the work of Christ that you must react in service to your most-worthy God?

~ Jared

July 15

RUN TO THE LORD

Chronological Bible Reading Plan: (Day 196: 2 Kings 16-17; 2 Chronicles 28)

"In the time of his distress he became yet more faithless to the LORD--this same King Ahaz. For he sacrificed to the gods of Damascus that had defeated him and said, 'Because the gods of the kings of Syria helped them, I will sacrifice to them that they may help me.' But they were the ruin of him and of all Israel."
2 Chronicles 28:22-23 (ESV)

When tough times come into our lives, we have a choice: we can either run to the Lord or run from Him. For Ahaz, instead of repenting before the Lord and begging for His favor over Judah after being defeated by the army from Damascus, he instead began worshiping their gods, seeing his defeat as the work of the hands of greater gods instead of judgment from the one, true God of Israel. He failed to learn the lesson God was trying to teach him in this difficult time, and, as a result, led the people of God astray toward a path of impending destruction.

When bad things happen in your life, how do you react? Do you see these moments as opportunities for you to know the Lord more, experiencing His grace and peace in ways that you possibly never would have otherwise? Or do you feel the need to punish God for allowing this event to come into your life by "robbing" Him of your worship and giving it to some other created thing?

Allow moments of trouble and testing to be moments to learn more about God. Run to Him, not from Him. See that He is our present help in a time of trouble. Taste and see that He is good.

In tough moments, our true faith is revealed. How will you respond?

~Jared

July 16

The Lord is Our Defender

Chronological Bible Reading Plan: (Day 197: Isaiah 13-17)

"For the LORD will have compassion on Jacob and will again choose Israel, and will set them in their own land, and sojourners will join them and will attach themselves to the house of Jacob. And the peoples will take them and bring them to their place, and the house of Israel will possess them in the LORD's land as male and female slaves. They will take captive those who were their captors, and rule over those who oppressed them." Isaiah 14:1-2 (ESV)

The Lord is our defender. Sometimes in the midst of what we see to be injustice, we try to take matters into our own hands and fix the situation on our own. This kind of mentality, however, fails to appreciate the sovereignty of God and his orchestrating of all things for His glory and our good. If we are able to get ourselves out of a troubling situation, then we receive the glory for it. If, however, we rely upon the Lord to deliver us and He does so miraculously, in ways we could have never even imagined, then He alone receives the glory.

Do you allow the Lord to defend you, or do you try to defend yourself? When someone says something negative against you, do you try to explain it away or are you so blameless in the situation that people will eventually come to see the falsity of those statements? Are you so secure in the Lord, that fixing the words of people takes a back seat to pleasing the Lord?

We must be careful to not "defend" ourselves out of learning what God is trying to teach us in difficult moments. Rather, in the midst of these times, continue to seek the Lord and trust that when the time is right He will deliver you and, further, will have made you a better follower of Christ.

~ Jared

July 17

God's Sovereignty Over the Nations

Chronological Bible Reading Plan: (Day 198: Isaiah 18-22)

"An oracle concerning Egypt. Behold, the LORD is riding on a swift cloud and comes to Egypt; and the idols of Egypt will tremble at his presence, and the heart of the Egyptians will melt within them. And I will stir up Egyptians against Egyptians, and they will fight, each against another and each against his neighbor, city against city, kingdom against kingdom; and the spirit of the Egyptians within them will be emptied out, and I will confound their counsel; and they will inquire of the idols and the sorcerers, and the mediums and the necromancers; and I will give over the Egyptians into the hand of a hard master, and a fierce king will rule over them, declares the Lord GOD of hosts." Isaiah 19:1-4 (ESV)

A common theme throughout the prophets of the Old Testament is God's sovereign control over the nations. He appoints the rulers of nations and uses them for His ultimate purposes. He gives victory to even the enemies of Israel in order to remind His people of His ultimate power and their need for Him. The Lord through the prophet, Isaiah, is calling down judgment over a number of nations, including Egypt. In bringing judgment against Egypt, the Lord is speaking to Judah, who turned to Egypt to save them from the attacks of the Assyrians. Judah must remember that as the people of God, their first place of refuge must be to run to the Almighty, who controls the fate of even the most powerful of nations, which in this case is Egypt.

For us today, we must also be mindful of God's sovereign control over the nations to bring about His will. Let us be mindful that our government is ordained by the Lord and that we should pray for those who represent us to seek to glorify the Lord through their actions rather than detract from His glory. Further, may we remember as a nation to look to the Lord for help first rather than some other government, as He is sovereign over every human institution. Take a moment and pray for our country, that we would turn to the Lord first for His provision and protection.

~ Jared

July 18
Our Almighty God

Chronological Bible Reading Plan: (Day 199: Isaiah 23-27)

"O LORD, you are my God; I will exalt you; I will praise your name, for you have done wonderful things, plans formed of old, faithful and sure."
Isaiah 25:1 (ESV)

In chapter 25 of the book of Isaiah, we see the elders of Jerusalem mentioned in 24:23 singing a new song to the Lord of admiration and awe. The Lord has displayed His might and His glory, and His people have been humbled. How could they not be? Nations are falling around them at the pleasure of the Lord. He has faithfully provided for the needy in their land, countering the oppressive work of those who have misused their earthly authority. He has proven once again His sovereignty over all things and His plans to bring about His will for His glory and our good.

Seeing the work of the Lord is a humbling experience and should cause us to respond in adoration. How has the Lord worked mightily in your life? How has He shown Himself faithful in the midst of injustice? How has He protected you?

May we not lose sight of the power of the God we serve. He spoke and everything that is happened. Think of this kind of power. We have not seen anything close to the might of God, and yet with all of that power, the Lord does not reign over us without love and mercy. He comes as a Servant-King, calling us to worship as we are overwhelmed by His pursuit of us and faithful provision for us. The might of God served as a source of hope for the people of Israel in the Old Testament, promising to restore them to their land, and it has also proven valuable to us, as He used that power on display in Christ to overcome the comparatively impotent powers of sin and death.

Be overwhelmed by the might of our God and worship Him for how He has used it to save you!

~ Jared

July 19

That You May Tell the Next Generation

Chronological Bible Reading Plan:

(Day 200: 2 Kings 18; 2 Chronicles 29-31; Psalm 48)

"Walk about Zion, go around her, number her towers, consider well her ramparts, go through her citadels, that you may tell the next generation that this is God, our God forever and ever. He will guide us forever." Psalm 48:12-14

As people who have experienced the provision and protection of the Lord, we have a responsibility to proclaim to those who come after us the legacy of our God. Our generation should pray and hope that generations after us will avoid the mistakes we made in turning our worship to created things and keep their focus on the only worthy object of worship, Christ. The way they know of His goodness is by our declaration. We have a responsibility to shout the good news of Jesus.

How are you entrusting God's faithfulness to the generation coming after you? Statistics show that a significant number of students who grow up in the church will not stay faithful between the ages of 18-22. We cannot afford to lose them. We must fight for them. We must entrust the love of the Lord within them.

Paul gave his life to the Church, but he also gave his life to Timothy to build and instruct him for the future of the Church. A large responsibility of parents in the nation of Israel was teaching their children the miraculous works of God for their people, so that their generation would not turn to a false hope in times of trouble. Time and time again in scripture we see this call to entrust the wisdom given to us in the next generation. The question is, "Are you entrusting?"

Take a moment and pray for the generations that are coming after us. Further, commit to disciple and mentor someone in younger generations, entrusting to them your knowledge of the Lord.

~ Jared

July 20

An Unusual Call

Chronological Bible Reading Plan: (Day 201: Hosea 1-7)

"When the LORD first spoke through Hosea, the LORD said to Hosea, 'Go, take to yourself a wife of whoredom and have children of whoredom, for the land commits great whoredom by forsaking the LORD.' So he went and took Gomer, the daughter of Diblaim, and she conceived and bore him a son."
Hosea 1:2-3 (ESV)

Can you imagine Hosea's response to the Lord when He spoke this command? "Excuse me, Lord? What did you say? Can you repeat that?" What man of God would ever be called to marry a prostitute, much less one that is promised to be unfaithful even after marriage?

Gomer is impure and seemingly unworthy of someone like Hosea's affection, and, yet, that is precisely God's point. You see, you and I are unfaithful to the Lord every day, as we choose to give our worship to other things He created instead of Him. We violate our covenant with Him and are worthy of being rejected. But, see how the Lord responds. Does He reject us? No! He pursues us. He comes after us in our unfaithfulness and buys us back, as Hosea did for Gomer. He is faithful even when we are not.

We should be overwhelmed by the ridiculousness of the love God has for us! Yes, the Lord may call us to do some crazy things, as He did Hosea, but remember that nothing He could call us to is more absurd than His intimate, persistent love for us.

Be overwhelmed by the love of God for you today. Think specifically of God's love for you displayed on the cross of Christ. Truly, He forsook everything to pursue you!

~ *Jared*

July 21

The Goal of Repentance

Chronological Bible Reading Plan: (Day 202: Hosea 8-14)

"I will heal their apostasy; I will love them freely, for my anger has turned from them. I will be like the dew to Israel; he shall blossom like the lily; he shall take root like the trees of Lebanon; his shoots shall spread out; his beauty shall be like the olive, and his fragrance like Lebanon." Hosea 14:4-6 (ESV)

The goal of repentance is always restoration. The Lord promises His people when they return to Him and repent of their idolatry and transgressions, He will forgive them and bless them. Both elements of restoration are important here. Forgiveness is important in that it communicates the healing of a fractured relationship. The Lord, though, doesn't stop there. Not only does He forgive Israel; He blesses them.

Consider for a moment the significance of this duality within restoration. The Lord could have simply forgiven them and let them dig themselves out of their self-imposed hole. Yet, He goes above and beyond. He forgives completely, as should we.

When we have been wronged by those around us, how do we respond? Often we may speak forgiveness, but fail to work toward full restoration with the other person.

When someone wrongs you, do you seek to bless them after they repent? Are you able to move forward in grace and love as the Lord has done for us time and again?

May we seek to act toward one another as the Lord has acted toward us. Once someone has asked for our forgiveness, let us not try to make them feel the pain we have felt. Rather, let us move forward in grace and seek to bless them as fellow brothers and sisters in covenant with Christ. The Lord has acted graciously toward us; may we act graciously toward each other.

~ *Jared*

July 22

Repentance Leads to Destruction

Chronological Bible Reading Plan: (Day 203: Isaiah 28-30)

"Then you will defile your carved idols overlaid with silver and your gold-plated metal images. You will scatter them as unclean things. You will say to them, 'Be gone!'" Isaiah 30:22 (ESV)

True repentance leads to the destruction of the idol in your life that is stealing your affection for the Lord. The goal of repentance is not for you to manage your sin nor keep it under control; the goal is for you to destroy your sin. For the Israelite people, when they repented they could not afford to keep the carved idols overlaid with silver nor the gold-plated images, for doing so would have left open the door for another transgression. They had to remove the temptation altogether in order to turn from their sin completely.

We must treat the idols in our lives the same way. When we recognize that they are interfering with our covenant relationship with God Almighty and we repent of them, we must destroy the idols and say to them, "Be gone!" Don't be so naive to think that you can keep the source of your sin near and not stumble. Destroy it or it will destroy you.

For many of us, this act of destruction is a very hard thing to do. Our idol can be a relationship, a sport we have spent years trying to perfect, a secret sin kept hidden for decades, or even an act of service in the church that we think is earning the favor of our Lord. While we must not be unwise in the way we dispose of our idol, we must also not wait forever in hopes that how we react to this particular stimulus will change.

What do you need to destroy in your life? What is stealing your affection from the Lord? What could you fill the void left by its absence with to lead you to greater intimacy with the Lord? Throw out the idols and taste of the satisfaction of the Lord. See that He alone is good!

~ Jared

July 23

The Lord, Our Firm Foundation

Chronological Bible Reading Plan: (Day 204: Isaiah 31-34)

"The LORD is exalted, for he dwells on high; he will fill Zion with justice and righteousness, and he will be the stability of your times, abundance of salvation, wisdom, and knowledge; the fear of the LORD is Zion's treasure."
Isaiah 33:5-6 (ESV)

Over the past few days we have looked at the Lord's plan for repentance, resulting from a period of discipline. We have seen our need to emulate Him in how we forgive and to destroy those things that cause us to take our eyes off of Him and His greater purposes for the nations. Today, we see how the Lord provides stability for us in the midst of His discipline. While we are being disciplined for the sin in our life, we may feel injustice or self-pity, but we must remember that there is purpose in discipline. Sometimes the covenant people of God must face instability in the physical world to remember God's ultimate control, thereby finding stability in Him alone.

When instability comes in your life, where do you turn? Do you turn to the Lord and cry out for His salvation, or do you blame Him for even allowing such discomfort in your life? In the midst of spiritual pain or loss, first ask the cause of this discomfort. Is this the enemy at work in order to discourage you from something the Lord has clearly called you to, or is this a consequence from persistent sin or disobedience in your life? If the former, run to the Lord and seek His grace to press forward in obedience. If the latter, seek the Lord's revelation in your life to know what needs to be removed. In either case, remember that the Lord is our foundation and the place we should run toward in every circumstance.

~ *Jared*

July 24

A Trusting Heart or an Anxious Heart

Chronological Bible Reading Plan: (Day 205: Isaiah 35-36)

"Say to those who have an anxious heart, 'Be strong; fear not! Behold, your God will come with vengeance, with the recompense of God. He will come and save you.'" Isaiah 35:4 (ESV)

The beginning of chapter 35 of the book of Isaiah begins with a joyous promise of restoration revealing the glory of God. As the Lord waters the dry land and His people once again begin to sing His praise, they will "see the glory of the Lord, the majesty of our God" (Isa. 35:2b ESV). Once they have beheld the glory of God in His faithfulness, Isaiah says their anxiety or fear should turn to confidence, for God is bigger than any temporary difficulty.

When we behold the glory of God, we should be emboldened, losing fear and gaining confidence. His glory reveals His strength and ability to accomplish His purposes through the instrumentation of all of creation. Nothing is too big for Him. So, why would we worry? Why would we fear? Why would anxiety ever enter into our lives, knowing that even in our darkest moments the Lord is working all things for our good and within His divine plan?

Do you have an anxious heart? An anxious heart reveals a lack of trust in God's power and sovereignty. Take comfort in knowing the biblical truth that God will do what He says He will do. Do not worry, but rest in His faithfulness. Remember the glory of God displayed on the cross of Christ and know that you have been saved from the greatest threat to your eternal happiness, so what else is there really to be anxious about? You can be eternally secure in your God, who has come to save you!

~ *Jared*

July 25

A Fool for Flattery

Chronological Bible Reading Plan: (Day 206: Isaiah 37-39; Psalms 76)

"At that time Merodach-baladan the son of Baladan, king of Babylon, sent envoys with letters and a present to Hezekiah, for he heard that he had been sick and had recovered. And Hezekiah welcomed them gladly. And he showed them his treasure house, the silver, the gold, the spices, the precious oil, his whole armory, all that was found in his storehouses. There was nothing in his house or in all his realm that Hezekiah did not show them." Isaiah 39:1-2 (ESV)

Hezekiah was in the prime of his reign over Judah. He had stood firm in the face of Sennacherib and his boisterous Rabshakeh, relying on the Lord to display His glorious might in their deliverance from the Assyrians. He had been seriously ill to the point of death and, then, miraculously healed by the word of the Lord through the prophet Isaiah and had his life extended. Just when you think things are perfect for Hezekiah, he does something dumb. He allows the flattery of a foreign government, in this case Babylon, to weaken his defenses and leave himself and his country exposed. When the Babylonians came to check on him, showing him great honor, he did not stop in welcoming, showing them everything in his house and in his realm. The Babylonians certainly would have been impressed, perhaps too much so. Isaiah confronts Hezekiah for his foolishness and speaks over him a promise: his desire to receive the praise of men will ultimately aid in the destruction of his beloved kingdom.

Beware of flattery because it can make you look foolish. Hezekiah never once stopped to ask if this foreign government had ulterior motives in coming to visit them because his vanity liked the attention. As a result, he made himself and his kingdom vulnerable. When someone comes with a flattering tongue, remember you are to boast in Christ alone. Keep your eyes on Him, not allowing the enemy to gain access to your heart.

~Jared

July 26
Behold My Servant

Chronological Bible Reading Plan: (Day 207: Isaiah 40-43)

"Behold my servant, whom I uphold, my chosen, in whom my soul delights; I have put my Spirit upon him; he will bring forth justice to the nations. He will not cry aloud or lift up his voice, or make it heard in the street; a bruised reed he will not break, and a faintly burning wick he will not quench; he will faithfully bring forth justice. He will not grow faint or be discouraged till he has established justice in the earth; and the coastlands wait for his law." Isaiah 42:1-4 (ESV)

Isaiah 40 marks a transition in the writings of Isaiah from warnings about exile to words of comfort in exile. The people of God have now been conquered by the Babylonians, as foretold in the previous chapters, and now Isaiah offers them a message of hope that actually foreshadows a greater hope for all of us. In chapter 42, we find the first of four "Servant Songs" in this epic prophetic work that promise the restoration of the Jewish people and foreshadow a coming messiah, who will achieve greater things for the good of the nations. This "chosen servant" will carry the favor of God and His Spirit and will establish justice upon the earth.

What an incredible message this is! When you look at this world and you see all of the injustice that exists, know that we are not without hope as the people of God in Babylonian captivity were not without hope. We have hope in this coming servant, Jesus Christ. He will establish justice and hold all of mankind accountable for their response to the one, true God of Israel and for their stewardship over what He has created.

When you see injustice, do not lose heart. The Lord has not forgotten us, for His Son suffered far greater injustice than we can see or imagine so that you and I could experience peace.

~ *Jared*

July 27
Refined for His Glory

Chronological Bible Reading Plan: (Day 208: Isaiah 44-48)

"For my name's sake I defer my anger, for the sake of my praise I restrain it for you, that I may not cut you off. Behold, I have refined you, but not as silver; I have tried you in the furnace of affliction. For my own sake, for my own sake, I do it, for how should my name be profaned? My glory I will not give to another."
Isaiah 48:9-11 (ESV)

The refining process is sometimes a painful one, but in the end it is worth it to better reflect the glory of God. The People of Israel forget their ultimate purpose in life: to represent God faithfully to the surrounding nations. The Lord, as a result, sent them through a period of refinement in order to remind them of their great need for Him and His ultimate control over all things. He would not allow His covenant people to transgress their promise and defame His holy name, which the Lord establishes as His chief concern. His holy name is the name by which we are saved. His holy name is the name to which every knee will bow and which every tongue will confess. His name represents the fullness of His being and we are not to take it nor our devotion to it in vain. We are to hold the name of God sacred and defend it, as He Himself does, for in His name is His glory upheld.

Would you give yourself completely to the Lord, allowing Him to shape and mold you into the image of Jesus through a refining process to better represent His name? Are you ok with walking through times of hardship and discipline for the sake of the glory of God?

If God's chief concern is His name, then that should be our chief concern as well, and we should seek to bring glory to it regardless of the cost. He certainly spared no cost in pursuing and saving us.

~Jared

July 28

Be Still and Know

Chronological Bible Reading Plan: (Day 209: 2 Kings 19; Psalms 46, 80, 135)

"Come, behold the works of the LORD, how he has brought desolations on the earth. He makes wars cease to the end of the earth; he breaks the bow and shatters the spear; he burns the chariots with fire. 'Be still, and know that I am God. I will be exalted among the nations, I will be exalted in the earth!' The LORD of hosts is with us; the God of Jacob is our fortress. Selah"
Psalm 46:8-11 (ESV)

In the midst of the chaos of life, it is good for mankind to be still and recognize God's ultimate control and plan for all things. We must continually stop and remind ourselves of our dependence upon Him and our responsibility to praise Him for His faithfulness, knowing that as we praise Him others will hear of His goodness and be blessed as they too look to Him alone for salvation.

In the church we often teach the need for a time of daily devotion, usually in the morning, wherein an individual studies the scriptures and reflects on their impact in his or her life. The purpose of this time, though, is more than simple obedience; it's also preparation. If we do not take time to be still before the Lord, we will miss the Lord's activity among the nations, seeing defeat instead of ultimate victory and complain or worry in situations where we should be praising. As we walk through our day, we will forget that the Lord is with us and is our mighty fortress and fail to give Him the glory for His provision.

The reality is that times of trouble will come. In being still before the Lord and reflecting upon His secure hold over our lives, we can truly hold onto the promise that He alone is our certain refuge and strength. Commit to be still before the Lord and know!

~ *Jared*

July 29

Our Promised Savior

Chronological Bible Reading Plan: (Day 210: Isaiah 49-53)

"Surely he has borne our griefs and carried our sorrows; yet we esteemed him stricken, smitten by God, and afflicted. But he was wounded for our transgressions; he was crushed for our iniquities; upon him was the chastisement that brought us peace, and with his stripes we are healed. All we like sheep have gone astray; we have turned--every one--to his own way; and the LORD has laid on him the iniquity of us all." Isaiah 53:4-6 (ESV)

In one of the most beautiful passages in all of scripture, the Lord through the prophet Isaiah sets forth a divine promise of greater salvation coming in the form of a servant. This servant, chosen and formed by the hand of God, will come to set the people of God free from a greater oppressive force than the Assyrian army. He will take on the oppression of sin and God's wrath against that sin, absorbing our full judgment as our Heavenly Father lays upon him the iniquity of us all. No longer will an animal pay the price for our sin; rather, God's chosen instrument will become our bearer of His wrath.

The promise here is unmistakable, as it clearly points to the work of Jesus Christ, who sacrificed the glory of heaven to pursue us and reconcile us to God by removing the stain of our transgression. We were rebellious in our devotion to the Lord as His creation, and yet for the sake of His glory, the Lord chose to rescue us and restore us as He did the people of Israel. From Genesis to Revelation, the Lord has been unfolding this ultimate plan of restoration, a small picture of which we see in Isaiah's prophetic work.

Our responsibility is the same as that of Isaiah. We are to proclaim Christ's redemptive work for the sake of the nations. Will you proclaim Christ's saving work today?

~ Jared

July 30

Return to the Lord

Chronological Bible Reading Plan: (Day 211: Isaiah 54-58)

"Seek the LORD while he may be found; call upon him while he is near; let the wicked forsake his way, and the unrighteous man his thoughts; let him return to the LORD, that he may have compassion on him, and to our God, for he will abundantly pardon. For my thoughts are not your thoughts, neither are your ways my ways, declares the LORD. For as the heavens are higher than the earth, so are my ways higher than your ways and my thoughts than your thoughts." Isaiah 55:6-9 (ESV)

The gospel, the good news of Jesus Christ, calls us to run toward the Lord in times of despair (even in times of sin) rather than run from Him. We are to trust in His goodness and His forgiveness if our hearts are repentant and committed to change. Isaiah speaks that truth over the people of Israel here. Do not remain far from the Lord; rather, forsake what you forsook Him for and return so that He may pardon you.

Does it make sense that a holy God would forgive an unholy people, who have so incredibly offended the core of His Being? No, but His ways are higher than our ways and His promise is that when we return, we will find His arms wide open.

How do you respond when you have sinned against the Lord? Do you run from Him, hoping to hide your guilt from His omniscience and omnipresence? Or do you embrace the sacrifice of this suffering servant, who has already borne our iniquity, and run toward your true place of solace and forgiveness?

Seek the Lord while He may be found and find His arms wide open, waiting for you, dear child of God.

~ Jared

July 31

SIMPLIFY AND FOCUS

Chronological Bible Reading Plan: (Day 212: Isaiah 59-63)

"The Spirit of the Lord God is upon me, because the Lord has anointed me to bring good news to the poor; he has sent me to bind up the brokenhearted, to proclaim liberty to the captives, and the opening of the prison to those who are bound; to proclaim the year of the Lord's favor, and the day of vengeance of our God; to comfort all who mourn; to grant to those who mourn in Zion—to give them a beautiful headdress instead of ashes, the oil of gladness instead of mourning, the garment of praise instead of a faint spirit; that they may be called oaks of righteousness, the planting of the Lord, that he may be glorified."
Isaiah 61:1-3 (ESV)

What are you going to do with the time you have left? Don't waste your life. Don't delay in knowing and doing God's will. You are too valuable and your life is too vital to neglect living in the center of God's will.

As He stood in the synagogue in His hometown, Jesus quoted Isaiah's prophecy concerning Himself. "And he rolled up the scroll and gave it back to the attendant and sat down. And the eyes of all in the synagogue were fixed on him. And he began to say to them, 'Today this Scripture has been fulfilled in your hearing'" (Luke 4:20-21 ESV).

God has pursued you with His redeeming love and placed His divine purpose inside of you by His Holy Spirit so that you can continue the ministry of Jesus on earth. You are anointed by God for worship, evangelism, discipleship, ministry, and authentic community. Draw near to God and allow Him to sensitize you to His redemptive activity. You are God's workmanship and you have been created by God and for God. Make yourself completely available for God's use today!

~ *Stephen*

August 1

Revival Awaits

Chronological Bible Reading Plan: (Day 213: Isaiah 64-66)

"Oh that you would rend the heavens and come down, that the mountains might quake at your presence—as when fire kindles brushwood and the fire causes water to boil—to make your name known to your adversaries, and that the nations might tremble at your presence!" Isaiah 64:1-2 (ESV)

We are desperate for revival in America. The slippery slope of sin has eroded the landscape of morality and dulled the point of purity in our society. Defiance and drifting have marked the cultural current of casual Christianity. What was once abhorred in American history is now deemed the new normal. We have accelerated the vast array of sinful indulgence and have become preoccupied with self worship.

In the darkest of nights, the light of God's holiness shines the brightest. We are positioned for a great move of God. God is pursuing us with His redeeming love and we have the capacity to respond to His pursuit. This is not the time to be "at ease in Zion" and settle for mediocrity. Jesus has paid far too high a price for our salvation. Let's not accept the status quo and let's refrain from embracing the embers of idolatry.

In brokenness over our sin and in humility before the Creator of the universe, let's pray for revival. Pray that God would open the heavens and come down to reveal His glory, to reveal His holiness, and to usher in revival in America. May the mountains quake at His presence and may the nations tremble at His presence.

Confess known sin instantly and completely. Receive God's forgiveness and surrender to the Lordship of Christ. Passionately pursue God's agenda. Seek His face with all your heart. Abandon your all. Place your "yes" on the altar and allow God to have His way in your life. Revival awaits!

~ *Stephen*

August 2

Desperation and Prayer

Chronological Bible Reading Plan: (Day 214: 2 Kings 20-21)

"In those days Hezekiah became sick and was at the point of death. And Isaiah the prophet the son of Amoz came to him and said to him, Thus says the Lord, 'Set your house in order, for you shall die; you shall not recover.' Then Hezekiah turned his face to the wall and prayed to the Lord, saying, 'Now, O Lord, please remember how I have walked before you in faithfulness and with a whole heart, and have done what is good in your sight.'" 2 Kings 20:2-3 (ESV)

Have you ever been desperate for God's intervention? Have you ever been between a rock and a hard place and wondered how you would make it through? Hezekiah reached the breaking point as he neared the point of death. To make matters worse, the prophet Isaiah came to Hezekiah with a definitive word from the Lord concerning the reality of Hezekiah's sickness ending in death. In absolute desperation, Hezekiah cried out to the Lord in prayer. God responded to Hezekiah's plea.

- *"'Turn back, and say to Hezekiah the leader of my people, Thus says the Lord, the God of David your father: I have heard your prayer; I have seen your tears. Behold, I will heal you. On the third day you shall go up to the house of the Lord, and I will add fifteen years to your life. I will deliver you and this city out of the hand of the king of Assyria, and I will defend this city for my own sake and for my servant David's sake.'"* 2 Kings 20:5-6 (ESV)

What do you need to take to the Lord in prayer? What are you agonizing over? Bring your burdens to the Lord. Entrust your life to His care.

~ Stephen

August 3

God Answers Prayer

Chronological Bible Reading Plan: (Day 215: 2 Chronicles 32-33)

"The Lord spoke to Manasseh and to his people, but they paid no attention. Therefore the Lord brought upon them the commanders of the army of the king of Assyria, who captured Manasseh with hooks and bound him with chains of bronze and brought him to Babylon. And when he was in distress, he entreated the favor of the Lord his God and humbled himself greatly before the God of his fathers. He prayed to him, and God was moved by his entreaty and heard his plea and brought him again to Jerusalem into his kingdom. Then Manasseh knew that the Lord was God." 2 Chronicles 33:10-13 (ESV)

How long can a person run from God? Manasseh refused to heed the voice of God and to demonstrate obedience. Instead, Manasseh rebelled against God and led his people to do the same. The Lord delivered severe consequences by bringing Manasseh into Babylonian captivity.

In humility, Manasseh chose to cry out to God in prayer. God was moved by Manasseh's entreaty and chose to bring him back into his kingdom in Jerusalem. Manasseh came to know the Lord by experience as the Lord his God.

Sometimes God will allow us to experience the consequences of our personal sin in order to forge brokenness and humility within us. As we turn from sin and turn to the Lord in brokenness and humility, God responds by restoring our love relationship. His abiding peace becomes our reality.

Learn to pray before you are tempted to compromise your convictions. Seek God's face perpetually and choose to practice God's presence. Be conscious of His activity and surrender to His Lordship. Don't allow anything to come between you and God. Keep a close eye on the priorities God as established in your life.

~ *Stephen*

August 4

Take Refuge in Him

Chronological Bible Reading Plan: (Day 216: Nahum)

"The Lord is good, a stronghold in the day of trouble; he knows those who take refuge in him." Nahum 1:7 (ESV)

Where do you turn when you need refuge? The world offers many choices. You can lose yourself in the stream of entertainment. You can anesthetize your pain with busyness. You can dive into your work and allow your energy to be consumed by that pursuit. Another option is to embrace worldliness and allow the current of the culture to take you places you haven't been.

The only choice that delivers on the promise is the choice to turn to God. When you call out to God, the response is that of mercy. God does not give us what we, in our sin, truly deserve. God lavishes us with His love and provides us with His peace. His mercy is evidenced as your soul takes refuge in Him.

What disaster has come your way? Take refuge in the shadow of His wings. Whenever you go through a season of uncertainty, take refuge in God. When the path is unclear, take refuge in your merciful God. As you wait for the answer to your prayers, take refuge in the God who hears and responds. The enemy will not thwart God's will. Nothing will separate you from the love of God.

As you take refuge in the Lord, thank Him for being merciful in your past, your present, and your future. Give God glory for His consistent measure of comfort during your seasons of desperation. Rely upon God's provision to see you through. God will make a way when there seems to be no way. He is your stronghold in the day of trouble. He knows you and knows what you need most. Take refuge in Him.

~ *Stephen*

August 5

Contagious Conduct

Chronological Bible Reading Plan:
(Day 217: 2 Kings 22-23; 2 Chronicles 34-35)

"In the eighth year of his reign, while he was still young, he began to seek the God of his father David. In his twelfth year he began to purge Judah and Jerusalem of high places, Asherah poles, carved idols and cast images."
2 Chronicles 34:3 (ESV)

What caused Josiah, at the age of sixteen, to begin to seek God? When you look at his family tree, you find that both his father, Amon, and his grandfather, Manasseh, did evil in the eyes of the Lord. It is obvious that Josiah did not receive his spiritual heritage from them. When you look into the life of his great-grandfather, Hezekiah, you find a much different portrait.

- *"And he did what was right in the eyes of the Lord, according to all that David his father had done."* 2 Chron. 29:2 (ESV)

I wonder if Josiah was influenced by the godly life that his great-grandfather, Hezekiah, lived. Another possibility is that Josiah began to seek God when he became a dad, at the age of sixteen, to Jehoahaz. For me personally, when I became a dad my understanding of God's love and my pursuit of God intensified. There's something about seeing your own flesh and blood and embracing the awesome responsibility of parenthood that draws you to God. You recognize your dependency upon God.

Regardless of your age or life stage, assess your level of thirst for God? Are you passionately seeking God daily and allowing Him to have full access to your mind, emotions, and will? Is there anything or anyone you desire more than you desire God? I have discovered in my walk with God, whatever you feed grows and whatever you starve dies.

~ *Stephen*

August 6

DAY OF THE LORD

Chronological Bible Reading Plan: (Day 218: Zephaniah)

"The Lord your God is in your midst, a mighty one who will save; he will rejoice over you with gladness; he will quiet you by his love; he will exult over you with loud singing." Zephaniah 3:17 (ESV)

As a child of the living God, you can look forward to the day of the Lord. In Christ, you have eternal security and you have a perpetual responsibility to invite others into a saving relationship with Jesus. The day of reckoning is approaching when every human being will stand before God to give an account for his or her life. If you are a follower of Jesus Christ, God will rejoice over you with gladness. He will quiet you by His love and exult over you with loud singing. You will experience the culmination of your salvation and hear the reassuring words, "Well done, good and faithful servant" (Matt. 25:21 ESV).

- *"But the day of the Lord will come like a thief, and then the heavens will pass away with a roar, and the heavenly bodies will be burned up and dissolved, and the earth and the works that are done on it will be exposed." 2 Pet. 3:10 (ESV)*

Choose to live in the readiness mode. Live in light of the day of the Lord. We have a limited amount of time to share God's love and to shine God's light in this dark and decaying world. Those who do not have a personal love relationship with Jesus will experience the dreadful day of the Lord where God's righteousness will expose the evil deeds of every unregenerate individual.

God is in our midst. Join Him in His redemptive activity to rescue the perishing. You are armed with the Good News of Jesus Christ. Put on the full armor of God and go to war for souls!

~ *Stephen*

August 7

Before You Were Born

Chronological Bible Reading Plan: (Day 219: Jeremiah 1-3)

"'Before I formed you in the womb I knew you, and before you were born I consecrated you; I appointed you a prophet to the nations.'" Jeremiah 1:5 (ESV)

What is your date of birth? How many birthdays have you celebrated up to this point? Now imagine the fact that before you were formed in your mother's womb, God knew you. Before your date of birth, God consecrated you unto Himself. In other words, God set you apart as a unique treasure for His unique purpose. Before you were born, God appointed you to continue the ministry of Jesus on the earth.

Your life matters. Every decision you make matters. God has pursued you with His redeeming love so that you could come into an intimate and eternal relationship with Him that is authentic. You are not an accident. You are God's idea and you are God's workmanship.

Just as God knew Jeremiah before He formed him in his mother's womb, God knew you. Just as God set Jeremiah apart and appointed Him as a prophet to the nations before he was even born, so God has intricately purposed your life and He has positioned you for eternity.

God has created you and re-created you in His image so that you can fulfill His purposes on the earth. Walk in the light God gives you and practice instant obedience. Obey what God has already shown you. Practice His presence through moment-by-moment full surrender to His Lordship and His leadership. Abandon your personal agenda and embrace God's agenda.

Get to know the heart of God. He loves you so much and His plan includes you. You are vital to God's kingdom economy. Your life will continue beyond what you see in the here and now. Yield to His prompting. Follow His lead. Finish strong.

~ *Stephen*

August 8

Dislodge Wicked Thoughts

Chronological Bible Reading Plan: (Day 220: Jeremiah 4-6)

"O Jerusalem, wash your heart from evil, that you may be saved. How long shall your wicked thoughts lodge within you?" Jeremiah 4:14 (ESV)

Your thought-life determines your walk-life. It matters how you think and it matters what you think. Your thoughts prompt your behavior. When impure thoughts linger, your life becomes contaminated. Impure thoughts can stain a pure heart.

The word of the Lord came through Jeremiah for the people to wash their hearts from evil so they could be saved. Jeremiah confronted them for their wicked thoughts lodged within them. The same word of the Lord could be spoken over us in our contemporary context in our culture saturated with sinful indulgence.

- *"Thus says the Lord: 'Stand by the roads, and look, and ask for the ancient paths, where the good way is; and walk in it, and find rest for your souls.'" Jer. 6:16 (ESV)*
- *"Do not be conformed to this world, but be transformed by the renewal of your mind, that by testing you may discern what is the will of God, what is good and acceptable and perfect." Rom. 12:2 (ESV)*

Dislodge wicked thoughts. Take every thought captive. Remember when you put garbage in, you get garbage out. Protect your mind and guard your heart. Find the good way and walk in it. Take paths that are firm and that are in alignment with God's purposes and plan. Find rest for your soul.

Instead of conforming to the pattern of this world, be transformed by renewing your mind. Replace falsehood with the truth of God's Word. Delete deception and embrace truth. Run from sin and run to Jesus. Flee sin and follow after the things of God. Feed on God's Word and maintain daily intimacy with God. Deliberately draw near to God.

~ Stephen

August 9

Boast in the Lord

Chronological Bible Reading Plan: (Day 221: Jeremiah 7-9)

"Thus says the Lord: 'Let not the wise man boast in his wisdom, let not the mighty man boast in his might, let not the rich man boast in his riches, but let him who boasts boast in this, that he understands and knows me, that I am the Lord who practices steadfast love, justice, and righteousness in the earth. For in these things I delight, declares the Lord.'" Jeremiah 9:23-24 (ESV)

What have you achieved thus far in this life? What are your accomplishments? How much success have you attained? You can answer these questions and before you know it, pride seeps in. You can easily pat yourself on the back and affirm yourself for how far you have come in this life.

God rewards obedience and He expects us to give our very best effort in the endeavors of this life. However, we must guard against boasting in our wisdom, in our might, or in our riches. Boasting in our accomplishments places the credit on ourselves and bypasses the gracious activity of God.

- *"But far be it from me to boast except in the cross of our Lord Jesus Christ, by which the world has been crucified to me, and I to the world." Gal. 6:14 (ESV)*

Celebrate the reality of your love relationship with God through Christ. Boast in the wondrous gift of having a personal intimate love relationship with the Creator of the universe. If you boast, boast in the precious privilege of understanding and knowing the Lord. Without God's pursuit of your life with His redeeming love, you would have nothing to boast about. Without the cross of our Lord Jesus Christ, your life would be empty, directionless, and hopeless. Boast in the Lord for allowing you to be the recipient of His marvelous grace and invite others into the same privilege.

~ *Stephen*

August 10

A Holy People Called to Represent a Holy God

Chronological Bible Reading Plan: (Day 222: Jeremiah 10-13)

"Hear the word that the LORD speaks to you, O house of Israel. Thus says the LORD: 'Learn not the way of the nations, nor be dismayed at the signs of the heavens because the nations are dismayed at them, for the customs of the peoples are vanity.'" Jeremiah 10:1-3a (ESV)

The covenant people of God were called to transform the cultures around them, not be transformed by those cultures. Instead of representing God and His holiness to their neighboring nations, Israel chose to become consumed with their vain pursuits. They worshiped false gods and transgressed their covenant with the Lord. As a result, the Lord promised a reminder in the form of judgment.

We have the same calling as God's new covenant people in Christ. We are called to proclaim the gospel and transform our culture, calling all people back to a right relationship with God. The same danger that entrapped the Israelites, however, still exists for us. We must be careful to not stumble into their vanity while trying to give them the gospel. Be sure you are the one transforming rather than being transformed.

In order to maintain your focus and abstain from the vain pursuits of man be sure you are walking in community with both the Lord and holy men. Spend time with the Lord so that you remember how He has delivered you and satisfied you in ways that the things this world offers never could. Further, have men and women around you who are pursuing the Lord in the same way so that if you are tempted, they can call you back into obedience.

The calling on our lives to represent God is of the utmost importance, because in representing Him we offer hope of fulfillment and purpose in Christ!

~ Jared

August 11

Beware of False Prophets

Chronological Bible Reading Plan: (Day 223: Jeremiah 14-17)

"And the LORD said to me: 'The prophets are prophesying lies in my name. I did not send them, nor did I command them or speak to them. They are prophesying to you a lying vision, worthless divination, and the deceit of their own minds. Therefore thus says the LORD concerning the prophets who prophesy in my name although I did not send them, and who say, 'Sword and famine shall not come upon this land': By sword and famine those prophets shall be consumed. And the people to whom they prophesy shall be cast out in the streets of Jerusalem, victims of famine and sword, with none to bury them--them, their wives, their sons, and their daughters. For I will pour out their evil upon them.'"
Jeremiah 14:14-16 (ESV)

Beware of false prophets, who gain success by telling you what you want to hear rather than the truth. In the midst of impending judgement upon the people of God, some prophets began telling the Israelites that God did not want to send famine or an army to destroy them. Rather, He wanted them to prosper as His beloved, covenant people. These prophets, though, did not receive this word from the Lord; they proclaimed this word for their own good, probably coming forth from their own hopes. But these prophets did not know the heart of God for His holy name and the severity of His offense toward those who defame that name and their covenant. Judgment was coming whether or not the people of God wanted it, because they needed it and deserved it.

False prophets, unfortunately, still proclaim false words, claiming them to be from the Lord, today. They communicate words sinful man wants to hear rather than what they need to hear, which ultimately does them no good. As the new covenant people of God, let us make sure that the words we allow someone to speak over us match the character of God as it is revealed in scripture. Do not be deceived by what you want to hear; be devoted to what you need to hear, flowing forth from the mouth of the Almighty.

~ Jared

August 12

Potter's Touch

Chronological Bible Reading Plan: (Day 224: Jeremiah 18-22)

"So I went down to the potter's house, and there he was working at his wheel. And the vessel he was making of clay was spoiled in the potter's hand, and he reworked it into another vessel, as it seemed good to the potter to do."
Jeremiah 18:3-4 (ESV)

One of my Sunday School teachers who flew an A-10 fighter jet in the Air Force used to say, "The closer you get to the enemy, the greater the conflict." When you are living to please God, be ready for that spiritual motion to cause friction and spiritual warfare.

The safest place for you to be is in the center of God's will. The most dangerous place for you to be is in the center of God's will. When you are living in the center of God's will, you experience His provision and protection. However, you are the greatest threat to Satan when you are living in the center of God's will. When you think about it, being on Satan's radar is an indication of being a threat to his kingdom. You cannot walk in the center of God's will unopposed.

Jeremiah, known as the weeping prophet, experienced the painful reality of being on the potter's wheel. God placed Jeremiah on the potter's wheel to demonstrate His loving and corrective touch. God demonstrated the value He places on purity, holiness, and full surrender. God expects that of every generation and every nation.

Don't resist those seasons of being placed on the potter's wheel. Remember that God is the Potter and you are the clay. God tenderly and lovingly molds you and shapes you for His glory. God removes the impediments in your life that restrict His flow through you. Be still! Rest! Give God access to every area of your life. Allow God to shape you for His eternal significance.

~ *Stephen*

August 13
Our God is at Hand

Chronological Bible Reading Plan: (Day 225: Jeremiah 23-25)

"Am I a God at hand, declares the LORD, and not a God far away? Can a man hide himself in secret places so that I cannot see him? declares the LORD. Do I not fill heaven and earth? declares the LORD. I have heard what the prophets have said who prophesy lies in my name, saying, 'I have dreamed, I have dreamed!' How long shall there be lies in the heart of the prophets who prophesy lies, and who prophesy the deceit of their own heart, who think to make my people forget my name by their dreams that they tell one another, even as their fathers forgot my name for Baal? Let the prophet who has a dream tell the dream, but let him who has my word speak my word faithfully." Jeremiah 23:23-28a (ESV)

As representatives of the Lord, let us be careful to follow that calling faithfully, not claiming a word from the Lord for our own glory but sharing that which He has revealed for His glory and our good. The leadership of the Israelite people had themselves fallen away from the Lord and had begun to lead the people entrusted to them away as well. The Lord in this passage marvels at the audacity of these prophets and priests, claiming the authority and blessing of the Lord while defaming His holy name. Had these leaders fallen so far out of God's presence that they failed to remember His nature and His resolve to defend His character and covenant?

As the people of God today, let us be sure that we are not claiming revelation from the Lord simply because of convenience. As the people of God today, and certainly those of us in leadership positions, may we hold in the highest esteem revelation from the Lord, using it with the holiest of intentions so that those around us do not come to question the integrity of God while questioning ours, because He will defend His name.

Know that God is all around us. Do not think you can slip something by Him that detracts from His glory rather than enhances it! Be aware of God's presence and live in light of it.

~ Jared

August 14

Seek the Welfare of the City

Chronological Bible Reading Plan: (Day 226: Jeremiah 26-29)

"Thus says the LORD of hosts, the God of Israel, to all the exiles whom I have sent into exile from Jerusalem to Babylon: Build houses and live in them; plant gardens and eat their produce. Take wives and have sons and daughters; take wives for your sons, and give your daughters in marriage, that they may bear sons and daughters; multiply there, and do not decrease. But seek the welfare of the city where I have sent you into exile, and pray to the LORD on its behalf, for in its welfare you will find your welfare." Jeremiah 29:4-7 (ESV)

Jeremiah is addressing the false prophecy of Hananiah, who proclaimed to the Jewish people that within two years of his prophecy, the Lord would release His people from the yoke of Babylon. Jeremiah proclaims that the Lord would not only leave them in captivity for longer than two years, but would leave them there for generations.

Jeremiah delivers an interesting challenge from the Lord to His people, urging them to engage with the city of Babylon for its welfare and for their own. The likely reaction for many of the Jewish people would be to simply ride out the storm of captivity and never have anything to do with Babylon, creating a bubble of sorts to shield themselves from these gentiles. Yet, God commands them to act otherwise, knowing that if the people of God give benefit to their captors, they will receive benefits as well.

For us today, a similar challenge exists. We are not in bondage to a foreign government as a people, but we do live in a culture that does not honor the Lord. We have a choice as God's people about how to interact with that culture. Do we simply wait for God to come rescue us and live in a bubble or do we engage the culture for our mutual good? I believe we should engage God's established, secular institutions for our mutual good rather than resisting the city altogether. In fighting for the welfare of the city we too may find benefit for the Kingdom of God.

~ Jared

August 15

God's Everlasting Love

Chronological Bible Reading Plan: (Day 227: Jeremiah 30-31)

"Thus says the LORD: 'The people who survived the sword found grace in the wilderness; when Israel sought for rest, the LORD appeared to him from far away. I have loved you with an everlasting love; therefore I have continued my faithfulness to you.'" Jeremiah 31:2-3 (ESV)

The presence of discipline does not indicate a lack of love; rather, discipline when given by the Lord is always motivated by love for the good of His children. As we have seen throughout the prophets, the people of God had wandered from the Lord and had begun to turn to other things to find satisfaction. The Lord calls them back to Himself in discipline, knowing that if His people continue to pursue the favor of idols or satisfaction in the world, they will come up empty. The best thing He can give His people is Himself. They have no need to turn elsewhere, if they remember that He truly is the perfect solution to every need they have. The discipline the Lord gives, then, is not only given out of anger, although there is a since in which the Lord is rightly offended by their sin. This discipline is ultimately given out of love for His glory and their good.

God's everlasting love for you has an inherent long-range perspective that allows for discipline in the present to protect you in the future. Parents surely understand this relational dynamic, knowing they must discipline their children in order to help them know how to act appropriately for their future success.

When discipline comes, don't become resentful toward the Lord; rather, seek out the truth behind the discipline, knowing God simply desires to root out ungodliness for His glory and your good.

~ Jared

August 16

The Price of Truth

Chronological Bible Reading Plan: (Day 228: Jeremiah 32-34)

"The word that came to Jeremiah from the LORD in the tenth year of Zedekiah king of Judah, which was the eighteenth year of Nebuchadnezzar. At that time the army of the king of Babylon was besieging Jerusalem, and Jeremiah the prophet was shut up in the court of the guard that was in the palace of the king of Judah. For Zedekiah king of Judah had imprisoned him, saying, 'Why do you prophesy and say, 'Thus says the LORD: Behold, I am giving this city into the hand of the king of Babylon, and he shall capture it;'" Jeremiah 32:1-3 (ESV)

Occasionally, speaking truth can have consequences attached to it. In this case, the Lord had spoken through His prophet a word about the future of Judah and, thus, its king. Needless to say, the king was not happy about what Jeremiah had spoken over his kingdom and imprisoned him as a result. Jeremiah's obedience to speak the truth cost him his freedom and put his life in danger.

We are charged today to speak forth the truth of the gospel of Jesus Christ, and while certainly the gospel is good news, it is also offensive. Inherent in our message is that people are bad, sinful, lost, and in need of a savior. We must point out the flaws of men in order to show them their need for a savior. Sometimes people respond negatively to this, and while they may not have the power to imprison you or threaten your life, they can be hurtful in their rejection. The question you must ask yourself, though, is whether or not this temporary rejection is worth their eternal good. Certainly for Jeremiah he thought the message of impending judgment was worth the risk because he loved his people.

Are you willing to risk your freedom in order to proclaim God's truth? Are you willing to love someone enough to let them reject you in order to tell them about their great need and Christ's glorious provision? What are you willing to sacrifice to spread the good news?

~ Jared

August 17

The Word of the Lord Stands Forever

Chronological Bible Reading Plan: (Day 229: Jeremiah 35-37)

"Take a scroll and write on it all the words that I have spoken to you against Israel and Judah and all the nations, from the day I spoke to you, from the days of Josiah until today. It may be that the house of Judah will hear all the disaster that I intend to do to them, so that every one may turn from his evil way, and that I may forgive their iniquity and their sin." Jeremiah 36:2-3 (ESV)

Once again we see the prophet, Jeremiah, coming against an ungodly king with the word of the Lord. In this particular instance, the Lord commands Jeremiah to write down all that He has revealed concerning His people and present the document to the king. Upon hearing the prophetic word, the king commands the seizure of both Jeremiah and his secretary, Baruch, and burns the word of the Lord. In response to this rash act of the king, the Lord simply instructs Jeremiah to recreate the scroll and speak over Jehoiakim a vision of wrath.

The word of God stands forever and cannot be destroyed. God has given us His revealed word to display His glorious nature and direct our steps as His creation. The words written by Jeremiah were not simply Jeremiah's words or ideas regarding God's people; they were inspired by God Himself and, therefore, carry His authority. Jehoiakim missed the point. Instead of seeing the scroll as God's way of allowing him to repent, the king responded in anger, attempting to destroy that which he did not like. God's word, though, is eternal and will stand against any attempt to destroy it.

May you and I both marvel at and respect the eternal word of God! God has spoken over mankind His will for all of creation, and we must choose to respond faithfully rather than reject that truth in anger simply because we don't like it. Treasure God's word for in it you will find blessing and hope as you obey its commands.

~ *Jared*

August 18

We Give Thanks Forever

Chronological Bible Reading Plan: (Day 230: Jeremiah 38-40; Psalms 74,79)

"But we your people, the sheep of your pasture, will give thanks to you forever; from generation to generation we will recount your praise." Psalm 79:13 (ESV)

We were created to worship the Lord! Look how He has provided for us as His sheep. Look at the pasture He has laid forth for us. He has satisfied us in every way. He has taken upon Himself the penalty for our sin. He has restored us into life abundant and everlasting. He has made us into a people for His own possession to represent Him to the nations. He has filled us with His Holy Spirit, allowing us to experience its fruit fully. What a blessing it is to have the Lord as our Shepherd, for under His care we truly shall not want.

The difference between the people of God and the enemies of God, according to this psalm, is our praise. The enemies of God question His name and make a mockery of His people. His covenant people, though, by proclaiming this psalm step forth with confidence in their Lord to redeem and protect.

Let not the nations question where our allegiance lies. May we as God's people proclaim boldly the affection we have for our Great Satisfier, and may we further remember that this is only the beginning! As God's children, our eternity will be a beautiful continuation of our faithful obedience here to ascribe worth to our worthy Creator.

Give thanks to the Lord, today, for He is good! Perhaps take a moment and write down the many ways you have experienced His provision personally and take a moment today to tell someone about it as a witness to His goodness.

~ Jared

August 19

A Futile Rebellion

Chronological Bible Reading Plan: (Day 231: 2 Kings 24-25; 2 Chronicles 36)

"In his days, Nebuchadnezzar king of Babylon came up, and Jehoiakim became his servant three years. Then he turned and rebelled against him. And the LORD sent against him bands of the Chaldeans and bands of the Syrians and bands of the Moabites and bands of the Ammonites, and sent them against Judah to destroy it, according to the word of the LORD that he spoke by his servants the prophets. Surely this came upon Judah at the command of the LORD, to remove them out of his sight, for the sins of Manasseh, according to all that he had done, and also for the innocent blood that he had shed. For he filled Jerusalem with innocent blood, and the LORD would not pardon." 2 Kings 24:1-4 (ESV)

Jehoiakim sought to rebel against the rule of Nebuchadnezzar over the people of God and bring about freedom by his hand. The problem that Jehoiakim faced, however, was that he was not simply rebelling against the rule of a foreign king; he was rebelling against the prophecy of God Himself. His failure to acknowledge the Lord's sovereign hand over his people was the problem of the majority of the kings in this time. They rejected the dictate of the prophets and, therefore, rejected the authority of the Lord, which is why they were in danger of falling in the first place. They did not rely upon the Lord to guide their reigns, seeking glory for themselves alone. The wise move for Jehoiakim would simply have been to fall on his face in repentance before the Lord, since only this kind of response would have led his people into freedom.

How do you respond in times of hardship before the Lord? Do you try to take matters into your hands, organizing plans for victory in your own strength and by your own hand? Or do you seek the Lord, asking Him to be your great defender? If it is true that we exist for the glory of God, then we must in every circumstance rely fully upon Him for His deliverance, knowing that when He acts He will receive the full credit. The Lord wants to be the defender of His people; may we seek Him to be and give Him the glory when He shows Himself faithful.

~ Jared

August 20

God's Timing is Perfect

Chronological Bible Reading Plan: (Day 232: Habakkuk)

"For still the vision awaits its appointed time; it hastens to the end--it will not lie. If it seems slow, wait for it; it will surely come; it will not delay 'Behold, his soul is puffed up; it is not upright within him, but the righteous shall live by his faith.'" Habakkuk 2:3-4 (ESV)

Have there been times in your life where you wanted something to happen and you couldn't figure out why it wouldn't? God, why won't you give me this job? God, why won't you give me a husband or a wife? God, why don't we have children? God, how long will my son or daughter run from You before they realize how pointless life is without You? God, how long will it take for my friends to get the gospel and come to a trusting faith in You?

We have all been there at some point in our life, asking why God's timing isn't our timing. The Lord spoke over Habakkuk a promise that His people would see defeat at the hands of the Chaldeans, otherwise known as the Babylonians. Habakkuk couldn't believe it. Why would God allow this to happen? Why would he allow His own people to suffer? How long would He allow evil to have victory?

The Lord's answer to Habakkuk regarding his questions is also our answer today. In Habakkuk's case, God had something He needed to teach His people to insure His plan. Habakkuk's complaint of evil being victorious was simply nearsighted; God had a much bigger plan. God would vindicate His people and His name but in His timing once His purposes had been fulfilled. In the mean time, the Lord commanded Habakkuk, as a righteous man, to live by faith and trust in the goodness of God.

Whatever question you may have, trust in the goodness of God. The answer to your prayer might not be in the timing you would have preferred, but remember when it does come, its timing is God's timing and His timing is always perfect.

~ Jared

August 21

A Source of Wisdom

Chronological Bible Reading Plan: (Day 233: Jeremiah 41-45)

"Then all the commanders of the forces, and Johanan the son of Kareah and Jezaniah the son of Hoshaiah, and all the people from the least to the greatest, came near and said to Jeremiah the prophet, 'Let our plea for mercy come before you, and pray to the LORD your God for us, for all this remnant--because we are left with but a few, as your eyes see us--that the LORD your God may show us the way we should go, and the thing that we should do.' Jeremiah the prophet said to them, 'I have heard you. Behold, I will pray to the LORD your God according to your request, and whatever the LORD answers you I will tell you. I will keep nothing back from you.'" Jeremiah 42:1-4 (ESV)

Do people within the sphere of your influence run to you in times of trouble for wisdom from the Lord because they know of how closely you walk with Him? Jeremiah was a man who walked closely with the Lord and the leadership of Judah knew it. In a moment of panic after the assassination of Gedaliah, the leadership runs to Jeremiah to have him intercede on their behalf. Jeremiah promises to pray for them and communicate whatever word the Lord gives him to them without reservation. Jeremiah was their connection to the Lord because of his faithfulness in every circumstance.

What about you? Are you known for your faithfulness to the Lord? Do those who are far from the Lord come to you for help and prayer? May we be a people so in-tuned with the Spirit of God that whenever those around us at work, school, or in our neighborhoods have trials and tribulations, they immediately come to us for wisdom and prayer. May the Spirit of God flow from us as we have sought Him continually in prayer and in His word. Become a place of hope for those in need as you radiate the fruit of the Spirit, having been transformed by the gospel.

And as a final thought today, thank the Lord for the Jeremiah's in your life, whom you run to in times of distress to find wisdom and discernment from the Lord.

~ Jared

August 22

The Folly of the Proud

Chronological Bible Reading Plan: (Day 234: Jeremiah 46-48)

"We have heard of the pride of Moab-- he is very proud-- of his loftiness, his pride, and his arrogance, and the haughtiness of his heart. I know his insolence, declares the LORD; his boasts are false, his deeds are false."
Jeremiah 48:29-30 (ESV)

The Lord opposes the proud, recognizing that to represent His character faithfully demands humility. As a result, when His people or even neighboring nations boast in the "might" of other gods and give the praise due our one, true God to graven images, He brings about the required humility of His creation through defeat.

In our case, as those saved by the glorious message of the gospel, we certainly know that we have no reason to boast save in the work of Christ on the cross. Why? For when we deserved God's righteous wrath because of our rebellion, He gave us grace and mercy by the sacrifice of His beloved Son. We did nothing to deserve this and have nothing of merit to give in return. This act is God's alone and, therefore, we boast alone in Him. When we forget this truth, the Lord has a way of humbling us, knowing that the aforementioned requirement of humility is as much for us today as it was back then. Every great leader of God in the Bible, save Jesus who did not need it, faced a moment of humility, in which the Lord gently or not so gently reminded them of their complete dependence upon Him to accomplish that to which they had been called.

In your own life, what do you boast in? Do you boast in your own abilities or accomplishments? Or do you simply boast in the cross of Christ, knowing how truly lost you were without it? May we be a people who continually deflect the accomplishments of this life to the glory of the next, reserved in Heaven for a God Who is sovereign over all things. His provision is our blessing, and we find pride only in His work in and through us.

~Jared

August 23

OUR REDEEMER IS STRONG

Chronological Bible Reading Plan: (Day 235: Jeremiah 49-50)

"Their Redeemer is strong; the LORD of hosts is his name. He will surely plead their cause, that he may give rest to the earth, but unrest to the inhabitants of Babylon." Jeremiah 50:34 (ESV)

Our redeemer is strong! He pursues us and rescues us, calling us to repentance and dependance as an act of worship to our God, who alone is worthy of praise! What is He rescuing us from? Why has He redeemed us? Certainly, you and I have no need to be rescued from a foreign national power in order to fulfill a Zionist prophecy in which we will be restored to our land of promise. We are, however, in bondage to sin and subject to this same wrath about which we read in the latter part of Jeremiah. Our offense before the Lord in rejecting His provision and worshiping created things demands His judgment; so, He is saving us from Himself in a way.

How can God be both redeemer and judge? That is the beauty of the character of God. Yes, He is righteous. Yes, He is just. Yes, He is Holy. But He is also merciful. He is also loving. He is also gracious. He is composed of all of these traits in their perfect and balanced form. His character demands justice but it also allows for redemption, but on His terms! Our redeemer is strong in that He alone can break the bondage of sin, having overcome all of its affects in the person and work of Christ. Do not be a slave to sin any longer. Do not let a foreign power, as it were, rule over your life. Run to the Lord, the light of our salvation, and find freedom from that which oppresses you!

~ *Jared*

August 24

God's Word is Sure

Chronological Bible Reading Plan: (Day 236: Jeremiah 51-52)

"And in the thirty-seventh year of the exile of Jehoiachin king of Judah, in the twelfth month, on the twenty-fifth day of the month, Evil-merodach king of Babylon, in the year that he became king, graciously freed Jehoiachin king of Judah and brought him out of prison. And he spoke kindly to him, and gave him a seat above the seats of the kings who were with him in Babylon. So Jehoiachin put off his prison garments. And every day of his life he dined regularly at the king's table, and for his allowance, a regular allowance was given him by the king according to his daily need, until the day of his death, as long as he lived." Jeremiah 52:31-34 (ESV)

The Lord never forgets His promises and His promises never fail. Even in the midst of the promised exile, for no explicit reason, the king of Babylon, Evil-merodach, invites the king of Judah, Jehoiachin, out from prison to his dining table. Whatever could have caused a foreign king to show mercy and favor to the king of his servants? Undoubtedly, the Lord is at work in this passage, remembering His covenant with David in which He promised him a permanent kingdom resulting in a messiah to fully deliver the people of God.

Even in hard times when we can't explicitly see the presence of God, may we not forget that He is faithful and His words never fail. Yes, in this chapter we see Him upholding the hard words of judgment but also the beautiful words of redemption. His promises are true and they will always bring about His glory and our good.

Do you know the promises of God? If not, how can you hold on to them when you are sitting in prison as a king? Do you speak the promises of God over times of trouble, taking refuge in His ultimate provision and plan for you and all things? God's word is sure! Know it and take refuge in it. Further, when you see His promises come true in your life, take a minute and thank Him for His faithfulness.

~Jared

August 25

The Steadfast Love of the Lord

Chronological Bible Reading Plan: (Day 237: Lamentations 1-3)

"The steadfast love of the LORD never ceases; his mercies never come to an end; they are new every morning; great is your faithfulness. 'The LORD is my portion,' says my soul, 'therefore I will hope in him.'" Lamentations 3:22-24 (ESV)

Every morning, including this very morning, we as the children of God must rise to the fresh and glorious provision of God's faithfulness, relying upon it and nothing else for our spiritual sustenance. Like manna from heaven, the Lord lavishes us with the fullness of His character in order for our souls to be completely satisfied. We never have to worry if the provision will cease nor whether or not it will be able to fill. The Lord has promised His mercy every morning, and, as we have seen in chapters past, His promises never fail.

What do you rely on, dear child of God, to face the worries of each day? What source of hope do you have in the midst of uncertainty? As the Lord Himself said in a parable to us all, rain comes into every life and threatens the foundation of our spiritual house. The key for the house's survival is the strength of its foundation. Is your foundation built upon the rock? Do you trust Him alone to daily see you through the floods that come your way?

Although your path may seem dark, although there may seem much to lament, find hope in these beautiful, inspired words. The Lord's love never ceases and His mercies never come to an end. They are tied to His eternal character and are, thus, eternal themselves. He showers them upon us every morning, as He promised He would. Therefore, may we look to Him alone for satisfaction and endurance, following faithfully His calling upon our lives as He faithfully blesses His beloved.

~ *Jared*

August 26

OUR GOD IS ETERNAL

Chronological Bible Reading Plan: (Day 238: Lamentations 4-5)

"But you, O LORD, reign forever; your throne endures to all generations." Lamentations 5:19 (ESV)

God is wholly different than that which He created. Whereas all of creation is confined to space and time, God exists beyond them. Time is a consequence of His Being. He is, and, therefore, everything else is, progressing toward that which He has predestined and decreed. We must never lose sight of this remarkable truth about the nature of God, knowing that we, as His beloved, can become overwhelmed by the present and lose perspective. What an encouragement it is, however, for His children in the midst of doubt to remember the sovereign hand of the Lord by which our steps are directed and our lives secured.

Child of God, take comfort in the nature of God. Remember His eternality and rest in His authority for all time over that which He created. Further, as a subject in the Kingdom of God, never fail, regardless of circumstance, to serve with gladness our King of glory. Building His Kingdom is our chief concern, knowing that in building His Kingdom we bring about peace and security as we destroy the effects of sin and death.

The Lord is a mighty King, who reigns for all of eternity. May we take comfort in our protector and serve gladly our gracious sovereign.

~Jared

August 27

Feast on the Word of God

Chronological Bible Reading Plan: (Day 239: Ezekiel 1-4)

"And he said to me, 'Son of man, eat whatever you find here. Eat this scroll, and go, speak to the house of Israel.' So I opened my mouth, and he gave me this scroll to eat. And he said to me, 'Son of man, feed your belly with this scroll that I give you and fill your stomach with it.' Then I ate it, and it was in my mouth as sweet as honey. And he said to me, 'Son of man, go to the house of Israel and speak with my words to them.'" Ezekiel 3:1-4 (ESV)

After receiving one of the most glorious visions ever recorded in scripture, Ezekiel now receives his calling. The Lord speaks over him a prophetic mission to go to the rebellious house of Israel and call them to repentance. Within this prophetic calling, the Lord also delivers Ezekiel a promise that the words he speaks will not be his own; rather through the anointing of the Holy Spirit, Ezekiel will proclaim "thus says the Lord." The Lord so passionately wants Ezekiel to recognize the importance of proclaiming His word that He calls him in the vision to actually eat the scroll before him containing His written words. Ezekiel must feast on the word of God before he can adequately proclaim the word of God.

Ezekiel's preparation, while not as dramatic, is an example for us today. We too have been called to proclaim repentance to a rebellious household, but in order to proclaim faithfully we must first have an intimate knowledge of God's truth. Otherwise, what would we proclaim? Human wisdom or intuition? Opinions of men based on experience? The words of man cannot help those in rebellion, but the words of God certainly can. Know the word of God and pursue truth. Then, having feasted on the word of the Lord, call others to join you at His bountiful table.

~ Jared

August 28

Be Careful Who You Follow

Chronological Bible Reading Plan: (Day 240: Ezekiel 5-8)

"And he brought me into the inner court of the house of the LORD. And behold, at the entrance of the temple of the LORD, between the porch and the altar, were about twenty-five men, with their backs to the temple of the LORD, and their faces toward the east, worshiping the sun toward the east. Then he said to me, 'Have you seen this, O son of man? Is it too light a thing for the house of Judah to commit the abominations that they commit here, that they should fill the land with violence and provoke me still further to anger? Behold, they put the branch to their nose. Therefore I will act in wrath. My eye will not spare, nor will I have pity. And though they cry in my ears with a loud voice, I will not hear them.'" Ezekiel 8:16-18 (ESV)

Beginning in chapter 8 of the book of Ezekiel, the prophet is given another vision of various abominable acts taking place in the temple of God, the culmination of which is 25 priests worshiping the sun at an altar built for the Lord. As a result of the defamation taking place in God's holiest place on the earth, the Lord promises wrath upon not only the leadership of Israel, but indeed all of its people.

When the leadership of a people forget their God and begin to worship created things rather than the Creator, all those under the influence of the leadership are also led astray. This passage serves as a reminder for us to be careful whom we follow. Do the leaders you follow and trust love the Lord with all their heart, soul, mind, and strength or do they claim He has forsaken us? Do they lead you into worship of the Most High, or do they focus on created things and the wisdom of man? Are they more concerned about lifting up the name of the Lord or their own name?

Be guarded about who you allow to speak into your life, making sure that your leaders are leading you toward the Lord rather than into judgment, for ultimately we are all accountable for our actions regardless of who led us there.

~ *Jared*

August 29

I Have Been a Sanctuary to Them

Chronological Bible Reading Plan: (Day 241: Ezekiel 9-12)

"Therefore say, 'Thus says the Lord GOD: Though I removed them far off among the nations, and though I scattered them among the countries, yet I have been a sanctuary to them for a while in the countries where they have gone.'"
Ezekiel 11:16 (ESV)

This morning we arrive at a turning point both in the prophecy of Ezekiel and, to a larger extent, for the people of Israel. After seeing the impending destruction of his people, Ezekiel cries out in 11:13 to the Lord asking Him if He will fully eradicate the "remnant of Israel." In response, the Lord introduces a new dynamic in terms of His relationship with His people. No longer will His presence be confined to a place; rather, in the midst of their dispersion, the Lord will still be a sanctuary for His people. He will be with them even in their judgment; He will be with them in the absence of a temple. This truth is a very important truth for a people whose identity was tied to this sacred building. How could they be the people of God without the presence of God in their midst, signified by the temple? The temple does not matter any longer, though, for the Lord is omnipresent and His people are more than a building. They are His people because of His presence upon them, and He can go with them anywhere.

We must be careful as God's people to not fall into the same trap into which Israel fell, equating God's presence with a building. Too many times we characterize the "church" as the place where God's presence resides, seeing it as a sacred place unto itself. We must remember, though, that the only reason the buildings in which we meet have any significance is because of its sanctified inhabitants. We are the Church and the presence of God is in us! He is our sanctuary both inside our walls and without. Recognize the presence of God in your life today. Everywhere you go is a holy place, for the Lord, your God, is with you.

~ *Jared*

August 30

Fruitfulness Comes from Faithfulness

Chronological Bible Reading Plan: (Day 242: Ezekiel 13-15)

"And I will make the land desolate, because they have acted faithlessly, declares the Lord GOD." Ezekiel 15:8 (ESV)

The Lord declares over His people through His prophet, Ezekiel, that He will take the land of promise, bountiful and flowing with milk and honey, and make it desolate as a result of Israel's unfaithfulness. The people of God are compared to a vine without fruit, for they have been disconnected from their source of blessing and life. Their rebellion, which they thought would bring ultimate joy, has left them rather barren and desolate.

Certainly, the impact upon us today from this prophecy of old is no less biting. The relationship between faithfulness and fruitfulness still rings true. When you and I faithfully pursue the Lord, we will bear fruit. When we minister faithfully, relying upon both the calling of God and the empowering of the Spirit, our ministries will bear fruit. Fruit-bearing is that simple; it simply happens when you are connected to the source of life! When we walk in rebellion, however, our lives and our ministries suffer as we quench the presence of the Spirit of God upon us.

Consider your life for a moment this morning. Are you relying upon the Lord fully as you prepare for your day? Are you seeking Him in His word? Are you taking the hard truths of scripture and applying them to your life, being conformed into the image of Jesus? Consider the ministries you oversee or in which you are involved. Do you ask the Lord's presence and blessing upon them, signifying your total reliance upon Him? Or are you like the princes of the people who fear failure more than the favor of God? If you rely upon anything other than the Spirit of God in both your personal life and ministry life, you will be fruitless for fruitfulness only comes with faithfulness.

~ Jared

August 31

I Am the Lord; I Have Spoken, and I Will Do It

Chronological Bible Reading Plan: (Day 243: Ezekiel 16-17)

"And all the trees of the field shall know that I am the LORD; I bring low the high tree, and make high the low tree, dry up the green tree, and make the dry tree flourish. I am the LORD; I have spoken, and I will do it." Ezekiel 17:24 (ESV)

You never have to worry if the Lord will follow through with what He promises. Time and time again, throughout the scripture, we see the Lord speak a promise over His people and bring that promise to fruition. Why? Because, God's character demands that He uphold His word! The Lord is holy in every way, and as a result there is no darkness within Him. His perfect holiness demands that what He says also be perfect. His "yes" will always be "yes" and his "no" will always be "no." The Lord does not take into account circumstance nor opposition when following through with His promises, because nothing is more important to Him than protecting the reputation of His holy name.

As the people of God, we should seek to emulate the Lord in this. As we seek to display the character of God, may we hold fast to our word when we give it, knowing that our actions as Christians say something about the God we serve. That was Israel's problem. Their actions didn't match their words nor their covenant. Therefore, the Lord, for the sake of His holy name, had to call them to repentance through judgment. May we be more wise than our predecessors. May we commit to speak in truth at all times, holding our promises in the same esteem with which the Lord holds His. We are His people and we are to put on display His character to the nations. Today, make a commitment to do what you have spoken as God Himself would do.

~ *Jared*

September 1

If a Man is Righteous, He Shall Surely Live

Chronological Bible Reading Plan: (Day 244: Ezekiel 18-20)

"If a man is righteous and does what is just and right-- [9]walks in my statutes, and keeps my rules by acting faithfully--he is righteous; he shall surely live, declares the Lord GOD." Ezekiel 18:5, 9 (ESV)

God has a standard for us. This standard is not some power-play from on high, in which the Lord seeks to show His creation just how much authority He has over them. Rather, this standard is for the good of creation. The best thing that God can give to His creation is Himself, knowing that He is the fulfillment of everything that we seek. If a man needs love, he should turn to the Lord because the Lord is the perfect and infinite source of love. The same truth applies to all of our most basic needs. The problem, though, arises when you and I fail to remain holy, for when any sinfulness comes into our lives it affects our access to the fullness of God. When we don't act as God indicates above and throughout the law, we defile ourselves and become unworthy of the presence of God and, thus, are unable to find true fulfillment.

This dilemma, however, reveals to us once again the beauty of Christ, who did do what was right and just. He never lifted His eyes to idols nor became ritually impure as directed by the law. He came not to oppress but give freedom and restoration. He never robbed anyone, forsook anyone in need, nor sought to harm someone in order to advance Himself. He was the perfect picture of righteousness, and because of that we can surely live! You see, He, in spite of His righteousness, took upon Himself our punishment for our shortcomings and gave us His righteousness. Because of that, we can now find true satisfaction and, having been satisfied, seek to communicate that truth to those in need around us.

~Jared

September 2

Grieving for the Lost

Chronological Bible Reading Plan: (Day 245: Ezekiel 21-22)

"'As for you, son of man, groan; with breaking heart and bitter grief, groan before their eyes. And when they say to you, 'Why do you groan?' you shall say, 'Because of the news that it is coming. Every heart will melt, and all hands will be feeble; every spirit will faint, and all knees will be weak as water. Behold, it is coming, and it will be fulfilled,' declares the Lord GOD." Ezekiel 21:6-7 (ESV)

Wrath was coming for the people of God and Ezekiel was the man given the unenviable task of proclaiming that impending reality. What a terrible message to have to proclaim! Can you imagine the people Ezekiel offended, frightened, or worried? Can you consider the weight Ezekiel must have felt bearing this heavy burden for his people? Of course Ezekiel grieved. Of course he was overwhelmed. Anyone who has this kind of message to proclaim and doesn't feel grief doesn't truly understand the message. The important lesson to learn from Ezekiel here, though, is that just because a message grieves you or is unpopular doesn't mean that you don't proclaim it! You have to proclaim it in spite of the possible offense for the sake of those who need to hear this life-altering truth.

Are you grieved for the future of those around you who do not know Christ? You see, we too have been given a message of impending wrath. The wrath of God is coming to account for the sinfulness of man, and without the wrath-bearing work of Jesus Christ to remove this wrath, those around you will have a very dark future. We must remember this reality and we should be broken over it, motivating us to spread the gospel or "good news" of Jesus. Yes, we were children of wrath, but God, abundant in mercy, made us alive in Christ Jesus and adopted us as His children! Wrath is coming, but we have hope in Christ. Now, we must proclaim, as Ezekiel did, the need for repentance and salvation alone in Jesus.

~ *Jared*

September 3

Does God Truly Have Your Everything?

Chronological Bible Reading Plan: (Day 246: Ezekiel 23-24)

"The word of the LORD came to me: 'Son of man, behold, I am about to take the delight of your eyes away from you at a stroke; yet you shall not mourn or weep, nor shall your tears run down. Sigh, but not aloud; make no mourning for the dead. Bind on your turban, and put your shoes on your feet; do not cover your lips, nor eat the bread of men.' So I spoke to the people in the morning, and at evening my wife died. And on the next morning I did as I was commanded." Ezekiel 24:15-18 (ESV)

This was not like Abraham's call. The Lord had asked for great sacrifices of godly men before, but in Abraham's case He supplied an alternative. Would this call on Ezekiel's life be like Abraham's or like Job's? If like Job's, would he have his fortune restored to him, or would it matter? How could losing a wife be restored? Yet, the Lord had asked; no, He declared! He would take the life of Ezekiel's wife as a foretaste of what was to come for the people of God.

On the face of it, this calling simply sounds cruel and unjust. Ezekiel comes across as completely powerless, not even begging for his beloved's life! What right does the Lord have to demand such sacrifice?

God has never asked us to sacrifice more than He has sacrificed. He gave His only begotten Son so that you and I could be saved! He sacrificed His beloved for those who hated Him, thereby showing the greatest kind of love ever exhibited. God has sacrificed, so shouldn't we have to as well? A change happens for the mature believer, in which everything that we have or love becomes an object for the Lord to use to teach His grace.

Let us never forget that the call to follow Christ is one of sacrifice (sometimes incredible sacrifice). And as you remember that truth, also remember that God has sacrificed more than we could ever give so that we who were far off could now be called children of God!

~ Jared

September 4
God's Justice

Chronological Bible Reading Plan: (Day 247: Ezekiel 25-27)

"For thus says the Lord God: Because you have clapped your hands and stamped your feet and rejoiced with all the malice within your soul against the land of Israel, therefore, behold, I have stretched out my hand against you, and will hand you over as plunder to the nations. And I will cut you off from the peoples and will make you perish out of the countries; I will destroy you. Then you will know that I am the Lord." Ezekiel 25:6-7 (ESV)

God's judgment would equal Ammon's sin. The nation rejoiced over Judah's misfortune when attacked by Nebuchadnezzar. Ammon hoped to benefit from Judah's destruction. Ammon rejoiced over the destruction of the temple. God demonstrated His justice by sending them to the people of the East as a possession. These nomads would overtake the Ammonites and turn their capital city into pasture for camels and Ammon into a resting place for sheep. However, rest would cease for the Ammonites.

God's love demands the demonstration of His justice. Without justice, there is no love. Without love, there is no justice. In spite of our rebellion, God chose to pursue us with His redeeming love. In spite of our sin, God chose to provide the only acceptable sacrifice to satisfy His justice and to eradicate the consequences of our sin.

- *"My little children, I am writing these things to you so that you may not sin. But if anyone does sin, we have an advocate with the Father, Jesus Christ the righteous. He is the propitiation for our sins, and not for ours only but also for the sins of the whole world." 1 John 2:1-2 (ESV)*

Pause to thank God for His mercy in your life. Rejoice over the immeasurable grace God has extended to you. In Christ, you are a new creation because of the awesome price Jesus paid for your deliverance.

~ *Stephen*

September 5

Other Side of Pride

Chronological Bible Reading Plan: (Day 248: Ezekiel 28-30)

"You were an anointed guardian cherub. I placed you; you were on the holy mountain of God; in the midst of the stones of fire you walked. You were blameless in your ways from the day you were created, till unrighteousness was found in you. In the abundance of your trade you were filled with violence in your midst, and you sinned; so I cast you as a profane thing from the mountain of God, and I destroyed you, O guardian cherub, from the midst of the stones of fire. Your heart was proud because of your beauty; you corrupted your wisdom for the sake of your splendor. I cast you to the ground; I exposed you before kings, to feast their eyes on you." Ezekiel 28:14-17 (ESV)

Ezekiel's third message against Tyre was directed to the ruler, Ethbaal III. His heart was filled with pride and he identified himself as a god. Ethbaal III self-proclaimed that his wisdom was greater than that of Daniel. Interestingly, Daniel was serving in the kingdom of Nebuchadnezzar, the king of Babylon, which God would raise up to destroy Tyre. Ezekiel prophesied that the death of Ethbaal III would be a shameful death, namely, "You shall die the death of the uncircumcised by the hand of foreigners" (Ezek. 28:10).

A parallel between Ethbaal III and Satan is established. Clearly the influence of Satan was at work in the prideful heart of the king of Tyre. Pride eroded the position that Lucifer had as the guardian cherub. He was a perfect creation by God until pride seeped in.

As a child of God, keep pride on the slide. Don't allow pride to gain access to your life. Embrace the way of humility by acknowledging your dependency upon the Lord. Be grateful for what God has done to deliver you out of the kingdom of darkness when He placed you in the kingdom of light.

~ *Stephen*

September 6
Sound the Alert

Chronological Bible Reading Plan: (Day 249: Ezekiel 31-33)

"So you, son of man, I have made a watchman for the house of Israel. Whenever you hear a word from my mouth, you shall give them warning from me." Ezekiel 33:7 (ESV)

God positioned Ezekiel as the watchman for the house of Israel. Ezekiel had a mandate from God to receive and declare God's Word to the people. The divine responsibility was placed upon Ezekiel to sound the alert of God's impending judgment. Ezekiel was entrusted with the message from God.

- *"For our appeal does not spring from error or impurity or any attempt to deceive, but just as we have been approved by God to be entrusted with the gospel, so we speak, not to please man, but to please God who tests our hearts." 1 Thess. 2:3-4 (ESV)*

You have been approved by God to be entrusted with the gospel. God has armed you with the Good News of Jesus Christ so that you can join Him in His redemptive activity. What are you doing with the treasure you have been given?

Sound the alert. Everybody will spend forever somewhere. The only hope is for people to repent of their sin and place their faith in Jesus alone for salvation. You know the Truth! You have been delivered from the kingdom of darkness and placed in the kingdom of light. You are God's workmanship and He has established you as a watchman to sound the alert. You have been given the assignment to share the bad news and the Good News. The bad news is that a person without Christ will spend eternity in hell. The Good News is that Jesus died to pay the penalty of our sin so that we do not have to go to hell. Sound the alert!

~ Stephen

September 7

NEW HEART AND SPIRIT

Chronological Bible Reading Plan: (Day 250: Ezekiel 34-36)

"And I will give you a new heart, and a new spirit I will put within you. And I will remove the heart of stone from your flesh and give you a heart of flesh. And I will put my Spirit within you, and cause you to walk in my statutes and be careful to obey my rules." Ezekiel 36:26-27 (ESV)

Remove the activity of God and hope dissipates. God initiates the love relationship made available to us by His grace. The only way a person can come into a right relationship with God and be reconciled is by responding to God's redemptive activity. The only way to know God personally and to obey God completely is by God's enabling.

Ezekiel prophesied the Word of the Lord affirming God's redemptive activity. God said that He would give them a new heart and put a new spirit within them. God would remove their heart of stone and give them a heart of flesh. God would put His Spirit within them and cause them to walk in His statutes and enable them to obey His rules.

You cannot live the life God has for you outside of God's provision. God does not expect you to live the Christian life in your own strength. In fact, you will fail. To live in the center of God's will requires God's power.

At the moment of your conversion, God removes your sin, imputes the righteousness of Christ, adopts you into His family, and fills you with the Holy Spirit. You become the walking tabernacle of His presence. God empowers you to walk in His ways and to fulfill His will on the earth. Yield to the prompting of the Holy Spirit and allow Him to have His way in your life.

~ *Stephen*

September 8
Can Dry Bones Live?

Chronological Bible Reading Plan: (Day 251: Ezekiel 37-39)

"Then he said to me, 'Prophesy over these bones, and say to them, O dry bones, hear the word of the Lord. Thus says the Lord God to these bones: Behold, I will cause breath to enter you, and you shall live. And I will lay sinews upon you, and will cause flesh to come upon you, and cover you with skin, and put breath in you, and you shall live, and you shall know that I am the Lord.'"
Ezekiel 37:4-6 (ESV)

Imagine the level at which Ezekiel's faith was challenged when God told him to prophesy to the dry bones that were located throughout the valley. Ezekiel prophesied as God commanded and then witnessed the impossible become a reality. God reconnected the bones and sinews and made flesh appear covered with skin. Then God breathed life into them as Ezekiel witnessed the miracle personally.

Have you ever faced an impossible situation? Have you been confronted by a circumstance that seemed hopeless? Recall the desperation you felt and the sense of hopelessness that covered you like a dark cloud. You knew the only way to experience a breakthrough would be for God to intervene.

- *"But Jesus looked at them and said, 'With man this is impossible, but with God all things are possible.'" Matt. 19:26 (ESV)*

Trust God with the impossible situations that come into your path as you live on this broken planet. Remember that nothing happens without God's permission and He always has the final say. If God allows difficulty to come your way, He will use it for your good and for His glory. God will not waste the pain your endure. God will redeem your pain and He will make a way when there seems to be no way. Entrust your life and your circumstances to His care.

~ Stephen

September 9

EZEKIEL'S VISION OF THE NEW TEMPLE

Chronological Bible Reading Plan: (Day 252: Ezekiel 40-42)

"In visions of God he brought me to the land of Israel, and set me down on a very high mountain, on which was a structure like a city to the south. When he brought me there, behold, there was a man whose appearance was like bronze, with a linen cord and a measuring reed in his hand. And he was standing in the gateway. And the man said to me, 'Son of man, look with your eyes, and hear with your ears, and set your heart upon all that I shall show you, for you were brought here in order that I might show it to you. Declare all that you see to the house of Israel.'" Ezekiel 40:2-4 (ESV)

Ezekiel was transported via visions from God to the land of Israel. In the visions, Ezekiel was given a tour by an angel of the Lord whose appearance was like bronze. Ezekiel was shown exceptional details about the temple God would build. Once the details were made fully known to Ezekiel, he was to then declare all that he had seen to the house of Israel.

Since this exact temple has never been built, it must refer to a future time period whereby God will build His temple. Many scholars believe that Ezekiel's visions refer to the great millennial temple that will be filled with God's glory during the millennial reign of Christ on the earth.

As you read Ezekiel 40-42, be reminded of God's desire to be the focus of your worship. You are created by God to worship Him and Him alone. Eliminate idols. An idol is anything that comes between you and God. Reserve your allegiance and your affection for the One who has redeemed you from the empty way of life and brought you into the kingdom of light.

~ *Stephen*

September 10

Glory of the Lord

Chronological Bible Reading Plan: (Day 253: Ezekiel 43-45)

"And the vision I saw was just like the vision that I had seen when he came to destroy the city, and just like the vision that I had seen by the Chebar canal. And I fell on my face. As the glory of the Lord entered the temple by the gate facing east, the Spirit lifted me up and brought me into the inner court; and behold, the glory of the Lord filled the temple." Ezekiel 43:3-5 (ESV)

When Ezekiel experienced the glory of the Lord, he fell on his face. When Isaiah encountered God's holiness, he responded in humility by saying, "Woe is me! For I am lost; for I am a man of unclean lips, and I dwell in the midst of a people of unclean lips; for my eyes have seen the King, the Lord of hosts!" (Isa. 6:5). When the apostle John encountered the Lord in a vision from the island of Patmos, he fell at His feet as though dead.

How do you respond to the glory of the Lord? When you became a follower of Jesus Christ, you transferred your trust from yourself to Jesus alone for salvation. Your sins were removed and you became the righteousness of Christ. Instantaneously, you were filled with the Holy Spirit and became God's temple. God has chosen to take up permanent residence inside of you by the Person of His Holy Spirit.

You have been filled with the glory of the Lord. Are you walking with the full awareness of God's glory inside of you? Are you allowing the glory of God to be revealed through your conversation and through your conduct? Others can be drawn to Christ as you allow the glory of God to become evidenced through your life.

~ *Stephen*

September 11

Lamb Without Blemish

Chronological Bible Reading Plan: (Day 254: Ezekiel 46-48)

"You shall provide a lamb a year old without blemish for a burnt offering to the Lord daily; morning by morning you shall provide it. And you shall provide a grain offering with it morning by morning, one sixth of an ephah, and one third of a hin of oil to moisten the flour, as a grain offering to the Lord. This is a perpetual statute. Thus the lamb and the meal offering and the oil shall be provided, morning by morning, for a regular burnt offering."
Ezekiel 46:13-15 (ESV)

Ezekiel is pointing to the sacrificial system during the millennial temple worship that will serve as a memorial to the once-for-all sacrifice Christ made. Blood sacrifices will not be necessary since Christ has already provided the complete atoning work on the cross. His substitutionary atonement satisfied the justice of God and provided for the removal of our sins.

- *"But when Christ appeared as a high priest of the good things that have come, then through the greater and more perfect tent (not made with hands, that is, not of this creation) he entered once for all into the holy places, not by means of the blood of goats and calves but by means of his own blood, thus securing an eternal redemption."*
  Heb. 9:11-12 (ESV)

Jesus shed His blood so that we could come into a right relationship with God. In Christ, we are reconciled to God and the penalty of our sin has been paid in full. The blood of the sinless sacrificial Son of God has purchased your salvation. Jesus paid the debt you could not pay. Jesus took your place so that you could benefit personally from the redemptive activity produced by His obedience to death on a cross.

~ Stephen

September 12

Deliberate Decision

Chronological Bible Reading Plan: (Day 255: Joel)

"'Yet even now,' declares the Lord, 'return to me with all your heart, with fasting, with weeping, and with mourning; and rend your hearts and not your garments.' Return to the Lord your God, for he is gracious and merciful, slow to anger, and abounding in steadfast love; and he relents over disaster." Joel 2:12-13 (ESV)

Consider going to a part of your life that is somewhat private and assess your normal response when you let God down. What do you do when you choose to disobey God? How do you respond to the convicting work of the Holy Spirit in your life? Perhaps you seek to hide from God and try to work things out on your on. Maybe you choose to allow sufficient time to elapse so that your sensitivity to the convicting work of the Holy Spirit diminishes.

Satan seeks to convince us that we need to delay our return to the Lord. We rationalize our sin and try to justify our choices. Eventually, we come to our senses and realize the foolishness of procrastination. We don't need to wait to run back to God. We don't have to get our lives all cleaned up and ordered in order to return to the One who redeemed us with His love.

- *"But I have this against you, that you have abandoned the love you had at first. Remember therefore from where you have fallen; repent, and do the works you did at first. If not, I will come to you and remove your lampstand from its place, unless you repent." Rev. 2:4-5 (ESV)*

The moment you become conscious of sin, run to God. Don't hesitate! Confess your sin instantly, specifically, and then receive God's forgiveness completely. Don't give the devil a toehold, a foothold, or a stronghold in your life. As soon as you become aware of even a fraction of sin in your life, run to God!

~ *Stephen*

September 13

Fiery Faith

Chronological Bible Reading Plan: (Day 256: Daniel 1-3)

"Shadrach, Meshach, and Abednego answered and said to the king, 'O Nebuchadnezzar, we have no need to answer you in this matter. If this be so, our God whom we serve is able to deliver us from the burning fiery furnace, and he will deliver us out of your hand, O king. But if not, be it known to you, O king, that we will not serve your gods or worship the golden image that you have set up.'" Daniel 3:16-18 (ESV)

Has your faith ever been tested? Maybe your home is a place where your faith is put to the test. Maybe your work environment has been a difficult place for you to express your faith. Swimming upstream is always a challenge. Whenever you decide to go in the opposite direction of the cultural current, you will face resistance and opposition.

Shadrach, Meshach, and Abednego, in the midst of impending death if they chose not to abide by the king's command, were willing to obey God at all costs. They demonstrated their belief in God's ability to save them from the blazing furnace. They went a step further by declaring that even if God did not deliver them that they would not worship the image of gold.

Do you have that kind of "but even if God does not" faith? Are you willing to obey God in the face of opposition and in the face of being misunderstood by your family or peers? Even if God does not deliver you from your difficult circumstances, are you willing to obey Him and honor Him?

The good news is that God did deliver Shadrach, Meshach, and Abednego. They would not bow, they would not bend, they would not budge, and they would not burn! God rescued them through the blazing furnace. God allowed them to go through the fire unharmed. Now that's a life changing experience!

~ Stephen

September 14
Between the Lions

Chronological Bible Reading Plan: (Day 257: Daniel 4-6)

"Then the king commanded, and Daniel was brought and cast into the den of lions. The king declared to Daniel, 'May your God, whom you serve continually, deliver you!'" Daniel 6:16 (ESV)

Daniel had a track record of faithfulness to God. After the king signed a decree forbidding Daniel to pray to God, Daniel allowed his devotion to God to supersede his devotion to the king. Daniel was not willing to disobey God in order to obey the king. Daniel paid a hefty price for his obedience. He was thrown into the lions' den.

- *"Then, at break of day, the king arose and went in haste to the den of lions. As he came near to the den where Daniel was, he cried out in a tone of anguish. The king declared to Daniel, 'O Daniel, servant of the living God, has your God, whom you serve continually, been able to deliver you from the lions?'" Dan 6:19-20 (ESV)*
- *"Then Daniel said to the king, 'O king, live forever! My God sent his angel and shut the lions' mouths, and they have not harmed me, because I was found blameless before him; and also before you, O king, I have done no harm.'" Dan 6:21-22 (ESV)*

Your devotion and faithfulness to God may not ever lead you to be thrown into a literal lions' den. However, your lions' den may simply be having others misunderstand you or criticize you for your devotion to God. Your family members may not support you in your walk with God. Your co-workers or neighbors may not fully understand your commitment to serving God. Your lions' den may be when your peers fail to comprehend your level of loyalty to God.

Trust God completely! God can shut the mouths of the lions. God can redeem the hurt you endure. God knows right where you are and He knows exactly what you need to accomplish His plan.

~ Stephen

September 15

Praying for Our Nation

Chronological Bible Reading Plan: (Day 258: Daniel 7-9)

"Then I turned my face to the Lord God, seeking him by prayer and pleas for mercy with fasting and sackcloth and ashes. I prayed to the Lord my God and made confession, saying, 'O Lord, the great and awesome God, who keeps covenant and steadfast love with those who love him and keep his commandments, we have sinned and done wrong and acted wickedly and rebelled, turning aside from your commandments and rules.'" Daniel 9:3-5 (ESV)

Daniel prayed in brokenness and confession on behalf of his people. He took ownership for their spiritual health and vitality. Daniel sought the Lord God in prayer. He cried out with fasting and humility before the Lord for God's mercy to be extended.

Revival is for believers who have become apathetic toward the things of God. Revival is designed by God to restore a believer's passion and hunger for God and His agenda. When revival comes, it produces a byproduct known as a spiritual awakening. While revival is for believers, a spiritual awakening impacts unbelievers and brings them to the place of transformation.

The only way for our nation to genuinely change is for the lost to get saved and have a growing relationship with Jesus Christ. Pray for everyone, including national leaders and those in authority, that they may come to know the Lord personally and have a growing relationship with Him.

Can you imagine our nation fully yielded to the Lordship of Christ? Can you envision our nation passionate about pursuing God daily and living for His glory? Join me in praying for that vision to become a reality. Pray for our nation. Seek the Lord in brokenness and humility on behalf of our nation.

~ Stephen

September 16

THE WICKED SHALL ACT WICKEDLY

Chronological Bible Reading Plan: (Day 259: Daniel 10-12)

"Many shall purify themselves and make themselves white and be refined, but the wicked shall act wickedly. And none of the wicked shall understand, but those who are wise shall understand." Daniel 12:10 (ESV)

The book of Daniel, at least in the second, more apocalyptic part, seeks to affirm in the people of God both at the time of writing and today the sovereignty of God in difficult circumstances. For those who are righteous, who seek out the activity of God in the events of human history, the hand of God will be evidenced. Even when seemingly difficult to see, we as the people of God must trust that He is there and that He is at work. The unrighteous, or wicked in this case, however, do not have the luxury of acknowledging the hand of God in difficult circumstances because they do not readily acknowledge Him in any circumstance. They choose to seek their own path and in so doing bring destruction upon themselves, which is truly all they know how to do.

As the people of God, we must live in this tension of knowledge today. On the one hand, we are aware of God's blessing, our eyes having been opened by the gospel of Jesus Christ, and seek to find that blessing in any circumstance. The possible frustration for us, however, is found in those who do not know the Lord who act in wicked ways, as their nature leads them to do. We may want to force them into seeing the Lord through loud preaching or "Bible brow-beating," but we must not! We must remember that the wicked act wickedly in any circumstance because they do not know the hope of Christ. We must not presume upon the ungoldy godliness. Rather, we must continue to proclaim the gospel and let the transforming work of the Holy Spirit lead them to a place where the revelation of God gives them hope and calls them to obedience. May we not forget as God's people to be a gracious people to those who do not know Him, for we were once blinded to the beauty of our Lord.

~ Jared

September 17

A Conflicted Return

Chronological Bible Reading Plan: (Day 260: Ezra 1-3)

"And they sang responsively, praising and giving thanks to the LORD, 'For he is good, for his steadfast love endures forever toward Israel.' And all the people shouted with a great shout when they praised the LORD, because the foundation of the house of the LORD was laid. But many of the priests and Levites and heads of fathers' houses, old men who had seen the first house, wept with a loud voice when they saw the foundation of this house being laid, though many shouted aloud for joy, so that the people could not distinguish the sound of the joyful shout from the sound of the people's weeping, for the people shouted with a great shout, and the sound was heard far away." Ezra 3:11-13 (ESV)

The Lord's promise of restoration to Israel after their exile finally came to fruition. Having defeated the Babylonian Empire, the king of Persia, Cyrus, decrees (by inspiration from the Lord) that all the Jewish people may return to their home and rebuild the house of the Lord. As permission turns into reality, the laying of the foundation for the new temple is met with a mixed response. Some respond in joy toward the faithfulness of God to His people, recounting a praise first uttered by their great king, David. Others, however, are filled with sorrow by what they have lost and how far they have to go to reclaim it.

You and I have a choice in how we respond to God's faithfulness after times of discipline. We can come through the other side rejoicing for how God has faithfully walked us through this process of refinement or we can focus on all that we have lost. We must remember that loss is part of pruning. God indeed requires sacrifice as a reminder to us of His supreme sufficiency.

When you look back on your life, don't fret all that could have been. Learn from those lessons and walk forward in the joy that comes from obedience. Maybe you don't have the old temple, but that doesn't mean you can't build a new one! Are you ready to lay your foundation?

~Jared

September 18
Joy is the Heart of Worship

Chronological Bible Reading Plan: (Day 261: Ezra 4-6: Psalm 137)

"And they kept the Feast of Unleavened Bread seven days with joy, for the LORD had made them joyful and had turned the heart of the king of Assyria to them, so that he aided them in the work of the house of God, the God of Israel."
Ezra 6:22 (ESV)

Joy is the heart of worship. In fact, I like to define worship as "joy expressed." The heart of the feast mentioned above for the people of God was joy found in God's faithfulness to them in allowing them to return to their land of promise and begin the process of rebuilding their temple. They were so overwhelmed by the provision of God that they could not contain their joyous response any longer.

Is worship for you fueled by joy? When you join your church to corporately praise the name of the Lord, are you motivated to sing those words and hear that teaching because of the inexpressible joy and satisfaction you have found in the saving work of Christ? When you serve on the mission field or in a local ministry near your home, are you doing so out of response to how Christ has so selflessly served you? If joy is not at the heart of your worship, then is it truly worship? Even in times of despair, our joy rises above that circumstance and allows us to sing hymns in the midst of prison cells.

Consider today all that you have to rejoice in from the Lord. Think about how faithfully He has guided you back to His promises and empowered you to do the work of ministry. Remember all the times that in the midst of adversity the Lord encouraged you and helped you to overcome. Write those remembrances down and use them as instruments of joy to fuel your worship today and every day as the people of God did upon returning to their home.

~ *Jared*

September 19

CONSIDER YOUR WAYS

Chronological Bible Reading Plan: (Day 262: Haggai)

"Thus says the LORD of hosts: Consider your ways. Go up to the hills and bring wood and build the house, that I may take pleasure in it and that I may be glorified, says the LORD. You looked for much, and behold, it came to little. And when you brought it home, I blew it away. Why? declares the LORD of hosts. Because of my house that lies in ruins, while each of you busies himself with his own house." Haggai 1:7-9 (ESV)

We must not neglect the building of God's house in building our own. Haggai prophesied during the return of Israel back to their land of promise, in which they initially began to rebuild the Temple but stopped when opposition arose. While there was a stoppage of work on God's house, the people of God began to focus on their own needs and desires, ultimately neglecting their original purpose for returning! They became so side-tracked with their own lives that they neglected the calling of God to build His house.

The same tragic oversight happens to many of us today. We become so consumed with building our own houses that we neglect the Church of God. We will spend time investing in our companies and in our families, which in and of themselves are not bad things, at the expense of our ultimate calling to grow the Kingdom of God through the gospel and His Church.

Let us remember that any success we have as a businessman or woman is meant to aid us in building the Church. Any success we have as a family is meant to put on display the gospel for those around us to see in order to build the Church. Everything we do is meant to glorify God by building His Church! Is that your focus? As Haggai challenges us in the text, we should consider our ways if it is not. Be purposeful today in building the house of God.

~ Jared

September 20
"BY MY SPIRIT, DECLARES THE LORD OF HOSTS"

Chronological Bible Reading Plan: (Day 263: Zechariah 1-4)

"Then he said to me, 'This is the word of the LORD to Zerubbabel: Not by might, nor by power, but by my Spirit, says the LORD of hosts.'" Zechariah 4:6 (ESV)

The people of God were discouraged. It had been nearly twenty years since their return and, yet, the temple was still only a foundation. Powerful opposition had prevented them from rebuilding the hallmark of their faith and a symbol of God's favor and presence among them. Zechariah, though, comes with powerful visions and a powerful word to help them overcome the devastation they felt as a people who had failed to accomplish their mission. He says to them (in my own words), "Do not fear what mortal men can do to you. They only have conventional powers at their disposal. The Lord, however, has no need for those things because He has the Spirit, and the Spirit is mightier than any force this world has!" His encouragement to them was also a reminder that if God wants something accomplished, He will accomplish it in His own time and with His own power. His people must simply trust and exhibit faith in that power as they obediently follow His calling.

Have you ever been discouraged in your walk with the Lord? Have you ever felt like He called you to a task surrounded by opposition and that you failed? Do not let the enemy or any conventional wisdom dismantle your sure faith in God's ability in the midst of your obedience. If God gave you a vision to accomplish something for His Kingdom, then faithfully walk forward in that vision regardless of the conflict, knowing that you have the Spirit of God behind you and He will not be stopped!

~ *Jared*

September 21

From Fasts to Favor

Chronological Bible Reading Plan: (Day 264: Zechariah 5-9)

"And the word of the LORD came to Zechariah, saying, 'Thus says the LORD of hosts, Render true judgments, show kindness and mercy to one another, do not oppress the widow, the fatherless, the sojourner, or the poor, and let none of you devise evil against another in your heart.'" Zechariah 7:8-10 (ESV)

The destruction of the temple was a defining moment for the people of God in that they saw their identity called into question. Without the temple, who were they? Undoubtedly, they asked themselves why God would allow such a heinous act to be performed. In remembrance of the temple's destruction and in hopes of the Lord forgiving their trespass, His people fasted and wept. Now that they had returned, however, and were in the process of rebuilding, were they still required to mourn? Were they still required to fast?

The Lord answered their question with our present text. All of the punishment, all of the fasting, and all of the mourning were meant to engender in the people of God a right heart toward each other. The question was not whether or not the actions should continue but rather whether the actions had led to a change of heart.

"Are you prepared to think of others as greater than yourself? Are you willing to sacrifice for the name of the Lord? Are you willing to live with less so that others can have some?"

The Lord does not desire vain action in an attempt to win His favor, especially for us today, since our action could never compare to the glorious act of Christ on the cross. Our actions must be in response to a right heart within us, having been overwhelmed by His mercy and grace toward us. Why are you living morally today? Why are you praying and fasting? Are you doing it to gain His favor or in response to the favor He has already displayed?

~ *Jared*

September 22
The Good Shepherd

Chronological Bible Reading Plan: (Day 265: Zechariah 10-14)

"And I will pour out on the house of David and the inhabitants of Jerusalem a spirit of grace and pleas for mercy, so that, when they look on me, on him whom they have pierced, they shall mourn for him, as one mourns for an only child, and weep bitterly over him, as one weeps over a firstborn."
Zechariah 12:10 (ESV)

Repentance, returning in a state of brokenness over sin to the Lord, comes when we look upon the suffering of our good Shepherd and recognize our role in causing His pain. We have traded a Shepherd who cares for us and protects us for one who devours us and uses us for his own purposes. To rescue us, His wandering sheep, our Good Shepherd gave Himself completely, beaten and pierced for our iniquity. He became what we could not so that in Him we might be redeemed and restored. For His sheep, He was broken so we could be healed. For His sheep, He was condemned so we could find freedom. For His sheep, He was abandoned so we could find acceptance.

The incredible thing about these incredible truths is that they were motivated not by merit nor debt; rather, our Shepherd was motivated by grace and mercy! Simply because of the love that He had and has for His sheep did He lay down His life in such a profound way.

Today, consider the goodness of your Shepherd. Look upon His piercing and remember why it happened. Have you repented of your sin? Are you broken over how He was broken? Are you encouraged to know that in your repentance you will find grace and mercy?

We serve a Good Shepherd; may we respond as good sheep.

~ *Jared*

September 23

Embracing the Absolute Fast

Chronological Bible Reading Plan: (Day 266: Esther 1-5)

"Then Esther told them to reply to Mordecai, 'Go, gather all the Jews to be found in Susa, and hold a fast on my behalf, and do not eat or drink for three days, night or day. I and my young women will also fast as you do. Then I will go to the king, though it is against the law, and if I perish, I perish.'" Esther 4:15-16 (ESV)

Esther sensed the heaviness of the reality of her circumstances and was willing to invite her people to fast for her. She committed to a three day absolute fast along with them in preparation for standing before the king. Esther was willing to put her life at risk by standing before the king. Her boldness was fueled by the abiding connection she had with God through the spiritual discipline of fasting.

There are times when God will lead you into an absolute fast. This type of fast is characterized by abstaining from food and drink for a set amount of time. You have to be very careful with this kind of fast and make certain that God has called you to it. Going any extended length of time without water can be detrimental to your health. Be certain that God has called you into this type fast.

Fasting and prayer go together. You can pray and not fast, but you cannot fast without praying if it is to be a biblical fast. God calls you to a fast so that you can passionately pursue Him and place your dependency upon Him.

Do you need to hear from God concerning a situation you are facing? Are you in need of God's wisdom and guidance? God may call you to an absolute fast to remove your dependency upon other things and to enable you to focus your attention on His provision.

~ *Stephen*

September 24

PROMOTED BY GOD

Chronological Bible Reading Plan: (Day 267: Esther 6-10)

"For Mordecai the Jew was second in rank to King Ahasuerus, and he was great among the Jews and popular with the multitude of his brothers, for he sought the welfare of his people and spoke peace to all his people." Esther 10:3 (ESV)

Esther was willing to risk her life in order to benefit her people. The favor of God was evident as Esther obeyed the Lord and followed His lead. God positioned her to influence the king and to orchestrate justice for the Jews. Esther seized the opportunity and recognized that God had raised her up for such as time as this.

- *"For if you keep silent at this time, relief and deliverance will rise for the Jews from another place, but you and your father's house will perish. And who knows whether you have not come to the kingdom for such a time as this?" Esth. 4:14 (ESV)*

Through the courageous decisions Esther made, God promoted Mordecai with both affluence and influence. Mordecai became great among his people and popular among his peers. God's favor was upon Mordecai as he sought the welfare of his people and as he spoke peace to all his people.

Will you allow God to position you to bless and benefit others? Be generous with your time and energy. Look to see where God is at work so that you can join Him. As you practice instant obedience, God will promote you in His perfect timing. You are created by God to continue the ministry of Jesus for such a time as this. Make yourself completely available for God's use. Value what God values and care about what God cares about. The next person you come into contact with may be your next divine appointment.

~ *Stephen*

September 25

Set your Heart to Study the Law of the Lord

Chronological Bible Reading Plan: (Day 268: Ezra 7-10)

"For Ezra had set his heart to study the Law of the LORD, and to do it and to teach his statutes and rules in Israel." Ezra 7:10 (ESV)

The narrative of Ezra jumps fifty-seven years between chapters 6 and 7, introducing now the titular character of Ezra. The hand of the Lord is obviously upon him, as he approaches the King of Persia, Artaxerxes, and receives permission to return to Jerusalem and once again instruct the people of God in how to live according to the Law. Notice in our verse for today, though, that his motivation in doing this was not power nor prestige but rather a love for the Law and for the Lord. The Lord raises him up and puts His hand upon Him to once again provide a mediator between He and His people, and this mediator will not lead others astray as so many other leaders have done because of His passion for the Law of the Lord.

If you and I are to lead the people God has placed in our lives to a deeper understanding of what it means to walk in relationship with the Lord, then we must set our hearts to study the Law of the Lord, to practice it, and to teach it. Firstly, we must study the Word of God. Too many of us rely upon others to feed us instead of investing ourselves in concentrated meditation upon the riches of scripture. When we study, we grow in relationship and the Spirit cultivates our heart after Christ's. Secondly, once we have studied, we must live out what we have studied. The Word of God is transformative, and how it transforms us displays its power and usefulness for when we proclaim it, which is our third responsibility. What we learn, we must entrust to others, who need to know what it means to walk worthy of the calling of God upon their lives.

Are you studying as Ezra did? Are you practicing? Are you teaching? Commit today to grow in one of these areas for your own good, the good of those around you, and, of course, for the glory of God!

~ Jared

September 26

Can You See It?

Chronological Bible Reading Plan: (Day 269: Nehemiah 1-4)

"Then I said to them, 'You see the trouble we are in, how Jerusalem lies in ruins with its gates burned. Come, let us build the wall of Jerusalem, that we may no longer suffer derision.' And I told them of the hand of my God that had been upon me for good, and also of the words that the king had spoken to me. And they said, 'Let us rise up and build.' So they strengthened their hands for the good work." Nehemiah 2:17-18 (ESV)

Nehemiah's vision to rebuild the walls of Jerusalem was birthed out of his burden for his people. As the cupbearer to King Artaxerxes, Nehemiah was the most trusted man in that kingdom. He had job security and a solid future serving in the palace in Susa. Upon receiving news concerning the plight of the Jews, Nehemiah brought his burdens to the Lord in prayer. After a season of praying, Nehemiah shared his burden with King Artaxerxes. God's favor was poured out on Nehemiah as the king was prompted to finance the mission.

Many people have vision, but a smaller number of people know how to implement their vision. God gave Nehemiah a clear and compelling vision to rebuild the walls of Jerusalem and Nehemiah took action. Having a vision was not sufficient; executing the vision was essential.

One of my mentors, Dr. Johnny Hunt, has often said in reference to vision, "If you don't see it, before you see it, you'll never see it!" What vision has God given you for your life and ministry? What burden has God placed inside of you? What troubles you? What needs your attention and your leadership? Can you see it?

~ *Stephen*

September 27

Vision and Opposition

Chronological Bible Reading Plan: (Day 270: Nehemiah 5-7)

"So the wall was finished on the twenty-fifth day of the month Elul, in fifty-two days. And when all our enemies heard of it, all the nations around us were afraid and fell greatly in their own esteem, for they perceived that this work had been accomplished with the help of our God." Nehemiah 6:15-16 (ESV)

God blessed Nehemiah's obedience and the walls of Jerusalem were finished in fifty-two days. Nehemiah had brought his burden to the Lord in prayer and then joined God in His activity. The vision to rebuild the walls in Jerusalem became a reality as God provided for Nehemiah every step of the way.

Nehemiah had to overcome obstacles and had to advance through adversity. Nehemiah was falsely accused and misunderstood.

- *"Now when Sanballat and Tobiah and Geshem the Arab and the rest of our enemies heard that I had built the wall and that there was no breach left in it (although up to that time I had not set up the doors in the gates), Sanballat and Geshem sent to me, saying, 'Come and let us meet together at Hakkephirim in the plain of Ono.' But they intended to do me harm."* Neh. 6:1-2 (ESV)

Motion causes friction. When you are on mission with God, you can anticipate the motion of obedience to generate friction from the enemy. Satan opposes God's will and he hates God's children. When you choose to implement the vision God has given you, be ready for opposition.

Don't come down from the wall God has called you to in order to try to alleviate the opposition. Reserve your energy for the task God has called you to so that the vision can become a reality. Remember that people are not the enemy, but the enemy uses people. Don't allow anyone to keep you from fulfilling the vision God has given you. Keep your eyes on the prize!

~ *Stephen*

September 28
Sacred Assembly

Chronological Bible Reading Plan: (Day 271: Nehemiah 8-10)

"Now on the twenty-fourth day of this month the people of Israel were assembled with fasting and in sackcloth, and with earth on their heads. And the Israelites separated themselves from all foreigners and stood and confessed their sins and the iniquities of their fathers. And they stood up in their place and read from the Book of the Law of the Lord their God for a quarter of the day; for another quarter of it they made confession and worshiped the Lord their God." Nehemiah 9:1-3 (ESV)

The walls of Jerusalem had been rebuilt and the people of Israel had gathered for a sacred assembly. Ezra read the Book of the Law in the hearing of the people. In brokenness and humility, the people of Israel assembled with fasting and consecrated themselves before the Lord. They chose to separate themselves from all foreigners and stood to confess their sins and the iniquities of their fathers. In this sacred assembly, they experienced the reading of the law, confession, and worship.

What does your worship look like in private? How do you commune with God personally and privately? Spend a few moments assessing your private worship. Do you spend time feeding on God's Word? Do you spend unhurried time alone with God in prayer and contemplation?

Now think about your public worship. When you gather with other believers to worship God, what does your worship experience entail? Are you conscious of your own sin and cognizant of the holiness of God? Is there a spirit of brokenness and humility as you worship God?

Ask God to take your private and public worship to a new level of intimacy. Invite the Lord to take you on a journey in worship that enables you to encounter Him in all of His fullness and holiness.

~ *Stephen*

September 29

Our Mourning Into Dancing

Chronological Bible Reading Plan: (Day 272: Nehemiah 11-13; Psalm 126)

"When the LORD restored the fortunes of Zion, we were like those who dream. Then our mouth was filled with laughter, and our tongue with shouts of joy; then they said among the nations, 'The LORD has done great things for them.' The LORD has done great things for us; we are glad." Psalm 126:1-3 (ESV)

Oh, the blessed promise the Lord gives to us of restoration! Yes, there are times, dear child of God, when hardship will come your way. Some of these will come as a result of poor choices and sinfulness, while others will come by the Lord's hand to teach or strengthen our faith. In either case, though, we can hold firm to the truth that God's grace is sufficient and that in time He will look down upon His children in love and turn our mourning into dancing. He will cause us to dream dreams and satisfy our eternal thirst as only He can. He will do great things for those who respond to times of distress with faith and obedience, once again making us glad!

Are you in dire straits today, beloved saint? Do you feel that you are sowing tears of sorrow? Call out to the Lord as the psalmist does and plead with Him to restore your fortunes! Do not stay in the valley, when the Lord is waiting for you on the mountaintop. Now, be sure you don't return to the reason for your valley; be careful to learn the lesson that the Lord wanted you to learn in your time of exile. Once learned, though, turn back to the Lord and see His faithful hand bring about an everlasting, unexplainable joy that will sustain you in any circumstance!

~ *Jared*

September 30
Worship that God Rejects

Chronological Bible Reading Plan: (Day 273: Malachi)

"Oh that there were one among you who would shut the doors, that you might not kindle fire on my altar in vain! I have no pleasure in you, says the LORD of hosts, and I will not accept an offering from your hand. For from the rising of the sun to its setting my name will be great among the nations, and in every place incense will be offered to my name, and a pure offering. For my name will be great among the nations, says the LORD of hosts." Malachi 1:10-11 (ESV)

Any worship that is offered for any other reason than proclaiming the greatness of the name of the Lord is vanity! In fact, the Lord suggests He would rather you not show up, if praising His name is not your chief concern. The people of Israel had forgotten this reality. Some eighty years after the promises of Haggai and Zechariah, the people of God found themselves impoverished and disillusioned. God's temple was rebuilt, but where was the promised blessing? Where was God's presence? Undoubtedly they had allowed their circumstance to encourage them to say things like, "Since He has not given us His best, we will not give Him our best. Surely, He would understand if we gave Him our worst livestock since we need our best ones for the best profit."

The Lord, however, takes exception to their insufficient offering. Our praise and worship of our Lord should never be dictated by circumstance. We must always seek to give Him our best, because His name is worthy of nothing less. We take in vain the name of the Lord when we don't come with our best. Think about your motivation for worship. Why do you come to sing songs and hear the word of God taught? Why do you serve daily in your neighborhoods or at the church? Is it to proclaim the greatness of the name of the Lord? If it is for any other reason, then it is in vain. You would be better to simply shut the temple doors.

~ Jared

October 1

We have Seen His Glory

Chronological Bible Reading Plan: (Day 274: Luke 1; John 1)

"And the Word became flesh and dwelt among us, and we have seen his glory, glory as of the only Son from the Father, full of grace and truth." John 1:14 (ESV)

Consider this profound truth for a moment, follower of Christ! Have you truly comprehended the enormity of this declaration by John in his beautifully written prologue? We have beheld the glory of God, the Father! That which would have immediately brought about death in us under the law because of our sinfulness has now become our source of hope and life. Jesus has come as the full revelation of God's glory to us, unveiling a plan established in eternity past in which the grace of God and the truth of His sovereign plan for all things would be profoundly revealed in the person and work of Christ.

Jesus is divine communication, and the Word among us communicates that our separation from God is not permanent. Further, our communion with Him is no longer confined to a building, for as Jesus lived among us, so now does the Holy Spirit live within us, imparting life in us to walk in beautiful fellowship with our God, having been redeemed by revealed grace and truth in Jesus.

Have you truly beheld the glory of the life of Jesus? Are you overwhelmed by the grace exemplified in His mission, death, and resurrection? Have you been transformed by the truth that in Him the glory of God gives us life rather than death? Dear child of God, called that by virtue of Christ's work, take a moment this morning and rejoice that God sent His son to reveal His glory and dwell not just among us but in us!

~Jared

October 2

GROW AS CHRIST GREW

Chronological Bible Reading Plan: (Day 275: Matthew 1; Luke 2)

"And Jesus increased in wisdom and in stature and in favor with God and man." Luke 2:52 (ESV)

Be careful not to be misled, dear friend, by what you read in today's verse. The critic of Christianity may ask what need has God of increase, for isn't God infinitely what He is? The answer, of course, is a resounding yes, but couched within that answer is the caveat of the incarnation, when God the Son took on flesh and dwelt among us. In His time of residence upon this earth, the Christ patterned for us what it means to live as God's representatives upon the earth, giving the truth of God flesh so that its impact may be personified.

The God-man, Jesus, in His humanity grew. Some of the growth described was of course natural, i.e. in His stature. The other growth described, however, that of wisdom and favor, was not natural but rather the effect of abiding in the presence of God. Jesus sought out truth and engaged that truth, displaying the fruit of the Spirit and a special anointing from God's hand that gave Him favor with man. He grew as we must grow, not simply in the natural way but also in the spiritual way as His legacy.

Can you say that you have grown in more ways than simply in stature? Have you engaged the truth of God's word so that it enhances your wisdom? Have you employed that wisdom for the glory of God, evidencing proclaimed favor while gaining favor with man? Seek today to do what Jesus did. Go to the Father's house, study the truth of scripture, and be about your Father's business. Grow as Christ grew so that you can accomplish what He desires you to accomplish.

~ *Jared*

October 3

Shine Like Stars

Chronological Bible Reading Plan: (Day 276: Matthew 2)

"And behold, the star that they had seen when it rose went before them until it came to rest over the place where the child was. When they saw the star, they rejoiced exceedingly with great joy." Matthew 2:9b-10 (ESV)

How did men so far away come to find the promised Messiah resting in a random house in the town of Bethlehem? Did they have some treasure map leading the way with clues, warning of imminent danger on their journey? Did they have scouts go before them and investigate what the local people had seen and/or heard about this special birth? No. They had a star. They had a marker placed by God, which led them beyond the snares of Herod and inside some seemingly unimportant house in Bethlehem to the fulfillment of their hopes and the object of their worship. They were undoubtedly aware of the promise and the prophecy regarding this deliverer and were searching for this proclaimed "king." In their searching, though, they were given an aid, which we must ourselves be today.

We are the modern day stars of Bethlehem. For those who are searching, who have the promise of God sealed on their heart as they bare His image, we are to be the lights that lead them to where Christ is so that they may join with all creation in appropriate worship. We must shine and lead so that all the world may see the fulfillment of scripture and the arrival of our once and future king!

Are you shining as a light in darkness? Are you engaging those who are searching? Are you resting over where Christ is so that when people find you they may also find Him? May we be lights today; may we shine like stars to a world searching for Jesus.

~ *Jared*

October 4

PREPARE THE WAY

Chronological Bible Reading Plan: (Day 277: Matthew 3; Mark 1; Luke 3)

"The beginning of the gospel of Jesus Christ, the Son of God. As it is written in Isaiah the prophet, 'Behold, I send my messenger before your face, who will prepare your way, the voice of one crying in the wilderness: 'Prepare the way of the Lord, make his paths straight.'" Mark 1:1-3 (ESV)

We are the beginning of the gospel for many of the people around us today. We are called to "prepare the way" as John the Baptist did for the message of Jesus to come into their lives and call them to a place of repentance. We are messengers, proclaiming the most important message ever to be proclaimed: "The Christ has come to take away the sins of the world."

This proclamation is a verbal proclamation, yes, but it is also a lived declaration. We are to make the path of Christ "straight," removing obstacles to the impact of this transformative message. In becoming like John the Baptist, then, in our prophetic role, we must be sure that we have not trivialized our message for temporary pleasures. John found his entire identity in speaking forth the gospel. He did not value material things, but rather only valued ministry. Let us be sure that our lives communicate as effectively the unique satisfying power of Jesus.

Are you preparing the way of Christ? Are you making the path of the gospel straight? Consider for a moment some things in your life that may hinder the spread of the gospel. Repent of those things even as you call others to repentance in light of the glorious reality of the good news of Jesus!

~ Jared

October 5

Our Talent, His Empowerment

Chronological Bible Reading Plan: (Day 278: Matthew 4; Luke 4-5)

"And when he had finished speaking, he said to Simon, 'Put out into the deep and let down your nets for a catch.' And Simon answered, 'Master, we toiled all night and took nothing! But at your word I will let down the nets.' And when they had done this, they enclosed a large number of fish, and their nets were breaking. They signaled to their partners in the other boat to come and help them. And they came and filled both the boats, so that they began to sink." Luke 5:4-7 (ESV)

Having just heard Jesus preach, these ordinary fishermen had already discerned something special in this man from Galilee. His words were not the words of an ordinary rabbi; no, there was something more pronounced and meaningful in His preaching. And, yet, there had to have been a moment of surprise when this carpenter/teacher told experienced fishermen to go back out to fish, having had no success that preceding night. Granted, Jesus was an incredible teacher, but what did He know about fishing?

The truth we encounter in this passage is a profound one indeed. In the Kingdom of God, the Lord has given us knowledge and ability, but both of those things are inept without the power of God fueling them. We may think we know how to fish, but unless we fish at the Lord's direction, we will work in vain with little to show for it. We are inherently dependent upon the Lord, and we must recognize that dependence even in activities at which we feel well-versed.

What talents and knowledge has the Lord given you? Are you using them in His empowerment for the building of His Kingdom? Or are you operating outside His empowerment, serving in vain and in frustration? Commit to submit today, responding to His clearly spoken direction rather than randomly throwing your nets into an unforgiving sea.

~ Jared

October 6

WHAT ARE YOU LIVING FOR?

Chronological Bible Reading Plan: (Day 279: John 2-4)

"Jesus said to them, 'My food is to do the will of him who sent me and to accomplish his work.'" John 4:34 (ESV)

God has a mission for you to fulfill. God created you to bloom where He plants you so that you can continue the ministry of Jesus. Your life matters to God. Stay on mission with God.

Jesus lived His earthly life to bring glory to God by doing His will and finishing His work. Jesus was on mission with God. His passion was to do God's will. When the disciples returned with food for Jesus to eat, Jesus clarified that His appetite was to do God's will. Jesus recognized the clear mission for which He was sent by God to the earth to fulfill.

- *"When Jesus had received the sour wine, he said, 'It is finished,' and he bowed his head and gave up his spirit." John 19:30 (ESV)*

Jesus completed His atoning work on the cross to purchase our salvation. He took the full wrath of God for our sin. Jesus was buried in a borrowed tomb and rose three days later. After forty days of post-resurrection appearances, Jesus ascended to heaven. On the Day of Pentecost, Jesus sent the Holy Spirit to indwell the believers as He promised (John 16:7 & Luke 24:49). Now Jesus is at the right hand of the Father making intercession for us (Rom. 8:34).

Will you embrace the mission of Jesus by doing God's will and finishing the work He wants to do through you? There are people who need the love of Jesus you possess. Multitudes stand in need of the gift of eternal life that you have received. Bring glory to God by living on mission with Him.

~ *Stephen*

October 7

Carry Your Corner

Chronological Bible Reading Plan: (Day 280: Matthew 8; Mark 2)

"And many were gathered together, so that there was no more room, not even at the door. And he was preaching the word to them. And they came, bringing to him a paralytic carried by four men. And when they could not get near him because of the crowd, they removed the roof above him, and when they had made an opening, they let down the bed on which the paralytic lay." Mark 2:2-4 (ESV)

These four men were convinced that Jesus was the answer. They were focused on the mission of getting the paralytic to Jesus. Even though the obstacles were vast and the house was full, these four men were willing to be creative and committed to bringing the paralytic to Jesus.

What if one of the four decided not to carry his corner? What if one of the four chose to give up and release his corner of responsibility? One of the remaining three would have had to take on double the load. Instead, the four men worked together as a team unified and devoted to bringing the paralytic to Jesus.

- *"And when Jesus saw their faith, he said to the paralytic, 'Son, your sins are forgiven.'" Mark 2:5 (ESV)*

Jesus rewarded their faith. These four men were willing to dig through the roof to lower the paralytic down. No barrier was big enough to penetrate their passion and to dilute their devotion. These men were willing to go beyond their own comfort and convenience in order to place the needs of this paralytic before their own.

Are you willing to carry your corner to bring people to Jesus? Are you willing to carry your corner to ensure the ministry of Jesus continues on the earth? Do your part to meet needs and to point people to Jesus.

~ *Stephen*

October 8
HEIGHTEN YOUR SENSITIVITY

Chronological Bible Reading Plan: (Day 281: John 5)

"So Jesus said to them, 'Truly, truly, I say to you, the Son can do nothing of his own accord, but only what he sees the Father doing. For whatever the Father does, that the Son does likewise. For the Father loves the Son and shows him all that he himself is doing. And greater works than these will he show him, so that you may marvel.'" John 5:19-20 (ESV)

Are you experiencing God? I remember the major shift that took place in my Christian journey after my wife and I went through Henry Blackaby's workbook, *Experiencing God*. Instead of seeking to do something for God, we began embracing the discipline of allowing God to do His work in us and through us.

The first of seven realities of *Experiencing God* is recognizing that God is always at work around you. If you want to see God at work, then ask God to heighten your sensitivity to His activity. Jesus was sensitive to God's activity. Even at age twelve, Jesus announced to His earthly mom and dad, "I must be about my Father's business."

Orient your life around God's activity. Remember, the Christian life is not about your story that you invite God into. The Christian life is about God's story that He invites you into. Jesus oriented His life around God's activity so that He could join God in His activity.

Place your "yes" on the altar and make yourself completely available for the Lord's use. Ride the wave God creates. Look to see where He is at work so that you can join Him in His activity. Seek to turn interruptions into opportunities to join God in what He is doing.

Pray this prayer with me: "Lord, I'm Yours! Help me to see where You are at work today so that I can join You!"

~ *Stephen*

October 9

Chosen By God and For God

Chronological Bible Reading Plan: (Day 282: Matthew 12; Mark 3; Luke 6)

"And he appointed twelve (whom he also named apostles) so that they might be with him and he might send them out to preach." Mark 3:14 (ESV)

Can you imagine the honor of being chosen by Jesus to serve as one of His twelve apostles? You would have a starting position on the varsity team that Jesus coached. You would have access to His life behind the scenes in the locker room and on the practice field. You would want to spend all your time in His shadow and under His personal touch ministry. To be like Him, you would want to watch His every move and to capture every word He articulated. It would be so refreshing to be that connected to the Son of God.

As a follower of Jesus Christ, you have that kind of connection with the Son of God. At the moment of your conversion experience, you were adopted into God's family and placed on the winning team. You have the privilege of drawing near to the Lord and learning how to enjoy His presence.

God did not save you so that you could stay in the huddle. God rescued you from eternal damnation and placed you into His forever family and filled you with His Holy Spirit so that you could continue the ministry of Jesus on the earth. You have been chosen by God to be sent out to portray His love and to proclaim the saving news of Jesus. You have been armed with everything you need to share the gospel. Every single person who places their faith in Jesus alone for salvation will be saved and adopted into the family of God. You are chosen by God to build that relational bridge to those who are lost.

~ *Stephen*

October 10

INSTEAD OF WORRYING

Chronological Bible Reading Plan: (Day 283: Matthew 5-7)

"Therefore do not be anxious about tomorrow, for tomorrow will be anxious for itself. Sufficient for the day is its own trouble." Matthew 6:34 (ESV)

Instead of worrying about tomorrow, focus on today. To worry is to be drawn in multiple directions. Worry causes you to feel fragmented and overwhelmed. Someone has said, "Today is the tomorrow you worried about yesterday." Where does worry take you? Worry takes you to an unhealthy place!

God gives you the grace you need for today. God gives you the provision you need for today. Focus on today. Release the fear and anxiety related to tomorrow. Jesus made it clear that tomorrow will worry about itself and each day has enough trouble of its own.

Aren't you thankful that there are 365 days in a year, twenty-four hours in a day, sixty minutes in an hour, and sixty seconds in each minute? Jesus does not want us to worry about tomorrow. Don't be anxious about the next installment of twenty-four hours. That's why Jesus did not teach us to pray, "Give us this month our monthly bread." Rather, Jesus taught us to pray, "Give us this day our daily bread."

- *"Let your reasonableness be known to everyone. The Lord is at hand; do not be anxious about anything, but in everything by prayer and supplication with thanksgiving let your requests be made known to God." Philippians 4:5-6 (ESV)*

Instead of worrying about tomorrow, choose to focus on what God wants to do in you and through you today. God is building you and developing you to fulfill His will for today. Don't waste one moment today. Every moment matters to God so make every moment count for God's glory.

~ *Stephen*

October 11

Does Your Love Match Your Forgiveness?

Chronological Bible Reading Plan: (Day 284: Matthew 9; Luke 7)

"'Therefore I tell you, her sins, which are many, are forgiven--for she loved much. But he who is forgiven little, loves little.' And he said to her, 'Your sins are forgiven.' Then those who were at table with him began to say among themselves, 'Who is this, who even forgives sins?'" Luke 7:47-49 (ESV)

Today we encounter one of the most beautiful stories in all of scripture, in which a sinful woman recognizes her indelible need to worship her worthy Savior. Luke does not provide us with much background story for this woman except for the note that she is a known "sinner." Because of her status, she is looked down upon by the "righteous," who call into question Jesus' righteousness for letting such a woman have any contact with Him. Upon recognizing their judgment, Jesus asks a simple question of His host, Simon, that carries a profound answer.

Why wasn't Simon treating the good "teacher" the way this sinful woman was? Why was she so broken and generous in her gift? Because she recognized her great need and the hope that rested for her alone in Christ.

The question for us today is, "Who do you most resemble in this story?" Are you broken over your sin? Do you bow before the Lord, desiring to give Him the very best you have because of what He has given you? Or do you judge those who have been forgiven much, thinking them unworthy of contact with you and your God?

The reality is that all of us have sinned greatly, whether we recognize it or not. The deeper we walk with the Lord and the greater we strive for holiness, the more junk we will find. May we not be accused of loving little for thinking we have been forgiven little. May we have the continual mindset of this brave woman, who saw her Savior and worshiped Him accordingly.

~ Jared

October 12

The Beautiful Rest of Christ

Chronological Bible Reading Plan: (Day 285: Matthew 11)

"Come to me, all who labor and are heavy laden, and I will give you rest." Matthew 11:28 (ESV)

Religion is hard. Trying to attain a righteousness that measures up to the God of the Bible is an impossible task, and yet we continually beat ourselves up for not attaining the impossible. Once we have failed enough at achieving perfection, we have two choices, humanly speaking: give up or change the standard.

In the midst of our frustration, though, Jesus gives us hope. Religion is not the answer; He is! He invites us to come to Him when we are defeated by religion and find that His yoke is easy and burden light. How is this so? Because He lived perfectly for you! He achieved righteousness and then offered it to you through the gospel. He is not asking you to try harder; He is asking you to surrender.

Will you quit trying to attain the impossible and enter into this beautiful rest? Or will you continue to live in frustration trying to achieve in vain that which Jesus already guarantees?

Dear child of God, remove the shackles of religious activity and find rest in the glory of the cross. Jesus has already paid it all. Let us not take His sacrifice in vain by trying to add to it, for it is more than sufficient!

~ *Jared*

October 13

The Importance of Need in Prayer

Chronological Bible Reading Plan: (Day 286: Luke 11)

"And I tell you, ask, and it will be given to you; seek, and you will find; knock, and it will be opened to you. For everyone who asks receives, and the one who seeks finds, and to the one who knocks it will be opened." Luke 11:9-10 (ESV)

The Lord has given us a blank check! At least, that's what our flesh wants to hear. We read this passage and think, "You mean, I can really ask for anything? The Lord is seriously promising to give me anything I want?" But we must read what Jesus is saying more carefully. Jesus is not teaching us that we can pray in His name and receive whatever we want. Rather, He is saying that our Father in heaven will meet every legitimate need you and I have. God is good, and He loves His children. Therefore, He will provide for them.

I have seen this first hand in my time in Africa. The children we work with there do not have much, but through the local church the Lord is providing. Consider this truth in your own life. Have you seen the Lord provide for you in times of great need? Have you given Him praise for His faithfulness?

When you pray in supplication, asking for something from the Lord, be sure you have asked yourself whether or not this request is a legitimate need or a selfish desire. The importance in this is striking, since you do not want bitterness to set in when the Lord does not answer your selfish request. See this beautiful promise for what it is, a statement of a Father's generosity toward His children, rather than an open door to an endless supply of extravagant things which we do not need.

~*Jared*

October 14

WE KNOW THE MASTER OF THE WIND

Chronological Bible Reading Plan: (Day 287: Matthew 13; Luke 8)

"And they went and woke him, saying, 'Master, Master, we are perishing!' And he awoke and rebuked the wind and the raging waves, and they ceased, and there was a calm. He said to them, 'Where is your faith?' And they were afraid, and they marveled, saying to one another, 'Who then is this, that he commands even winds and water, and they obey him?'" Luke 8:24-25 (ESV)

If you have ever been on a small boat in the midst of a torrential storm, then surely you know the reaction of the disciples in this passage is not a melodramatic one. Waves crashing over the sides, flooding the decks, and knocking people off of their feet would cause anyone to worry. These men were frightened and justifiably so. In their fear, they run to their "Master," Who for some reason is sleeping in the midst of this chaos and beg Him to save them. In response, Jesus stands up, calm and composed, and demands the elements reflect His nature rather than allowing His to be affected by them.

The Lord is our firm foundation. He is the calm and hope we need in times of great distress. He does not grow weary by circumstance nor worry about the future, for He establishes the circumstance and directs the future. He is sovereign over all things, and we must place our faith in that sovereignty, trusting that when times become difficult or our burden seems too large to bear that we have a Master, who calms the seas by simply speaking over them "Peace, be still."

How do you react in times of stress? Do you worry and run to the Lord in fear? Or do you remember the God you serve and take comfort in the knowledge that He is in control of all things and will work those circumstances for the good of those who love Him?

~ *Jared*

October 15

Let Your Light Shine

Chronological Bible Reading Plan: (Day 288: Mark 4-5)

"And he said to them, 'Is a lamp brought in to be put under a basket, or under a bed, and not on a stand? For nothing is hidden except to be made manifest; nor is anything secret except to come to light. If anyone has ears to hear, let him hear.'" Mark 4:21-23 (ESV)

The Kingdom of God is being established by the Church through the gospel of Jesus Christ all over the world. We, as God's ambassadors, are proclaiming hope and purpose as a result of the cross, demanding the darkness of depravity to recede in the glory of the light of God's beautiful revelation in Jesus. We are revealing God's purpose for all things and calling creation to restoration, enabling all things to worship the Lord and give Him the glory that He alone is due!

In light of these profound truths, how could we ever consider keeping the light within us as a result of the Spirit's regenerative work hidden? Why do we allow the darkness to demand authority over the light? When we walk into a room as God's chosen people, that room should be lit by the joy in our hearts, demanding the hearts of those who have not responded to Christ's sacrifice to consider the difference in our worldview and there's.

We have been called to be witnesses, which should not be a hard thing given this image from Jesus. Witnessing should be a natural thing, in that any time light steps into darkness the difference is noticeable. This was certainly true of Jesus, the ultimate light, whose radiance in the midst of darkness changed the course of human history! Will you follow His example? Will you let your light shine and build the Kingdom of God today?

~ *Jared*

October 16

Wisdom and Innocence

Chronological Bible Reading Plan: (Day 289: Matthew 10)

"Behold, I am sending you out as sheep in the midst of wolves, so be wise as serpents and innocent as doves." Matthew 10:16 (ESV)

The mission of the Church given by Christ is not an easy one. How could it be when it is itself a continuation of the ministry of Jesus that resulted in His crucifixion? Jesus in this passage is preparing His disciples and, by proxy, us for the reality of persecution on this side of heaven. To prepare them and us, Jesus charges His followers to be "wise as serpents and innocent as doves." For Him, wisdom and innocence are our greatest assets in the midst of persecution?

Why these two traits? Why do wisdom and innocence help us in the midst of maltreatment? Jesus helps us as the passage continues. He suggests that we must use wisdom to know which men to trust and which men not to trust. We must have a discerning spirit, knowing that when men are confronted with their depravity they sometimes react harshly. Further, when the day comes that you can no longer escape the hand of men through wisdom, innocence becomes your ally. As with Jesus, people will begin to question the legitimacy of the charges brought against you, seeing your pure heart and your accuser's malicious one.

Seek today to grow in wisdom by meditating on the Word of God and abiding in the Spirit. Ask the Spirit to open your heart to those men and women who are open to the gospel and to guard against those who are hardened. Secondly, commit to be above reproach. When we commit to this, we do more than ask if something is right or wrong; rather, we ask, "Is this wise?" If we commit to act only in the wisdom God gives, then truly who can be against us?

Be wary, sheep, for there are wolves around. Grow in wisdom and walk in innocence for your good and God's glory.

~*Jared*

October 17

The Complete Sustaining Nature of Christ

Chronological Bible Reading Plan: (Day 290: Matthew 14; Mark 6; Luke 9)

"He charged them to take nothing for their journey except a staff--no bread, no bag, no money in their belts--but to wear sandals and not put on two tunics." Mark 6:8-9 (ESV)

What an interesting command from Jesus found here in Mark's gospel. Jesus has called to Himself "those whom he desired" and allowed them to walk alongside Him as they learned (Mark 3:13 ESV). Now, as He is preparing to send them out, He commands them to take nothing with them except what they have on their back. Why would Jesus demand such a thing from His disciples? Why would He not allow them to "prepare" more thoroughly for the task at hand?

Jesus was teaching His disciples (and us) about the importance of fully relying upon Him and His provision for the purposes of ministry. If Jesus sends us under His authority and calling as His disciples, then He will sustain us as we go. If He sends you, He will provide for you. The disciples, like us, had to learn this truth in order to properly submit to the will of the Lord as His representatives, thereby allowing Him to receive all the glory for the work that He would do through them. Further, how could they communicate the complete satisfying nature of Christ without having experienced it themselves? In their mission, they were learning as they were going.

Do you fully rely upon the Lord to accomplish that to which He has called you? Or do you overcompensate, not fully trusting in His ability to work miraculously through you? When we fail to fully rely upon Him to sustain, we often miss the opportunity to be part of something extraordinary, since only in Him is such a work possible.

~ Jared

October 18
Why Do You Seek Him?

Chronological Bible Reading Plan: (Day 291: John 6)

"Jesus answered them, 'Truly, truly, I say to you, you are seeking me, not because you saw signs, but because you ate your fill of the loaves.'" John 6:26 (ESV)

Throughout the book of John, we see a progression of miraculous signs performed by Jesus through which He communicates to the world His authority over things both spiritual and physical. Earlier in this chapter, for instance, Jesus takes five barley loaves and two fish and feeds thousands of bystanders, proving His glorious and ample ability to provide and satisfy. The people in the crowd who experienced this miraculous work wake up the next day to find that Jesus and His disciples have crossed the Sea of Galilee (Jesus on foot and the disciples by boat) to Capernaum and decide to pursue Him.

The issue for Jesus, though, in this pursuit is their motivation for doing so. Why were they coming after Him? Were they coming because they had recognized this miracle as a "messianic sign"? Or were they coming after Him because He was a free meal ticket? Jesus suggests that the latter is their true motivation.

Why do you follow Jesus? Have you recognized Him as the Messiah, the only hope of the nations? Have you seen your depravity and great need for a savior and found Jesus alone able to satisfy that need? Or do you simply like what He can give you? Maybe you just like the idea of escaping Hell?

Oh, child of God, do not mistake the generosity of Christ as a license to feel entitled. Do not lose the humility that should accompany the recognition that Jesus is the Son of God, Who has come to take away the sins of the world. Yes, we will receive blessing and, yes, we will escape eternal judgement, but our sole motivation for seeking Jesus should be a result of His greatest miracle, when He overcame sin and death so that we could have life abundant!

~ *Jared*

October 19

WHERE DOES SIN COME FROM?

Chronological Bible Reading Plan: (Day 292: Matthew 15; Mark 7)

"And he called the people to him and said to them, 'Hear and understand: it is not what goes into the mouth that defiles a person, but what comes out of the mouth; this defiles a person.'" Matthew 15:10-11 (ESV)

The religious elite of Jesus' time were under the false understanding that sinfulness or unrighteousness is a state that comes from the inside of man being influenced by his outside. When they ate or partook of unholy things, those unholy things made them unholy. Jesus, however, had a different message for the Pharisees and scribes, proclaiming to them that sinfulness was a result of inward rebellion that no amount of action could either lessen or even increase? Depravity was (and is) depravity and while certainly the requirements of the law withheld God's judgement against that depravity, those actions in no way made the individual more holy.

This teaching is the dilemma for all mankind. We are sinful and there is no amount of religious activity that can fix that sinfulness. We can act holy and we can fake devotion, but that doesn't mean that the core of who we are has been transformed. We are simply white-washed tombs, as Jesus would say. But this also is the hope of the gospel, in that Jesus existed in a way that we could not. He was not depraved; rather, He was inherently holy. Through His sacrifice, He now offers His perfect holiness to us, replacing our sinfulness and transforming our hearts. We no longer have to pretend to be holy or fight to earn it; it has been earned for us and given to us freely as a response to our repentance. We are sinful, but Jesus is holy. Through Him we who were sinful can be declared holy and restored to a right relationship with God. Rejoice in that profound truth today.

~ Jared

October 20

Who Do You Say That I Am?

Chronological Bible Reading Plan: (Day 293: Matthew 16; Mark 8)

"He said to them, 'But who do you say that I am?' Simon Peter replied, 'You are the Christ, the Son of the living God.'" Matthew 16:15-16 (ESV)

Throughout the centuries following the coming of Christ, humanity has been forced to make a decision as to His true identity. Who was He really? Was He another great prophet like Isaiah or Jeremiah? Was He simply a charismatic leader? Or was He truly the second person of the Trinity incarnate? Where you fall in this debate is of the utmost importance as the answer forms the foundation of saving faith.

Jesus was more than simply a prophet, and He was more than another charismatic leader. He came proclaiming Himself to be Lord! He came as the Anointed One of God chosen to rectify the damage of sin and restore creation. Any other conclusion denies the testimony of Scripture. As C.S. Lewis famously wrote in *Mere Christianity*, anyone who claimed what Jesus claimed could not be considered a moral teacher, if indeed He was not the Son of God, for His morality would be rejected as He would be proclaimed either a liar or a lunatic. Lewis' "trilemma" is simply stated: either Jesus was a liar, a lunatic, or the Lord!

My friends, there can be no marginal or mild response to Jesus. Either you proclaim Him to be the Christ, repent, and follow Him with complete devotion, or you reject Him as the Lord and choose to continue to follow the path of self-exaltation. He cannot be just another voice in the volumes of history. Either He is unique or He is not. Who do you say that Jesus is? Moreover, do your life and actions reflect that sentiment as true belief?

~ *Jared*

October 21

The Problem with Miraculous Mountains

Chronological Bible Reading Plan: (Day 294: Matthew 17; Mark 9)

"And there appeared to them Elijah with Moses, and they were talking with Jesus. And Peter said to Jesus, 'Rabbi, it is good that we are here. Let us make three tents, one for you and one for Moses and one for Elijah.'" Mark 9:4-5 (ESV)

What an incredible event! Can you imagine experiencing what Peter experienced on this mountain? Can you imagine how you would react if you were to see Moses, Elijah, and Jesus all in their glorified form? Peter wanted to build a memorial. He wanted to stay there indefinitely and just revel in the miraculous moment. Isn't that exactly how we react to incredible, life-changing encounters with God? When we experience the Lord in this way, we want to stay there forever, and when we have to leave we immediately begin to long for the next mountaintop experience. Reacting in this way, though, completely misses the point of these impactful moments. These moments aren't meant to be ends unto themselves; rather, they are meant to be launching pads for ministry, motivating and encouraging us to continue our ministry as disciples. Jesus didn't let Peter build the tents because if he had, Peter would have missed all of the ministry He had for him in the valleys between the mountains.

May we not miss the ministry Christ has for us in our desire to experience the Lord in new and exciting ways. When the Lord reveals Himself to us so profoundly, the purpose is always to better enable us to accomplish the mission of the Church in building the Kingdom of God. Be thankful for these special moments, but don't allow the pursuit of them to become distractions. Seek the Lord while He may be found, but when you find Him, serve Him.

~*Jared*

October 22

The Necessity of Forgiveness

Chronological Bible Reading Plan: (Day 295: Matthew 18)

"Then Peter came up and said to him, 'Lord, how often will my brother sin against me, and I forgive him? As many as seven times?' Jesus said to him, 'I do not say to you seven times, but seventy times seven.'" Matthew 18:21-22 (ESV)

Forgiveness is a hard thing, no doubt, but it is also an essential thing for Christians. Peter in our passage this morning asks a question many of us have asked in our lives. How many times should we have to forgive someone? If someone keeps offending us or betraying us, should we continue to forgive them? Jesus answers from experience. While to the human mind forgiving someone so treacherous seven times may seem extraordinary, Jesus more than exceeds that expectation suggesting seventy times that!

Why should we keep on forgiving? Why should we forgive so freely? Well, consider the example of the gospel set before us. Consider how many times you and I have offended Jesus. Consider how many times we have rejected Him. Consider how many times we have rejected Him, and yet He forgave us. Not only did He forgive us, He made the forgiveness possible by taking on the penalty of our transgression Himself. He who knew no sin became sin so that we might be the righteousness of God! How incredible is that!

You and I must forgive because of how much we have been forgiven. I assure you nobody can do to you what we have done to the Lord, and yet in spite of our rejection He loved us enough to send Jesus to reconcile us. Do not be like the unforgiving servant, who having been forgiven chose not to extend that forgiveness to others. Rather, in light of what you have been forgiven, seek to extend that forgiveness to others as an act of worship to One Who has forgiven us so much.

~ *Jared*

October 23

Does the Truth Set You Free?

Chronological Bible Reading Plan: (Day 296: John 7-8)

"So Jesus said to the Jews who had believed in him, 'If you abide in my word, you are truly my disciples, and you will know the truth, and the truth will set you free.'" John 8:31-32 (ESV)

Do you know the truth of God? He has revealed it to you. The Scriptures offer us the complete revelation of God, concerning His character, His covenant, and His plan for all things. As a disciple of Christ, that truth should make you come alive. Simply by reading the Bible you can know the God of the universe more intimately and uniquely. Granted, the truth given to us may not always be easy to read or hear, but we welcome it because we know that in it lies freedom. Freedom is in this truth because of how we are shaped into the image of Jesus as a result of hearing it, thereby enabling us to be more fully satisfied by Him as opposed to the things of this world.

For those who are not children of God, however, the exact opposite is true. While for us, there is a welcome reward to hearing the truth of God, those outside of the family of God are offended, seeing the truth as an obstacle to their freedom rather than a gateway. They see the principles and precepts of scripture as restraints, whereas you and I see them as pathways to greater freedom.

Simply, how you respond to the truth of God spoken over you says a lot about your place as a disciple. If you welcome truth because of how it enables you to be more like Jesus, then take comfort, child of God. If, however, you resist that truth to pursue your own selfish endeavors, you may want to take a moment and see what part of your life you have yet to surrender fully to the Lordship of Christ.

~ Jared

October 24
God's Work on Display

Chronological Bible Reading Plan: (Day 297: John 9-10)

"And his disciples asked him, 'Rabbi, who sinned, this man or his parents, that he was born blind?' Jesus answered, 'It was not that this man sinned, or his parents, but that the works of God might be displayed in him.'" John 9:2-3 (ESV)

For me, this passage is one of the most challenging in all of scripture. Jesus and His disciples happen upon a man, who was born blind, and the disciples, influenced by the common belief of the day, asked what fault existed in this man or his parents that God would judge him by making him blind. Jesus, as He so often does, challenges the false assumptions of the disciples by suggesting to them the cause of this man's blindness was not his sinfulness nor that of his parents but rather so the glory of God might be displayed through him, which of course it was when Jesus healed him.

What an incredible question this passage presents! Are we, as disciples of Jesus, willing to allow our bodies, our resources, our talents, our failures, indeed everything we have to be used for the work of God to be displayed? When difficulties arise in our lives, when we lose that job or sickness befalls us, are we willing to say to the Lord, "Work through me in this time to display your glory and my ultimate satisfaction and trust in you," instead of asking, "Why me?" The tendency for us, like that of the disciples, is to ask what we have done to deserve such treatment. We want to know how we can fix it to regain that which we have lost, but what if the purpose is greater than that? What if we have been placed in that situation for God to do a miraculous work through us so that others may see Him and believe?

Are you willing to be used in that way? Are you willing to allow every circumstance in your life to be used for the glory of God? This teaching is challenging, yes, but I suspect our willingness to do so represents a new level of faith in our walk with the Lord.

~ *Jared*

October 25

THE DISTRACTION OF SERVING

Chronological Bible Reading Plan: (Day 298: Luke 10)

"But Martha was distracted with much serving. And she went up to him and said, 'Lord, do you not care that my sister has left me to serve alone? Tell her then to help me.' But the Lord answered her, 'Martha, Martha, you are anxious and troubled about many things, but one thing is necessary. Mary has chosen the good portion, which will not be taken away from her.'" Luke 10:40-42 (ESV)

Serving should be the natural response of someone who has been transformed by the gospel of Jesus Christ. Jesus Himself came to serve and to build a Kingdom that was others focused, as explicitly expressed in the "Sermon on the Mount" and various other teachings of Jesus. There is a potential danger, however, in this proclivity toward service. If we are not careful, we can begin to fall back into our "pre-gospel" understandings of how we relate to God and once again subconsciously use service as a way to gain His favor. You see, we like activity and we like busyness, because both of these things make us feel like we are contributing to the product. But the gospel expressly states that you and I cannot help ourselves and that salvation and the maintenance of salvation are entirely an act of the Spirit of God, enabled by the sacrifice of Christ.

We must, then, be careful in the midst of our serving to remember the reason we serve. We do not serve to gain, we serve because of what we have already gained in Christ. Further, in light of that realization, we must remember to sit and worship this Christ, who has given us so much! There is a time for service, yes, but there is also a time for meditation. We must have balance, a balance that only comes by a healthy understanding of grace as exemplified in the good news of Jesus.

~Jared

October 26

Do Not Be Anxious

Chronological Bible Reading Plan: (Day 299: Luke 12-13)

"And he said to his disciples, 'Therefore I tell you, do not be anxious about your life, what you will eat, nor about your body, what you will put on.'"
Luke 12:22 (ESV)

Have you worried about anything this week? Have you been anxious about an event or circumstance? Jesus has a word for you this morning: stop. But how can we stop worrying? Isn't worrying a part of having responsibility or being human? Worrying or anxiety at its core is a statement about our trust in the sovereignty of God. In this particular passage and also in Matthew's recording of the Sermon on the Mount, Jesus tells His disciples to consider the fullness of creation and how even the smallest birds are provided for by their Heavenly Father. They do not worry about where their food will come from because the Lord has taken care of them. The challenge for us is to trust in the same way, knowing that we are of more value to the Lord as His prized creation.

What kind of things have you felt anxious over this week? My guess is that for many of you food, clothing, or shelter were not chief among them. The Lord has provided for you, and yet in spite of all of these evidences we still allow relatively small things to captivate our minds and divert our attention from our meditation on the goodness of God. Today, choose to trust. Choose to walk in faith, knowing that the Lord will provide. And if you do find yourself in a situation worthy of concern, pray and ask the Lord to come to your rescue. Who knows? It may be that your request will be met by someone who in turn has recognized the abundance of blessing the Lord has given to them and in generous response wants to share that with someone else. That is how the body of Christ is supposed to work after all, proving another way that God has provided for His people.

~ Jared

October 27

A Father's Love and A Son's Response

Chronological Bible Reading Plan: (Day 300: Luke 14-15)

"'For this my son was dead, and is alive again; he was lost, and is found.' And they began to celebrate." Luke 15:24 (ESV)

Child of God, hear this beautiful promise today: you can never wander too far away from the loving arms of your Heavenly Father! There may be times in your life when the temptations of this world once again captivate your mind and call you back into the pig sty in which you were found by Jesus, but know that even in the mud and muck of depravity, your Father in heaven waits and longs for you to "come to yourself," repent, and return. A father's love is unending and unconditional.

For many of us, these times of spiritual defeat push us away from the Lord, causing us to think ourselves too unworthy to return. "How can I go back to Him and ask Him to forgive me again? Would He even recognize me?" While certainly, as a Christian, our desire should be to grow in holiness, reflecting in greater detail the nature of Christ in our lives, do not let moments of weakness once again define you as they did before you surrendered your life to Jesus. Remember who you are! Your are a child of the living God, made so by the sacrifice of Jesus and the regenerating work of the Spirit. Yes, you have fallen, but get back up and return home to the arms of your loving Father.

May we not allow the inevitability of failure to ensnare us in defeat. We are more than conquerors in Christ, guaranteed eternal victory over our battle with sin. Stand up today, dear friend, and walk forward in holiness. Return to your Father, confess your sin, and see the feast that awaits!

~*Jared*

October 28

Have You Been Faithful with Little?

Chronological Bible Reading Plan: (Day 301: Luke 16-17)

"One who is faithful in a very little is also faithful in much, and one who is dishonest in a very little is also dishonest in much." Luke 16:10 (ESV)

The natural tendency of sinful man is to seek greater and greater glory for himself. We strive for more responsibility typically because it means more recognition and praise. We must be careful as redeemed followers of Christ, saved from our sinfulness, to not let this proclivity toward self-glorification seep its way into our service in the Kingdom.

Do you seek greater things? Do you seek greater responsibility? Why? Do you seek it because you wish to hear the applause of men? Do you seek it because you find security in success regardless of the source? Or do you desire to see God's glory grow? Are you happy with that with which you have been entrusted, knowing that the Lord's name is being praised because of it, or are you constantly seeking more, feeling a sense of entitlement?

Take a moment today and see what God has already given you. What areas in your life or ministry do you have influence over? Be thankful for those and seek to make them better, knowing that in their excellence the name of the Lord will also be seen as excellent. As you walk faithfully in these things, also trust that the Lord will see your faithfulness and entrust more as any good lord would to a trustworthy servant. Now, remember that this inevitability is not a cunning way to sneak your desire for personal glory past the eyes of the Lord, as He is of course knowledgeable of both our actions and motivation, but it is a promise that our greatest happiness is found in the promulgation of His glorious name. Let that be your goal and whatever task He entrusts to you will be worth your life.

~ Jared

October 29

Come Forth

Chronological Bible Reading Plan: (Day 302: John 11)

"When he had said these things, he cried out with a loud voice, 'Lazarus, come out.' The man who had died came out, his hands and feet bound with linen strips, and his face wrapped with a cloth. Jesus said to them, 'Unbind him, and let him go.'" John 11:42-43 (ESV)

There is no more perfect picture of the process of salvation than is found here in the gospel of John, for the story of Lazarus is all our story. We, like him, were dead in our trespasses, bound by our ever-deepening entanglement in sin, and grieving the heart of our loving Lord. And, yet, when it seemed that all hope was lost, Jesus spoke life into us as He did the brother of Mary and Martha.

Do you remember that day? Do you remember when the Lord of heaven and earth gently but firmly spoke your name and called you to "come forth"? Do you remember when He released you from the binding of sin, free to walk in abundant life? Oh, child of God, never forget that day. Never forget that when Christ has set you free, you are free indeed.

And why must we remember? We must because of our tendency to wander back into the tomb. Every now and then we forget that we have this life within us and act as we did when we were dead, cold and unresponsive to the movement of God. We allow sin to find a place in our lives once again, forgetting the death it spoke over us.

When temptation comes or when you stumble, remember the voice of the Lord speaking over your life, for when you do you remember that sin has no victory and death no sting! Rejoice today that Christ called you to come forth.

~ *Jared*

October 30

WHAT DO YOU LOVE MORE THAN JESUS?

Chronological Bible Reading Plan: (Day 303: Luke 18)

"When Jesus heard this, he said to him, 'One thing you still lack. Sell all that you have and distribute to the poor, and you will have treasure in heaven; and come, follow me.' But when he heard these things, he became very sad, for he was extremely rich." Luke 18:22-23 (ESV)

We do not teach a "poverty gospel" in Christianity, meaning that we do not affirm that only in poverty can you truly live a life pleasing to the Lord, free from material distractions. While it is true that materialism is a dangerous foe to a Christian's proper devotion to the Lord, material things are not in and of themselves evil. So, what is Jesus teaching this "ruler" in Luke's gospel? If we are not affirming a poverty gospel, then why would Jesus command this drastic act of worship? Jesus asks this of the man because He knows where his true devotion lies. The rich ruler has been extraordinarily obedient to the requirements of the law, yet his heart still longs for the things of this world. He has yet to discover the central message of Christianity: true satisfaction is only found in God and God is only found in Christ.

This story is always a challenging one for the follower of Jesus, because it forces us to assess ourselves and see what things we are unwilling to sacrifice for Him. Are there things in your life that you would be unwilling to give up if Jesus asked you? If so, you have found a god greater than Him in your own mind. We all have idols that intermittently rise up in our lives; the trick for us, though, who desire to grow in Christ-likeness is to identify those things and put them to death so that they do not steal our affection for the Lord.

Dear friend, do not go away from the Lord sad as this rich ruler did. Remember that whatever it is that you must sacrifice in order to be obedient is far less satisfying in comparison to the greatness of our Lord.

~ *Jared*

October 31

Revenge or Restoration

Chronological Bible Reading Plan: (Day 304: Matthew 19; Mark 10)

"And Jesus called them to him and said to them, 'You know that those who are considered rulers of the Gentiles lord it over them, and their great ones exercise authority over them. But it shall not be so among you. But whoever would be great among you must be your servant, and whoever would be first among you must be slave of all. For even the Son of Man came not to be served but to serve, and to give his life as a ransom for many.'" Mark 10:42-45 (ESV)

James and John approach Jesus with an interesting request. They ask Him to grant them to sit at His right hand, presumably as a sign of special honor for them once Jesus has been raised and established as a political ruler (revealing a still false understanding of future events). Jesus challenges these two disciples, whom He loved, by rooting out the motivation for their request. Why did they want this honor? Why did they want this power? Was it to be in a position of influence to rule over people? Or was it to be in a position of power to help people?

You could understand, I think, why James and John would want earthly power, having been persecuted for following Jesus and likely economically or socially oppressed their whole lives as Jews under Roman rule. Yet, Jesus did not come in power to exact revenge; He came to serve and restore.

The tendency of mankind is to find new and ingenious ways to rule over one another, seeing subjection of people as affirmation of one's superiority to another. The more people we have looking to us, the more unique and special we feel. Truly, we seek to be like God. The message of Jesus, though, is not a means to get the same old thing, i.e. leverage over others. Rather, the message of Jesus suggests our chief goal is not ruling over one another but serving, knowing that ultimately God is the only one worthy of worship and devotion. Who will you serve today?

~ Jared

November 1

MORE THAN LIP-SERVICE

Chronological Bible Reading Plan: (Day 305: Matthew 20-21)

"'Which of the two did the will of his father?' They said, 'The first.' Jesus said to them, 'Truly, I say to you, the tax collectors and the prostitutes go into the kingdom of God before you.'" Matthew 21:31 (ESV)

What kind of faith do you truly have? Is your faith transformative? Does it cause you to live differently in light of the knowledge of Christ and His atoning sacrifice? Or is your faith empty? How do you know? James, the brother of Jesus, gives us some insight into the answer to this question in his New Testament work writing, "What good is it, my brothers, if someone says he has faith but does not have works? Can that faith save him?" (Jas. 2:14 ESV). Is James saying that works are a necessary part to a truly saving faith? No. He is saying, however, that true faith leads to obedience, working for the Kingdom of God.

In the "Parable of the Two Sons" in Matthew's gospel, Jesus essentially says the same thing to the chief priests and elders who are questioning His authority. These religious men may have the appearance of true faith, but their lack of obedience in spite of their language proves their heart is not fully devoted to the Lord. They say they love the Lord and will obey Him, yet they never truly act in alignment with their "faith," meaning that it is dead. True faith transforms us and leads us to action.

Christianity in America is in a dangerous place, composed of millions who claim a saving faith but relatively few who live out the gospel. Are you truly obedient? Are you truly driven to serve your Heavenly Father? Or is your Christianity more "lip-service" than substance? Commit today to serve the Lord, affirming your faith by your actions for the good of those around you and the glory of God.

~ Jared

November 2

Salvation Has Come To This House

Chronological Bible Reading Plan: (Day 306: Luke 19)

"And Zacchaeus stood and said to the Lord, 'Behold, Lord, the half of my goods I give to the poor. And if I have defrauded anyone of anything, I restore it fourfold.' And Jesus said to him, 'Today salvation has come to this house, since he also is a son of Abraham. For the Son of Man came to seek and to save the lost.'" Luke 19:8-10 (ESV)

The essence of salvation is restoration. Jesus came to restore that which had been broken or lost as a result of sin by taking upon Himself the penalty of that sin and overcoming its effect, which is ultimate death or separation from God. We are able to be restored as God's image bearers within His creation because of the sacrificial work of Jesus.

Once we have been restored, our desire, having experienced the glorious work of His salvation, should be to extend the same grace we have been shown to others. As Jesus made a way for our relationship to be restored, we should make every effort to restore broken, earthly relationships. How can we hold on to grievances or guilt in light of Christ's restorative work? Zaccheus provides us with a prime example of this. Having been forgiven so much and restored to right relationship with Christ, he declares his intention to restore that which he had broken. He says he will give the money he has earned illegitimately to the poor and restore money to those whom he defrauded fourfold. You see, it wasn't enough for Zaccheus to simply be forgiven; he wanted to bring about restoration as Jesus did.

What about you? Having been restored by the work of Jesus, do you seek to bring about restoration in the lives of those in your realm of influence? Do you seek out those whom you have offended and ask for forgiveness? Do you try to right wrongs from your past to show forth the transforming work of the gospel in your life? Remember, we are continuing fully the ministry of Jesus, so we must be about restoration as He was.

~ Jared

November 3

WE MUST LIFT JESUS HIGH

Chronological Bible Reading Plan: (Day 307: Mark 11; John 12)

"And I, when I am lifted up from the earth, will draw all people to myself." John 12:32 (ESV)

The way to draw people into the Kingdom of God is simple: we lift Jesus high and He will draw all people to Himself. How simple the plan of God truly is! Our responsibility as disciples is not to force people into a relationship with Jesus nor to convince them of gospel truth. We simply proclaim. We proclaim His unmerited death and our unmerited favor as a result of this work of grace. We proclaim His victory over sin in the resurrection and our impending victory as a result. We proclaim the abundant life He lived and has given us as a people transformed by His Spirit. We tell the gospel, the good news of Jesus, and as we proclaim Christ crucified and resurrected, people will come to Him.

Are you proclaiming the gospel of Jesus, the full good news? Or are you proclaiming only part? For many of us, we offer good biblical advice based on principles from the Bible, but we never get to the point of challenging people in their sin and depravity and revealing their need for repentance. Christianity is more than good advice. In fact, the advice we give is inherently tied to the gospel. Marriages and relationships only work when we recognize the sacrifice of Jesus and how He has loved and forgiven us. Only then will we work to show that kind of love and forgiveness to others. Advice, then, that is not rooted in the gospel is man-centered and lacks transformative power.

Dear friend, do not lose the message of Christ. Do not forfeit the gospel for an easier, man-centered philosophy. Proclaim this good news and watch as Jesus draws all people unto Himself and brings about restoration as a result.

~ *Jared*

November 4

The Greatest Commandment

Chronological Bible Reading Plan: (Day 308: Matthew 22, Mark 12)

"And he said to him, 'You shall love the Lord your God with all your heart and with all your soul and with all your mind. This is the great and first commandment. And a second is like it: You shall love your neighbor as yourself. On these two commandments depend all the Law and the Prophets.'"
Matthew 22:37-40 (ESV)

Our complete affection for the Lord and devotion to Him should be our primary concern as disciples, knowing that only as we love Him completely can we truly walk as we were created to walk. We must seek to love the Lord fully with every part of our being; it is not enough to only give Him part for He is worthy of the whole. Once we have learned to love Him completely, allowing Him to satisfy our every need, then, according to Jesus, every other commandment will make sense. Our ability, then, to walk in obedience cannot be motivated by simple obligation; rather, our ability to walk in faithfulness is directly proportional to the type of affection we carry for the Lord. Further, our ability to love others as Christ loved them and commanded us to is only possible once we have learned to love the Lord fully. We can love others because of how He has loved us.

Do you love the Lord fully? Have you completely surrendered the entirety of your self to Him, forsaking other temporary pleasures for the great reward found in Him? If you have not learned to love the Lord with all your heart, soul, mind, and strength, then the rest of discipleship is meaningless. Only when you have obeyed this greatest command can you truly walk forward as a sincere disciple and follower of Christ.

~ Jared

November 5

ARE YOU SOMEONE TO BEWARE OR BEHOILD?

Chronological Bible Reading Plan: (Day 309: Matthew 23; Luke 20-21)

"Beware of the scribes, who like to walk around in long robes, and love greetings in the marketplaces and the best seats in the synagogues and the places of honor at feasts, who devour widows' houses and for a pretense make long prayers. They will receive the greater condemnation." Luke 20:46-47 (ESV)

As the people of God, we are to put on display the character and nature of God, reflecting His goodness to a world in need. We are to love as Christ has loved us. We are to be peaceful, patient, and kind, following the example of our great Savior. We are to be good, faithful, and gentle to those around us, seeking the good of others above self, and we are to be self-controlled, testifying to the incredible satisfying power of Christ. When we live in this way, we are accomplishing our purpose of bringing glory to God as all creation was intended to do.

A danger, however, exists for those who have learned the actions but failed to experience transformation. As religious people, we can come to appreciate action or service over discipleship and true restoration. Such is the case with the scribes mentioned in Jesus' warning. They had the appearance of devotion, but were simply white-washed tombs (nice to look at on the outside but dead on the inside). They loved the honor of religion but lacked the heart of devotion reflective of the true, life-transforming love seen in Christ.

Where are you on this transformation spectrum? Have you truly been transformed by the gospel or is your relationship with the Lord more cultural or learned behavior? We are called to display the character and nature of God, and if we cannot do that in response to the gospel, then we are living lives Jesus says to beware of rather than behold. Seek to live faithfully in light of your calling today.

~ *Jared*

November 6

Stay Awake

Chronological Bible Reading Plan: (Day 310: Mark 13)

"Therefore stay awake--for you do not know when the master of the house will come, in the evening, or at midnight, or when the rooster crows, or in the morning--lest he come suddenly and find you asleep. And what I say to you I say to all: Stay awake." Mark 13:35-37 (ESV)

Jesus is coming again! What an incredible message of hope for us as believers. He has not forgotten us, nor abandoned us. He will come again to finish what He started, and He won't be coming on a donkey this time! This message of hope for believers is also a challenge to prepare the way of the Lord, continuing the proclamation of the gospel and the building of His kingdom in His temporary absence, for while this truth is a message of joy for us, for those who do not believe, the reality is far more sobering. The coming of Christ will secure a future of wrath for those outside of His grace, meaning that because we are uncertain of when He will come, we should do everything we can to prepare everybody we can until we hear that trumpet sound.

Dear Christian, are you awake to this reality? Or has the urgency of the second coming of Christ disappeared having been distracted by the business of your day to day schedule. Do not be found sleeping on the job. God has given you a purpose in your time here to proclaim His goodness, calling those around you to join in worship. Don't forsake this glorious purpose and eternal glory for temporary pleasures and vain rewards. Be on guard and stay awake, knowing that at any moment the Lord could return to reclaim His creation fully.

~ Jared

November 7
Will You Endure?

Chronological Bible Reading Plan: (Day 311: Matthew 24)

"But the one who endures to the end will be saved." Matthew 24:13 (ESV)

The world, indeed all of creation, is moving toward an end. There is a goal to creation and the Lord is working all things to bring about that desired end. That goal, of course, is His glory and every created thing is meant to reflect some divine attribute that displays more fully the glorious reality of our Lord. As the end draws near in which all things will once again glorify the Lord fully, there will be countless obstacles to the Christian's participation in building God's Kingdom, causing some to abandon ship as they decide the cost is not ultimately worth the reward. This abdication of Christian conviction and belief based on the circumstance of their time is a clear indication that these who have rejected the faith never truly had it at all.

The true believer, having been called from death to life, will cling to that life ultimately knowing that truly nothing else can satisfy them and that nothing this world offers has any meaning apart from its Creator. How could someone who truly met the Master reject Him? There are those, however, who have been converted in name only, never fully repenting of their sin and therefore never recognizing their great need for and provision from the work of Christ. These people should not make us fear that such apostasy is possible for the true convert but rather remind us of the difficulty of our task and the complete sufficiency of Christ in the midst of that difficulty.

Seek this morning to remember the gospel and your time of true repentance. Remember what Jesus has saved you from and how ultimately He will judge all of creation. Rest in that hope, enduring whatever comes your way, and be mindful of the future, remembering the need of those around you who will neither endure the tribulation to come nor the judgment thereafter.

~ *Jared*

November 8

To the Least of These

Chronological Bible Reading Plan: (Day 312: Matthew 25)

"And the King will answer them, 'Truly, I say to you, as you did it to one of the least of these my brothers, you did it to me.'" Matthew 25:40 (ESV)

The Kingdom of God is about overcoming every effect of sinfulness in the world. The work of Christ overcomes spiritual death, of course, but in so doing it also brings about the restoration of all things physical, repairing relationships, poverty, sickness, among other various effects of depravity. This restorative work is the responsibility of the Church, as we continue the ministry of Jesus. We are to be concerned with the least of these, caring for the oppressed, imprisoned, poor, and sick. We do this not as a means to gain God's favor or earn His grace but rather because we already have these things. This kind of heart for the less fortunate is characteristic of those who have been overcome by the gospel because of how Jesus cared for us. We were spiritually sick and poor; we were oppressed and imprisoned. Jesus, seeing us in this state, did not abandon us but rather in His mercy came to help us. His sheep will do the same.

Are you burdened by the less fortunate? Are you striving to overcome the effects of sin by building the Kingdom of God? Are you warring against poverty and oppression? Are you championing the less fortunate? These are not just things we do as humans who have empathy for other humans. No, we fight these battles because they are the battles Jesus fought. He healed the sick and helped the oppressed, and we must as well. The gospel is about the work of Christ, yes, but it is also about the restorative effects of that work. Today, rejoice in how you have been restored and work to bring about that restoration around you.

~ *Jared*

November 9

The Familiar Kiss of Betrayal

Chronological Bible Reading Plan: (Day 313: Matthew 26; Mark 14)

"Now the betrayer had given them a sign, saying, 'The one I will kiss is the man; seize him.' And he came up to Jesus at once and said, 'Greetings, Rabbi!' And he kissed him. Jesus said to him, 'Friend, do what you came to do.' Then they came up and laid hands on Jesus and seized him." Matthew 26:48-50 (ESV)

The picture painted by Matthew of Judas' betrayal of Jesus is especially tragic, given the intimacy of the scene. You don't just kiss anyone on the cheek. While certainly kissing on the cheek was a customary greeting in the old world, it was usually reserved for friends. Further, this wasn't just any random acquaintance of Jesus; rather, he was one of the twelve, specifically chosen by Jesus and given unique access to continue forth His ministry once He had ascended back into heaven. Judas was a friend; Judas was a confidant. He walked and talked with Jesus, witnessing countless miracles and displays of supernatural power, and yet in spite of all of that he chooses to betray Him.

Have you ever been there? Have you ever had someone near and dear to your heart abandon you in this way? I have and it is devastating. You move through a variety of emotions from despair to anger, all the while not knowing how they could have come to double-cross you in this way. If you're not careful, this despair can turn into bitterness, resulting in a robbing of joy and contentment in the midst of this circumstance.

Take comfort today, dear child of God, that you have an advocate in heaven with whom you can identify! Jesus was betrayed and felt, undoubtedly, everything you have felt, and yet He allowed His betrayal to be used for the glory of God. Do not remain embittered toward your betrayer; rather release the feelings of bitterness and allow the situation to be used for the glory of God. The Lord always redeems hurt, if you let Him.

~ Jared

November 10

A New Commandment

Chronological Bible Reading Plan: (Day 314: Luke 22; John 13)

"A new commandment I give to you, that you love one another: just as I have loved you, you also are to love one another. By this all people will know that you are my disciples, if you have love for one another." John 13:34-35 (ESV)

The distinguishing mark of a true disciple of Christ is not the ability to raise people from the dead nor heal the blind. Rather, Christ proclaims that our identity as Christians is inherently tied to our ability to love one another as Christ Himself loved us. How did Christ love us? He loved us sacrificially and humbly. Think about the act of service Jesus performs for His disciples earlier in this passage. He washes their feet, and He does this having full knowledge that the Father had "given all things into his hands" (John 13:3 ESV). These hands that hold divine power in their grasp are the very same hands removing the dust and dirt from the feet of those He loves.

Jesus did not allow power to cloud His affection for His people, and we must guard against the spirits of this world doing the same. We cannot fake the kind of love that Jesus is calling us to. This kind of love is more than tolerance or acceptance. This kind of love is transformative and self-sacrificing. This kind of love is only possible in light of the gospel. We must love one another in a supernatural way, and when those around us see people from such different backgrounds and ethnicities loving each other so completely, they will be astonished. They will wonder why these people are acting so differently toward one another, meeting each other's needs and bearing one another's burdens, and we will be able to tell them we are able to because of how Christ first loved us!

Dear family of God, we must love one another. The growth of God's Kingdom depends on it. Will you commit to love sacrificially today?

~ Jared

November 11

Jesus is the Way

Chronological Bible Reading Plan: (Day 315: John 14-17)

"Jesus said to him, 'I am the way, and the truth, and the life. No one comes to the Father except through me. If you had known me, you would have known my Father also. From now on you do know him and have seen him.'"
John 14:6-7 (ESV)

Jesus, proclaimed in John as the "Word of God in the flesh," is divine communication. He represents fully to us the character and nature of God, allowing us to behold our Creator and witness what it looks like to walk in complete intimacy with Him. Jesus, then, communicates our goal. We are to walk in fellowship with God as Jesus walked in fellowship with Him. We are to be one as the Father and the Son are one. The dilemma for us, unlike Jesus, is that we are sinful and, therefore, cannot be one with Him unless our nature is changed. We, who are dead, cannot have fellowship with the life that Christ embodies unless that sin is eradicated.

Jesus allows for this provision. He came to communicate to us, yes, but He also came to make a way for us to have fellowship with God, as we were created to do. Further, He was the only one who could have made this way. His unique incarnation and perfect fulfillment of the law makes Him the only way to the Father. We cannot earn this nor choose a different path, for only in Christ do we see the fullness of God displayed both in His life and in His resurrection.

Rejoice today, dear child of God, that the Lord did not abandon you. Rather, He loved you enough to send His only begotten Son, and in this sacrifice we find the ability to be fully satisfied and have our joy be made complete.

~ *Jared*

November 12

Give Us Barrabbas

Chronological Bible Reading Plan: (Day 316: Matthew 27; Mark 15)

"The governor again said to them, 'Which of the two do you want me to release for you?' And they said, 'Barabbas.' Pilate said to them, 'Then what shall I do with Jesus who is called Christ?' They all said, 'Let him be crucified!' And he said, 'Why, what evil has he done?' But they shouted all the more, 'Let him be crucified!'" Matthew 27:21-23 (ESV)

Oh, the depravity of man! As we read this passage, it would be very easy for us to look upon the chief priests, elders, and crowd with disgust at their choice. How could they choose a clearly innocent man over the "notorious prisoner," Barabbas (Matt. 27:16 ESV)? Barabbas, seen from the other gospel accounts, was notorious because he had committed robbery, insurrection, and murder! Truly, he was the danger to society, and, yet, with a unified voice the crowd demands for the crucifixion of Jesus.

"How could any sane man make this decision?," one may ask. Isn't it true, though, that we choose as ridiculously every day? Don't we compare seemingly terrible things to the glory and innocence of Christ on a daily basis and choose to indulge in them rather than in the complete sufficiency of Jesus? We choose to indulge our pride in the face of Christ's humility. We choose to value material things over those spiritual. We choose to lust after temporary pleasures rather than embracing the sacrificial love of Christ, and in so doing we legitimize the need for Jesus to be crucified. We are as guilty as they.

The beautiful news of the gospel, though, is that precisely because of His innocence and willing death upon the cross, now you and I have the ability to be forgiven of our guilt and restored in right relationship to the Lord. Today, commit to choose Jesus; don't get overwhelmed with sin and choose poorly, chanting as the crowd did so many years ago, "Give us Barabbas!"

~ *Jared*

November 13
What is Truth?

Chronological Bible Reading Plan: (Day 317: Luke 23; John 18-19)

"Pilate said to him, 'What is truth?'" John 18:38a (ESV)

At some level, every single person that has ever lived on this earth has asked the question we read Pilate asking today. "What is truth?" The importance of the answer to this question cannot be overstated, both in the narrative of the passion of the Christ in John and in the narrative of our own lives. In the case of the biblical account, Pilate finds (at least initially) no fault in Jesus, as He apparently is a teacher of abstract, philosophical ideas of which no person can truly know the merit. The one deciding truth, then, tries to release Jesus on the basis of the idea that abstract truth is unknowable. Does this rationalization sound familiar?

Jesus declares that He came to "bear witness to the truth" (Jn 18:37 ESV, emphasis mine). Jesus' own words, then, declare that there is an ultimate truth to which all of creation will be held accountable. This truth is accessible and knowable, although admittedly also convicting. The truth of the gospel is not an option in the pursuit of truth; it is THE truth.

We live in a culture of warring ideologies, reflective of the tension exposed in John's gospel. Many around us today will ask how we can know that the truth of Jesus is the truth, suggesting that any religious conviction is at best probable rather than certain. The challenge for us is to remember that there are truths that are absolute. There are plenty of things about which we can be certain, and the gospel of Jesus revealed to us by the work of the Holy Spirit is such a thing. Rest in the certainty of the work of Christ and give thanks, knowing (as is of course the purpose of John's gospel) that He is the way, the truth, and the life and that no man comes to the Father except through Him.

~ *Jared*

November 14

Go, Therefore

Chronological Bible Reading Plan: (Day 318: Matthew 28; Mark 16)

"And Jesus came and said to them, 'All authority in heaven and on earth has been given to me. Go therefore and make disciples of all nations, baptizing them in the name of the Father and of the Son and of the Holy Spirit, teaching them to observe all that I have commanded you. And behold, I am with you always, to the end of the age.'" Matthew 28:18-20 (ESV)

As Evangelical Christians, we often emphasize the need to proclaim the gospel of Jesus Christ to the ends of the earth. We must do this because the resurrection of Christ and the ensuing consequences of His resurrection (i.e. victory over sin and death) are the centerpiece to the beautiful, eternal plan of God to unite all things to Him in Christ Jesus. God is working all things for His glory and He has called us to be a part of this process, making disciples of all nations, baptizing them, and teaching them the overarching truths of scripture.

In order to do this effectively, however, we must remember the power that drives us. We are not proclaiming empty words; rather, we are going forth in the authority of Christ to speak Spirit-covered words that He uses to draw men unto Himself. Our task, then, should not be a source of fear nor an object of neglect, for Christ has empowered us to accomplish this great commission.

Are you proclaiming the truth of the gospel? Are you making disciples? Remember, disciple-making is a long process that continues long after conversion, and both are a part of the ministry Christ has given to us. Commit today to share the good news of Jesus with someone who needs it and help them walk worthy of the calling Christ has placed on their life.

~Jared

November 15

The Purpose of Scripture

Chronological Bible Reading Plan: (Day 319: Luke 24; John 20-21)

"Now Jesus did many other signs in the presence of the disciples, which are not written in this book; but these are written so that you may believe that Jesus is the Christ, the Son of God, and that by believing you may have life in his name." John 20:30-31 (ESV)

John reveals his purpose in recounting the works of Jesus in this gospel: that upon reading this account of Jesus the one who reads will be overwhelmed by its testimony and find abundant life. Incidentally, John also provides us with a larger purpose for Scripture generally. All Scripture functions in this way. The Word of God is meant to testify to the redemptive work of the Lord amongst first a particular people and now among all people. The Bible anticipates the need for a savior, reveals Jesus as that savior, and lays the groundwork for His ultimate victory over all things in His second coming. He is the promised hope for all of creation and John's gospel exemplifies in a microcosmic way that truth, showing Christ's authority over things both physical and spiritual.

Be thankful for the revealed truth of God's Word today. Treasure it, for it is meant to be used by the Spirit of God to seal up belief in your heart. As you read the accounts of God's redemptive activity, the Holy Spirit will open your eyes to how He has worked redemptively in your life in similar ways. Allow the Word of God to do what John desires to do in His gospel: affirm in you correct and saving belief in Jesus Christ. Read the Bible and be amazed at God's provision and miraculous work for His people.

~ Jared

November 16

We Have Work To Do

Chronological Bible Reading Plan: (Day 320: Acts 1-3)

"And while they were gazing into heaven as he went, behold, two men stood by them in white robes, and said, "Men of Galilee, why do you stand looking into heaven? This Jesus, who was taken up from you into heaven, will come in the same way as you saw him go into heaven." Acts 1:10-11 (ESV)

What a spectacle these disciples must have beheld as Jesus ascended into heaven! Can you imagine the thoughts running through their minds? Not forty days earlier their Savior, once thought dead, suddenly reappeared, displaying His victory over the power of sin and death. Now, this same Jesus, having equipped them to continue His ministry in His absence, suddenly ascends into the sky! No wonder they were amazed. Who wouldn't be amazed at such a display of the glory of God? If His first coming ended like this, what would His second coming look like?

While certainly the anticipation of Christ's return should be of significance for us, we must heed the warning of the messengers in today's passage and not become so focused on it that we miss the present. The Lord left us here with a purpose, and that purpose is comprised of so much more than simply trying to figure out when He will return. We are to "proclaim good news to the poor . . . to proclaim liberty to the captives and recovering of sight to the blind, to set at liberty those who are oppressed, to proclaim the year of the Lord's favor" (Luke 4:18-19 ESV). All of this continued ministry is of course predicated on Christ returning to finish what He started, but our focus must be on building the Kingdom until our King comes to ascend His throne. Dear child of God, be thankful for Christ's return, but don't stare in the sky waiting for it to happen. Rather, act and serve as Christ Himself did while He was here.

~ Jared

November 17

From Selflessness to Selfishness

Chronological Bible Reading Plan: (Day 321: Acts 4-6)

"But a man named Ananias, with his wife Sapphira, sold a piece of property, and with his wife's knowledge he kept back for himself some of the proceeds and brought only a part of it and laid it at the apostles' feet." Acts 5:1-2 (ESV)

Selfishness can have no place in the Church, for the calling of Christ upon it demands the sacrifice of the individual for the good of the whole. How could it not? Its founder and example personified this truth. Jesus sacrificed all for the good of God the Father's eternal plan to unite all things to Him through the sacrifice of Christ.

The early church understood this. In fact, in the book of Acts, the early church was holding all of their possessions in common, making sure none among them had need. They were sacrificing their material goods for the sake of the whole. One man in particular, Joseph, sold a field and brought all the money he had earned to the apostles to use for ministry. His sacrifice was immense and it was noticed.

This notoriety interested a couple named Ananias and Sapphira. They saw the recognition that accompanied Joseph's selfless act and desired such attention for themselves. So, they sold, like Joseph, a piece of property, but unlike Joseph they kept back part of the proceeds for themselves while claiming to have given them all. You see, their motivation was their exaltation, while Joseph's was the exaltation of Christ. Selfishness has no place in the body of Christ and Ananias and Sapphira were dramatically removed from the fellowship.

Why do you serve the Lord? If you were never recognized for the work you do for Him, would you be ok with that? Do you need the recognition as justification for your service or is the advancement of the Kingdom enough? To be a true imitator of Christ we must commit ourselves to selflessness, for only in that can we aid the mission of the Church.

~ *Jared*

November 18

The Proper Response to Rebuke

Chronological Bible Reading Plan: (Day 322: Acts 7-8)

"'Repent, therefore, of this wickedness of yours, and pray to the Lord that, if possible, the intent of your heart may be forgiven you. For I see that you are in the gall of bitterness and in the bond of iniquity.' And Simon answered, 'Pray for me to the Lord, that nothing of what you have said may come upon me.'"
Acts 8:22-24 (ESV)

Simon was a new believer. To this point in his life, he had been the envy of many men, drawing crowds to marvel at his magic. Yet, when he heard the message of Phillip, he was compelled by the gospel of Jesus Christ and repented. His repentance, though, did not make him perfect, for when he saw the power of Peter and John as they laid hands upon those who desired to receive the Holy Spirit, he desired the same type of power for himself. He wanted the same ability to impress a crowd as before, just with a different source of wonder. Peter immediately rebukes Simon's attempt to buy their power and favor, suggesting that such a gift was only for the pure in heart. His words were true and direct, and Simon heard them and repented yet again.

Just because we have given our lives to Christ does not mean that we have already attained perfection. In fact, we must guard against the comforts of the flesh taking up root once again in our hearts. As believers, may we not look at Christianity as a new way to get the same things we have always wanted. Rather, let us see it for the gift it is and passionately pursue it for the sake of God's glory rather than our own. Further, may we seek to have people in our lives to speak hard truth over us when we do begin to forsake the name of the Lord for our own.

Do you have someone in your life that can speak tough truth to you? Do you respond as Simon did here? Remember, the goal for us until Christ returns is progress; we seek perfection but only in as much as it is rooted in that of Jesus.

~ Jared

November 19

What God Has Made Clean

Chronological Bible Reading Plan: (Day 323: Acts 9-10)

"And there came a voice to him: 'Rise, Peter; kill and eat.' But Peter said, 'By no means, Lord; for I have never eaten anything that is common or unclean.' And the voice came to him again a second time, 'What God has made clean, do not call common.'" Acts 10:13-15 (ESV)

Is there a more glorious statement in all the New Testament than that spoken by the Lord to Peter in Acts 10? As Peter responds out of a sincere religious devotion regarding that which is regarded as ritually unclean, the Lord responds with a new vision of ritual purity. No longer is our cleanliness concerned with exterior things polluting us in the interior; rather, now our purity is seen from the inside out. The Lord through the sacrifice of Christ now can proclaim us clean, not from any ritual effort of our own but precisely because of the sufficient work of Jesus!

This is good news. We don't have to pick and choose what we eat nor which livestock to sacrifice, for the completed ministry of Christ has given us the opportunity, once seen as unclean, to now be proclaimed clean! We can have fellowship with the Lord. We can be free from a future of wrath and judgment. We can have abundant life both here and for all of eternity all because God has proclaimed us clean.

Now there are some, perhaps, that still want to proclaim you as unclean, whether because of some Pharisaical pride or the inability to see past your past. Remember, though, that they do not have the final say. If you have repented of your sin and submitted your life to the Lordship of Christ, your past no longer defines you nor does your lineage, for the gospel is sufficient for all! Give thanks today, dear friend, that you have been made clean!

~ Jared

November 20

The Gospel is for All People

Chronological Bible Reading Plan: (Day 324: Acts 11-12)

"'If then God gave the same gift to them as he gave to us when we believed in the Lord Jesus Christ, who was I that I could stand in God's way?' When they heard these things they fell silent. And they glorified God, saying, 'Then to the Gentiles also God has granted repentance that leads to life.'" Acts 11:18-19 (ESV)

We can easily be entrapped by our context. We assume, at least in the way that we act, that the world is everywhere as it is where we are and that people, generally, are the same as well. Within this assumption lies an ember of pride, suggesting that we are the center of the universe and everything that occurs is for our benefit. This is the nature of the self, to think the world is concerned with me above all else. The gospel must challenge that assumption within us, however. We are not more special than any other person God created, for He created us equal. We all have the same need of Him, both for satisfaction and salvation. We must not assume, as the early Jewish leaders of the Church, that the gospel is reserved for us alone; rather, we must give our lives to the realization that the gospel is for all people and all people need to hear it.

Are you engaging this tendency to consider yourself greater than the rest of humanity? How so? Are you actively seeking out friendships with people that are different than you? Are you descending or ascending the socioeconomic status ladder to show the equality of the gospel? Are you building relationships with nationals in other countries who are sacrificing to build the Kingdom of God in their context? Otherwise, you may say you believe that the gospel is for all people, but are you truly evidencing your belief in action?

~ *Jared*

November 21

Would You Send Your Best?

Chronological Bible Reading Plan: (Day 325: Acts 13-14)

"While they were worshiping the Lord and fasting, the Holy Spirit said, 'Set apart for me Barnabas and Saul for the work to which I have called them.' Then after fasting and praying they laid their hands on them and sent them off."
Acts 13:2-3 (ESV)

The church at Antioch was blessed, wouldn't you say? They had some incredible leaders, serving as prophets and teachers, not the least of which were Barnabas and Saul, also called "Paul." The church was growing and preaching the gospel to the Gentiles; they were actively building the Kingdom of God! In the midst of their growth, though, an interesting declaration comes from the Lord, in which He tells Antioch to set apart Barnabas and Saul for a new work, one that will take them away from their church.

Why was the church in Antioch so willing to do this? They sent out their best leaders because they had a larger view of the Kingdom of God. They knew that their growth wasn't dependent on any one man but rather on the favor and power of the Spirit at work within them. Further, if the Lord explicitly called these men out and they didn't send them, surely the favor of God would leave them in their disobedience.

May we be like the church in Antioch! May we recognize that our devotion is not to a man but rather to the Lord, and may we be willing to commission our best men to be sent out for the good of the gospel, if the Lord so commands. We must be willing to sacrifice our best and trust in the Lord's greater provision, as that is truly the heart of the message of Jesus displayed beautifully by the church at Antioch.

~ Jared

November 22

What Causes Fights Among You?

Chronological Bible Reading Plan: (Day 326: James)

"What causes quarrels and what causes fights among you? Is it not this, that your passions are at war within you?" James 4:1 (ESV)

In the midst of a disagreement or conflict, we very easily can point out the flaws in the individual or individuals with whom we are at odds. We can outline for anyone who will lend their ear to us their guilt and our innocence in the matter at hand. James challenges us, however, to consider another source for the tension: ourselves. James suggests that quarrels and fights within the church are motivated by selfish desires within the individuals themselves. The source of the battle is not the failure of the other, but rather the failure of me.

Think about his concept for a moment. When you "war" with someone in your life, what is the motivation for such hostile behavior? (As a side note, I use the words "war" and "hostile" intentionally here, as that is the image James is trying to create in the language of the New Testament.) Isn't your anger typically rooted in the loss of some fix to a self-centered desire? "He stole my position at the church." "He won't let me teach." "She always gets the solos and I never do." Have you heard any talk like this at your church? Inherent to each of these phrases is a perceived loss, a loss rooted in selfish desires, and if we allow that loss to linger it can transform into bitterness and appear in anger.

Is there conflict in your life? Are you causing conflict in your home or church? Take a moment this morning and do some reflection. Why are you so invested in this disagreement? What "passion" is motivating your participation? Once you recognize your motivation, submit that to the Lord and see how peace may appear at the most opportune time for you and your family, both at home and at church.

~ *Jared*

November 23

Joy is Bigger Than Circumstance

Chronological Bible Reading Plan: (Day 327: Acts 15-16)

"And when they had inflicted many blows upon them, they threw them into prison, ordering the jailer to keep them safely. Having received this order, he put them into the inner prison and fastened their feet in the stocks. About midnight Paul and Silas were praying and singing hymns to God, and the prisoners were listening to them..." Acts 16:23-25 (ESV)

How you respond to adversity matters. It matters because it communicates strongly about the source of your joy and contentment. Paul and Silas had been stripped, beaten, and thrown into prison. Then, they had been placed into stocks, likely stretching their legs out to the point where it popped their hips out of joint. They were undoubtedly in a tremendous amount of pain, not to mention the smells of a prison with no indoor plumbing.

While many of us would have responded to this with complaining, Paul and Silas responded with worship. Why would they do this? How could they respond in this way? They were able to worship in the midst of the worst circumstances because they had a holy perspective. They had already set their minds on heavenly things and knew that the Lord could use even this circumstance for His glory, which of course He did by allowing Paul and Silas to lead their jailer to the Lord. Imagine if they had complained or if they had run when they had the chance. This jailer likely would have committed suicide and the rest of the prison would have been no different. Yet, because of their joy being bigger than their circumstance, lives were genuinely changed.

Is your joy rooted in such a heavenly perspective? Are you fully satisfied by Christ, so that no circumstance can rob you of your need to worship? If not, spend some time this morning reflecting on what things you are more afraid of losing than your ability to praise. Chances are those things have an improper place in your life and need to be lost anyway.

~ *Jared*

November 24

A DIFFERENT GOSPEL

Chronological Bible Reading Plan: (Day 328: Galatians 1-3)

"I am astonished that you are so quickly deserting him who called you in the grace of Christ and are turning to a different gospel--" Galatians 1:6 (ESV)

Paul's epistle to the people of Galatia has a very different beginning than his other epistles. Paul typically encourages the church in its faithfulness to the gospel of Jesus Christ. Here, however, Paul includes no section of thanksgiving, preferring instead to immediately address a dangerous issue both to the church in Galatia and the advance of the gospel as a whole.

The Galatians found themselves in the midst of a familiar struggle in the early formation of the New Testament people, disagreeing about the place of traditional Judaism in the face of this new theology rooted in the grace of Christ. This disagreement was so profound that it was causing division and motivating some, so-called "Judaizers," to demand gentile converts to be circumcised in order to be considered a Christian. This act of man to secure salvation, however, is inherently opposed to the message of the gospel that Paul proclaimed. Salvation is entirely an act of God; man has no part in the securing of salvation, as he would then be able to share in the glory that is both God's alone and the primary motivation for the act of the gospel in the first place. To say, then, that someone must perform a ritual in order to add to Christ's salvation makes the gospel indifferent news rather than good news, for truly nothing has changed.

We must guard against adding to the message of grace inherent to the gospel of Jesus Christ. Either it is entirely a work of the Lord or it is not. Paul's concern is legitimate, for when we add to the simplicity of salvation by grace through faith, we truly change the central message of the New Testament, for earned salvation is inherently impossible, as we could never earn enough to satisfy the wrath of God. Rejoice in the grace given by the Lord through Jesus and seek to work in response to that grace rather than participate in securing it.

~ Jared

November 25

The Gift of Gentle Restoration

Chronological Bible Reading Plan: (Day 329: Galatians 4-6)

"Brothers, if anyone is caught in any transgression, you who are spiritual should restore him in a spirit of gentleness. Keep watch on yourself, lest you too be tempted. Bear one another's burdens, and so fulfill the law of Christ."
Galatians 6:1-2 (ESV)

As brothers and sisters in Christ, we have a responsibility to hold each other accountable, encouraging one another to greater Christ-likeness. We are to speak life into the areas of our fellow heirs to the Kingdom of God that are commendable, exhorting them to greater devotion, but we are also commanded to truthfully and graciously speak rebuke over those areas that are of the flesh and preventing growth in their walk with the Lord.

Firstly, we are to confront our fellow recipient of grace gently. When we point out sin in another, we must first remember the power of the gospel in our own lives, remembering the depths from which Christ so victoriously pulled us. When we have that proper perspective, we will not approach our fallen brother with pride or misplaced zeal but rather with humility and the goal of restoration. Secondly, we are to bear the burden of our spiritual sibling. We are not called to simply point out the flaw; we are called to struggle with them as they seek to overcome. Repentance is messy. Turning from sin can be a very hard process, full of both victory and failure. Let us remember, however, that we do not celebrate perfection in the redeemed but progress. The only perfection we praise is that of Christ.

Are you willing to graciously and gently help your brothers and sisters grow in Christ-likeness by speaking truth into their lives? Or will you allow them to continue down a path of destruction that you know will never satisfy them? Further, will you commit to do the hard work of ministry in restoring them to a place of victory over sin through the power of Christ? May we be a people committed to one another as we each seek to walk worthy of the calling of God on our lives.

~ Jared

November 26

KNOW YOUR CULTURE

Chronological Bible Reading Plan: (Day 330: Acts 17)

"So Paul, standing in the midst of the Areopagus, said: 'Men of Athens, I perceive that in every way you are very religious. For as I passed along and observed the objects of your worship, I found also an altar with this inscription, 'To the unknown god.' What therefore you worship as unknown, this I proclaim to you.'"
Acts 17:22-23 (ESV)

We are called to be evangelists, as followers of Christ, proclaiming the "good news" wherever an opportunity arises. The nature of this work changes in different environments and cultures. For instance, the way you would present the gospel in the middle of an impoverished, third-world country may be different from the way you would present the gospel to a professor on the campus of Oxford. I am not saying here that the message changes from place to place, by no means! The cross of Christ should form the center of our message, but how that message of hope impacts us as individuals certainly varies within cultures.

Paul took this principle of relevance to heart in his missionary journeys, as evidenced in his encounter with the people of Athens in Acts 17. Paul studied the culture of Athens. He knew the "Athenians and the foreigners who lived there would spend their time in nothing except telling or hearing something new" (Acts 17:21 ESV). He also knew that the Greeks prided themselves on their ability to discuss at length matters of philosophy and religion. So, as he begins sharing the gospel on the Areopagus, Paul recognizes his need to speak into the particular culture of Athens while also presenting a distinct message about Christ.

How well do you know your culture? Do you know how the gospel speaks into the generation coming after you? Do you know what areas of need your neighbors have for the gospel? Do the work of an evangelist today and see the beauty of the gospel as it comes alive in different environments to bring glory to the one, true God!

~ Jared

November 27

The True Heart of Ministry

Chronological Bible Reading Plan: (Day 331: 1 & 2 Thessalonians)

"So, being affectionately desirous of you, we were ready to share with you not only the gospel of God but also our own selves, because you had become very dear to us." 1 Thessalonians 2:8 (ESV)

Paul is writing to the church in Thessalonica in response to a number of issues, including a number regarding his character. In an effort to squelch the growing Christian church, the Jewish elites of the day who enjoyed the security and prosperity the Roman Empire provided for them began to suggest that Paul was only in Thessalonica for personal gain, not for the sake of the gospel. They wanted to call his character and motivation for ministry into question in order to protect their power. Paul responds by reminding the church of his devotion to them, not for monetary gain but in response to deep, convicting love.

Is there a more perfect picture of Christian community and ministry? We are not simply to share words with one another or passing salutations; we are called to invest our lives in one another. This, of course, means a greater commitment on our part but also a greater reward. The type of community Paul exhibits is what we all long for. We want people to know us fully and still accept us. We want to know we are valued, and what greater way can that be seen than by someone giving all of themselves to us?

Now, some people you invest in will leave; some will abandon you. This type of ministry almost guarantees you will get hurt, but for all the heartache, there is a beautiful silver lining knowing that many have come to a vibrant, joy-filled walk with the Lord because of your personal investment in them.

Will you fully invest your life in ministry? Will you love people as passionately as Paul did? I pray you will because deep inside you know that you need it and those around you need it.

~Jared

November 28

A Community of Confession

Chronological Bible Reading Plan: (Day 332: Acts 18-19)

"Also many of those who were now believers came, confessing and divulging their practices." Acts 19:18 (ESV)

The message of the gospel is essentially a great equalizer, calling us all to the recognition that we are by nature flawed. We give our affection and worship to created things that were meant to direct us toward the only pure object of worship, God. That sinfulness in our life is ever-present and must be uprooted in order for the grace inherent to the gospel to take its place and fulfill us as we were meant to be fulfilled.

We see this practice of confession in repentance in Luke's account of the rebuke of the sons of Sceva. Having been beaten up by the demonic force they were trying to expel, the power of these seven sons of a Jewish high priest was proven to be exponentially inferior to that of Christ and His disciples. Many who had practiced magical arts renounced both the practice of sorcery and any item attached to it. They wanted to both acknowledge their failure and walk forward in grace.

This should be the practice of every believer. Why are we so afraid to confess our failures? We all have them. We all have fallen short of the glory of God. Yet it seems that every time we gather together as the Church, we pretend those truths aren't taught in the Bible, preferring to allow people to see us as we want to be seen rather than how we really are. The danger is, though, that if we do not confess our sin and burn the remnants of it, it will linger and likely take us captive once again.

Test the gospel today, dear friend. Find a trustworthy friend or spiritual adviser and get that mess out of you, allowing them to help you burn all your instruments of sin and step back on the path of righteousness. Everybody knows you are a sinner; that's why Christ's sacrifice was necessary.

~ Jared

November 29

Gratitude for Spiritual Fathers

Chronological Bible Reading Plan: (Day 333: 1 Corinthians 1-4)

"For though you have countless guides in Christ, you do not have many fathers. For I became your father in Christ Jesus through the gospel."
1 Corinthians 4:15 (ESV)

Within the family of God, our Heavenly Father has seen fit to bless us with men and women who care for us spiritually as, hopefully, our earthly parents cared for us physically. Now, I am not speaking here of every single pastor or spiritual teacher with whom you have ever crossed paths, but rather a specific person or persons who have singled you out particularly to invest in your spiritual growth. Can you think of such a person in your life? Have you sought out someone to pour themselves into you, asking you to "be imitators of me" (1 Cor. 4:16 ESV).

Think about the man or woman that the Lord has particularly placed in your life to both encourage and admonish you. Say a prayer of thanksgiving to the Lord for His provision, but also take some time today to actually tell that individual how much their ministry has meant in your life. You see, this relationship goes both ways, for as it is true that your spiritual "father" loves to care for you and see you grow in your walk, it is also true that in communicating his or her value to you, you serve to encourage them to continue to pour out their lives.

Discipleship and ministry are not easy things to give your life to. They require countless hours of answering tough, life-altering questions, fighting for the purity of loved ones, and walking graciously through valleys of failure. These men and women who have signed up to fight the good fight need encouraging to continue as you needed them to help direct your path toward Christ. Today, return the favor and minister to those who have so graciously ministered to you.

~ Jared

November 30

My Brother's Keeper

Chronological Bible Reading Plan: (Day 334: 1 Corinthians 5-8)

"Therefore, if food makes my brother stumble, I will never eat meat, lest I make my brother stumble." 1 Corinthians 8:13 (ESV)

Christ has set us free from the burden of ritual purity. Yes, we have been called to live pure lives but that purity now comes from that of Christ imputed in us by the Holy Spirit. Our holiness and standing before God, then, is not threatened by the ingestion of created things declared impure by the law. The problem in Paul's day, however, as seen in the Corinthian Church was that some weaker brothers, who had not yet fully grasped the concept of grace, had not arrived at this conclusion and still viewed the eating of food sacrificed to idols as falling back into their previous sinful behavior. Paul suggests here that as the more mature believers, we have the responsibility to refrain from a known freedom so that the weaker brother can grow into that knowledge.

How does this apply to us today? Certainly, there are various applications, but the chief concern for us should always be the spiritual growth of our brothers and sisters around us. If we know they struggle with something that we do not struggle with, we should not in spiritual pride throw that temptation in front of their face; rather, we should seek to create safe environments for them in which they can experience in greater ways the ultimately satisfying nature of Christ. Nothing that is free for us to experience is more important than the sanctification of a fellow saved sinner.

Now there is a balance here in that we cannot allow legalism to prevail as it did in the time of Christ. For those who wish to create new rules under the freedom of grace, we must stand firm in remembering the cause of our salvation. Yet, when there is a legitimate concern for a fellow brother or sister on their way to Christ-likeness, may we freely give up our freedom for the sake of their freedom and for the good of the Kingdom.

~ *Jared*

December 1

The Lord's Supper

Chronological Bible Reading Plan: (Day 335: 1 Corinthians 9-11)

"When you come together, it is not the Lord's supper that you eat. For in eating, each one goes ahead with his own meal. One goes hungry, another gets drunk." 1 Corinthians 11:20-21 (ESV)

The Lord's Supper, an ordinance established by Christ Himself in His last days of ministry upon the earth, is meant to be a reflection of His tremendous provision and sacrifice for the good of all of humanity. As we take the elements, both the drink and the bread, we are to remember how Christ's body was broken for our sin and how His blood was poured out for our redemption. This event is a tremendously solemn occasion and should not be taken in vain, as doing so would communicate falsely about the most important act in all of human history.

It's no wonder, then, that Paul reacts so strongly in our passage for today regarding the Corinthian Church's mishandling of the supper. They were using it as a means to once again show the strong division between those who were rich and those who were poor, making the lesser of the two feel their inferiority. What act could be more contrary to the message of the gospel, in which He who was the richest of all became poor for the sake of the poor? Paul, then, says to these new believers that their supper is no commemoration at all, but rather an act of sinful indulgence.

The people of God should look different. Our rich and our poor should not have their economic status worn as a badge of either pride or shame, respectively. Rather, we must as the Church remember our common spiritual poverty before the Lord and His generous provision on our behalf. That message unites us in spite of any other earthly distinction. Commit today to see people as the Lord's Supper intends them to be seen: men and women all in need of a glorious and generous Savior!

~ *Jared*

December 2

Love Never Ends

Chronological Bible Reading Plan: (Day 336: 1 Corinthians 12-14)

"Love never ends. As for prophecies, they will pass away; as for tongues, they will cease; as for knowledge, it will pass away. For we know in part and we prophesy in part, but when the perfect comes, the partial will pass away."
1 Corinthians 13:8 (ESV)

The sinful need for distinction had infiltrated the Corinthian Church, and members within the church were arguing over who had the greatest gift. Was prophecy the greatest gift? Or was tongues preferable? The uproar was causing strong division and Paul spoke boldly into the contentious situation, reminding the people of God about the purpose of these gifts. All gifts are meant to edify the Church. Gifts are meant to build each other up, and the second these gifts become about the individual, we have turned these God-given gifts into sinful manifestations for the glorification of man.

The core of this argument is found in 1 Corinthians 13, a passage that is so much more profound than we often notice in weddings. Love must be the motivation for the use of spiritual gifts, because love is the only component of the Church that is eternal. When Christ returns, we will no longer need prophecy, as all its objects will have been fulfilled. Further, we will not need tongues nor interpretation, as we will fellowship with God fully in His Spirit in Heaven. Love, then, should be the chief concern for us as it will be the only gift we take with us forever.

Are you concerned with how you love your fellow man? Do you genuinely love your brothers and sisters in Christ or do you simply tolerate them? This kind of love is birthed from a true love for the Lord, knowing that if we love Him, we must love others since love is from God. Seek today to love better, rejecting the tendency to compare yourself to others and build up your own image and pride.

~ Jared

December 3

The Gospel is of First Importance

Chronological Bible Reading Plan: (Day 337: 1 Corinthians 15-16)

"Now I would remind you, brothers, of the gospel I preached to you, which you received, in which you stand, and by which you are being saved, if you hold fast to the word I preached to you--unless you believed in vain. For I delivered to you as of first importance what I also received: that Christ died for our sins in accordance with the Scriptures..." 1 Corinthians 15:1-3 (ESV)

The Church has one message: the gospel of Jesus Christ. We are to continually proclaim the substitutionary work of Christ on the cross for our sins and His unique ability to do so. We are further to proclaim His resurrection from the dead, demonstrating not only His atoning work but also His victory over every effect of sin including death. Every single issue we face as fallen humanity can be faced with the message of the gospel of Jesus Christ!

The danger for us is that we think if we talk about the gospel too much that people will grow tired of hearing it. We think we have to help the gospel out by making it flashier or more relevant. My friend, be weary of this trend, for the gospel has never been in danger of being irrelevant. No, as in the time of Paul, it is still of first importance. Do you have bitterness in your heart toward someone who wronged you? Look at the message of the gospel and seek to forgive as Christ forgave. Do you have strife in your marriage? Strive to be gracious to one another as Christ was gracious to us. Do you have a loved one in the midst of a terminal illness? Remember that Christ has overcome the grave, removing the sting from death!

When the Church stops proclaiming the gospel, it will have forfeited its power, for only in the gospel do we have anything of significance to say. Speak forward boldly this message today, delivering it as of first importance as you received it.

~ *Jared*

December 4

Are You a Recommendation to the Gospel

Chronological Bible Reading Plan: (Day 338: 2 Corinthians 1-4)

"You yourselves are our letter of recommendation, written on our hearts, to be known and read by all. And you show that you are a letter from Christ delivered by us, written not with ink but with the Spirit of the living God, not on tablets of stone but on tablets of human hearts. Such is the confidence that we have through Christ toward God." 2 Corinthians 3:2-4 (ESV)

Paul takes a moment in the middle of his accounting of his triumph in Christ over various trials to explicitly state his intention for such writing. He writes to the Corinthian Church that His purpose is not to commend himself in his apostleship but rather to commend Christ for His glorious provision in the midst of any circumstance. As for Paul, he needs no further commendation, such as a letter, for his efficacious work is evidenced in the men and women who are living transformed lives as a result of the message Paul shared and the resulting favor of the Holy Spirit.

Would your life be able to be used by Paul as a reference to the power of the Holy Spirit? If Paul's apostleship were being called into question today, could he point to you as evidence of the truth of the power of the gospel? We must be more than moral people; we must be more than people of good will. We must be a transformed people, acknowledging failures and our complete dependency upon the grace provided by the sacrifice of Christ. If we fail here, then we will fail to affirm the very message we say is unique. May we commit today to embody the truth of Christ's completely satisfying nature, forsaking all other things for the gift of knowing Him!

~ Jared

December 5

A Generous God Deserves a Generous People

Chronological Bible Reading Plan: (Day 339: 2 Corinthians 5-9)

"...for in a severe test of affliction, their abundance of joy and their extreme poverty have overflowed in a wealth of generosity on their part."
2 Corinthians 8:2 (ESV)

We are to be a generous people, reflecting the heart of our very generous God! The people of Macedonia knew this, demonstrating an unusual combination of joy in the midst of poverty. That coupling would for many of us lead to bitterness and doubt. For them, however, a different reaction was seen most certainly rooted in a proper gospel perspective. You see, the people of Macedonia knew that the same God who provided for their sins in the coming of Christ would most certainly provide for their earthly needs as well. They would give what they had, trusting that the Lord would do for them what He had done for His people in the time of the Exodus and countless other times as recorded in Scripture.

Do we have that same kind of trust in the Lord's faithfulness today? We often equate blessing with monetary blessings, but the Lord often asks us to sacrifice that which we value most dearly to remind us of our great need for and dependence upon Him. Would you still be joyful in the midst of extreme poverty? Or would you be like the rich, young ruler who could not bring himself to part with his possessions in order to inherit the Kingdom of God?

May we care more about the spreading of the gospel than our personal wealth! Now, we should not ignore our responsibilities as spouses and parents, but we should consider it a privilege to give sacrificially as an act of worship to our God who has so richly blessed us in the giving of His only Begotten! May we heed the word of Paul and follow the example of the gospel in being a generous people.

~ Jared

December 6

Live in Peace

Chronological Bible Reading Plan: (Day 340: 2 Corinthians 10-13)

"Finally, brothers, rejoice. Aim for restoration, comfort one another, agree with one another, live in peace; and the God of love and peace will be with you."
2 Corinthians 13:11 (ESV)

In the concluding remarks of this letter, Paul delivers an incredible recipe with four major ingredients for living in peace with your brothers and sisters in Christ. He begins by reminding the people of Corinth to rejoice. Part of living in peace with your fellow man is living in peace with God, remembering His incredible work displayed in the gospel. When you and I spend time rejoicing, we don't have as much time to focus on the failure or differences of others. Living in peace, then, begins with praise.

The second element that Paul encourages in the people of Corinth is aiming for restoration. Part of being a part of a community of people is cultivating healthy relationships. People are imperfect and they mess up, likely offending others, but our responsibility is not to abandon them. Certainly not! We are to aim for restoration, seeking out whatever means necessary to bring this division to a peaceful resolution. This is what Christ did for us, so how could we do any less?

The last two ingredients of which Paul writes are encouragements to the Corinthians to both comfort one another and agree with one another, shepherding them to both empathize with their fellow man and support them. We are on the same team as members of the Church of Jesus Christ, meaning we are fighting the same battles, winning the same victories, and suffering the same losses. There should be no contention among us, then, as that outside of us is already so great. We should not allow momentary mishaps to distract us from the greater purposes of God.

Today, take these words from Paul to heart and apply them to your life as you seek to live in peace with your fellow redeemed sinners.

~ Jared

December 7

The Face of Depravity

Chronological Bible Reading Plan: (Day 341: Romans 1-3)

"Claiming to be wise, they became fools, and exchanged the glory of the immortal God for images resembling mortal man and birds and animals and creeping things." Romans 1:22-23 (ESV)

The beginning of the gospel of Jesus Christ is a recognition of humanity's great need for salvation. The beauty of Christ's perfection and sacrifice loses some of its splendor if it is separated from the reality of mankind's hopelessness because of sin. Otherwise, what need would there have been for His act of redemption? Paul recognizes this and, thus, begins his discussion of the reality of the work of Christ with man's reality of depravity. Man, having been created to be fully satisfied by God and return that satisfaction to Him in praise, had rejected his reator and began instead to worship created things. As a result, a separation was created between God and man. No longer was pure fellowship available between the Creator and His creation because of His righteous and just need to account for such rejection through His wrath being poured upon the rebellious.

The depravity of man, then, demands the wrath of God, and this point highlights the beauty of the gospel. Our rejection of God led to Christ being rejected for us. He took upon Himself our deserved wrath and thereby enabled us to have fellowship with our Creator once again. Christ did not look down upon us in our helplessness and turn a blind eye; no, He acted for the good of all men by emptying Himself, taking on the form of a servant, and becoming obedient to death, even death on a cross.

As we mark the coming of Christ in the season of Christmas, take a moment and remember your great need for His incredible sacrifice and, then, turn the joy you feel as a result of His salvation back into praise to this worthy and generous God we serve!

~ *Jared*

December 8

Do Not Let Sin Reign

Chronological Bible Reading Plan: (Day 342: Romans 4-7)

"Let not sin therefore reign in your mortal body, to make you obey its passions." Romans 6:12 (ESV)

Because of the gospel, we are dead to sin and alive in Christ! As we read yesterday in Romans 1, before Christ we had no freedom in regards to our proclivity to sin as depravity led us toward greater and greater rebellion against God. Yet, in Christ, we have the freedom now to choose to reject sin and move toward greater obedience, finding satisfaction in the Lord and responding joyfully in praise.

If it is true that we have this freedom to finally find true satisfaction, why do we still return to the vanity of our transgression? Why do we continue to allow ourselves to be distracted by things that ultimately have no significance? Further, when we do fall short, why do we feel the need to punish ourselves incessantly, forgetting the propitiatory work of Christ? Paul's command to us in light of these perennial struggles within Christianity is to stop! He uses an imperative here in the language of the New Testament on purpose. You have the ability in Christ to stop. You can choose to reject sin and move forward in holiness. Further, when you do fail because you have not entered into the perfect yet, do not let sin reign in your mortal body by robbing you of the joy and abundant life secured for you in Christ! Repent of your failure and move forward.

Dear child of God, are you engrossed in perpetual sin? Are you living in guilt and defeat? Do not let sin reign in your mortal body! Claim the promise of Christ; claim the abundant life found in radical obedience to the gospel. You have the freedom to reject sin, so reject it for the promise of greater satisfaction in Jesus.

~ Jared

December 9

There is Now No Condemnation

Chronological Bible Reading Plan: (Day 343: Romans 8-10)

"There is therefore now no condemnation for those who are in Christ Jesus." Romans 8:1 (ESV)

Christ changed everything! This sweet truth provides the underlying message of all of Romans, no more clearly communicated than in this climactic statement in the beginning of chapter 8. Paul begins with "therefore," referencing all the material in the preceding chapters to proudly proclaim that now in Christ Jesus there is no condemnation. Of course, under the law, we were all condemned, as it revealed our unworthiness in light of God's holiness. Now, however, that Christ has given us life instead of death and released us from the law through His perfect obedience, we are freed from condemnation because He was condemned.

Child of God, rejoice, in this truth today! The wrath of God has been satisfied. The fear of death has lost its sting. The bondage to sin that we had in depravity has been eternally loosened, for Christ has set us free. When you and I submit our lives to His Lordship, we are protected eternally, as Paul later points out:

"For I am sure that neither death nor life, nor angels nor rulers, nor things present nor things to come, nor powers, nor height nor depth, nor anything else in all creation, will be able to separate us from the love of God in Christ Jesus our Lord" (Rom. 8:38-39 ESV).

Do you live in light of this truth? Do you live as if you are free? Are you filled with the joy that this news rightly demands? Far too many of us continue to live in condemnation of ourselves for failures when Christ has already overcome them. Do not diminish His great gift by living in defeat. Live today in the freedom of Romans 8:1!

~ *Jared*

December 10

Do Not Be Conformed, but Transformed

Chronological Bible Reading Plan: (Day 344: Romans 11-13)

"I appeal to you therefore, brothers, by the mercies of God, to present your bodies as a living sacrifice, holy and acceptable to God, which is your spiritual worship. Do not be conformed to this world, but be transformed by the renewal of your mind, that by testing you may discern what is the will of God, what is good and acceptable and perfect." Romans 12:1-2 (ESV)

The gospel of Jesus Christ is a transforming message, meaning that the truth contained therein is meant to be more than informative. This truth is meant to strike at the core of who we are and radically alter both the way we view the world and act in it. This type of reaction is very different from simple conformity. Conformity simply observes the rituals and practices of society generally and engages in them in order to be accepted. As you and I both know, however, this behavioral attestation can be very dangerous, as culture so often because of depravity leads one away from intimacy with the Lord rather than to it.

Paul's challenge to us is clear. As followers of Christ, no longer must we look to our culture and the norms of the day as our standard of acceptance; rather, we must continually sacrifice our need for human acceptance for a greater acceptance in the Lord. In order to do this, then, we must radically offer our very lives to Christ, shaping and molding them in light of the truth of the gospel, making decisions and thinking thoughts that demonstrate the Holy Spirit's power within us.

Today, commit to live a transformed life, looking only to the message of Christ as an example of salvific behavior. Do not become distracted by the interests of this world, once again conforming to its values and idols, but rather reject those for the supreme knowledge of Christ incarnate, crucified, and resurrected.

~ Jared

December 11

Unity

Chronological Bible Reading Plan: (Day 345: Romans 14-16)

"May the God of endurance and encouragement grant you to live in such harmony with one another, in accord with Christ Jesus, that together you may with one voice glorify the God and Father of our Lord Jesus Christ."
Romans 15:5-6 (ESV)

Unity in the body of Christ is important because of how diverse people from different backgrounds who have different interests come together in love to accomplish the overarching purpose of growing the Kingdom of God. As Christ Himself said, people know we are His children by how we love one another, as such love is impossible to possess without the spirit of God doing a transforming work within us (John 13:35). Unity is important.

Unity is also hard. Notice that Paul calls upon God to grant His people both endurance and encouragement. What an interesting combination of attributes Paul asks the Lord to share! Why would he ask for these things? Well, the second is rather obvious, as certainly we are constantly in need of encouragement to remember both the goal of the Christian and the motivation for seeing it through.

Endurance, though, seems to be a bit more unusual. Even though the true people of the Church are regenerate, they have not yet become perfect, meaning that they still sin and mess up. As a result, feelings get hurt, promises are broken, and relationships fall apart from unwarranted suspicions and careless words. To pursue unity, then, in the midst of such hurt is hard work.

We must extend grace to one another as the people of God, committing to live in harmony with our spiritual family no matter the difficulty, understanding that such unity in the midst of enormous diversity reflects the heart of our Heavenly Father and the power of the gospel over sin.

~ *Jared*

December 12

We Must Declare the Whole Counsel of God

Chronological Bible Reading Plan: (Day 346: Acts 20-23)

"...for I did not shrink from declaring to you the whole counsel of God."
Acts 20:27 (ESV)

The Ephesian Church was in danger. Paul speaks to the elders of the church and suggests to them that when he leaves, wolves will enter and try to devour the church. Paul's concern, though, is limited, knowing that he has done all he can to prepare them by preaching to them the full counsel of God's word. He did not choose to leave portions out, thinking that they would be too hard for them to digest or handle. No, he boldly proclaimed all of Scripture, knowing that even the hard truths were necessary for this church's success.

In America today, we face similar dangers as that of the Ephesian Church, yet many of our leaders have shied away from preaching the full counsel of God, choosing instead to focus on the more acceptable aspects of Scripture. The problem, though, that arises when you only teach a partial gospel is that when difficult times come or false teaching is presented, the people do not know how to respond and are likely either defeated or led astray. Certainly no pastor intends for this to happen, but when parts of God's Word and, thus, His character are ignored, the Church is ill-prepared to accomplish the purpose God has set before it.

My friends, may we commit to be a people who teach the full counsel of God. May we not shy away from topics such as God's wrath and His coming judgment even as we proclaim His sacrificial love. May we teach people how to be better citizens or our planet, yes, but may we be more concerned with teaching them how to embody the fullness of Christ and the sacrifice such embodiment demands. God revealed Himself fully in His Word; who are we to question which aspects of Him are acceptable and which are not?

~ Jared

December 13

Our God Raises the Dead

Chronological Bible Reading Plan: (Day 347: Acts 24-26)

"Why is it thought incredible by any of you that God raises the dead?"
Acts 26:8 (ESV)

The Resurrection of Christ is the most important event in all of human history, in that it secures our hope in a restored future. Jesus' rising from the dead clearly displays for us the possibilities for all of creation, which will likewise pass away and be made new as Christ Himself was made new. There will be a new heaven; there will be a new earth. There will be a new Jerusalem, and we all, who are in Christ, will be made new, joining together with all of creation in its redeemed form to eternally worship our merciful and gracious God.

If there is no resurrection, then none of this is possible, as Paul points out in 1 Corinthians 15. The resurrection is the foretaste of that which is to come. Certainly, such an event is possible. Some would say that it is not, and therefore dismiss Christianity as a whole, seeing its linchpin teaching as unreasonable. But given our belief about God, that He is the greatest possible being and the initiator of creation, then certainly it is within His power to breathe life back into that which is dead. Is a resurrection really that hard to accept, if God is Who He says He is in Scripture?

Do not shrink away from the teaching of Christ's resurrection, fellow Christian. Despite what modern conceptions may say, we cannot afford to give way on this subject, for in it rests our entire system of belief. There is no demythologizing that which is central to our belief. God is omnipotent and our Creator. He is certainly able to raise the dead, and by raising Christ, He has secured for us an everlasting hope.

~ *Jared*

December 14

The Trajectory of the Gospel

Chronological Bible Reading Plan: (Day 348: Acts 27-28)

"It happened that the father of Publius lay sick with fever and dysentery. And Paul visited him and prayed, and putting his hands on him healed him."
Acts 28:8 (ESV)

The gospel is a message of enormous significance on a number of levels. The gospel is certainly about the actions of Christ, providing a means by which we as sinners can be reconciled to God, the Father, worshiping Him as we were created to do, but it is also concerned with much more than simply the means of salvation. The gospel is further concerned with where such an act, i.e. Christ's resurrection, will take all of creation. The gospel is about the restoration of all things! As Paul himself writes in Eph.1:9-10, the gospel is about the Lord "making known to us the mystery of his will, according to his purpose, which he set forth in Christ as a plan for the fullness of time, to unite all things in him, things in heaven and things on earth" (ESV).

Paul wasn't just concerned with proclamation; no, he was about incarnation. He wanted the gospel to take up root in him, so that as with Christ the Word of God could dwell among all the peoples of the earth. He was concerned with poverty. He was concerned with sickness. He was concerned with every effect of the fall, seeing their eradication as further evidence of Christ's victory over all sin.

You and I have the same ministry. We are called to proclaim first, yes, as Christ's witnesses but we are also called to care. We are called to minister to the least of these as if we were ministering to Jesus Himself. Are you fully embodying the gospel? Or are you only partially concerned with its progression? We must be about telling people about Jesus, but we should also be concerned with showing them about the victory we have in Him.

~ Jared

December 15

How Do You Overcome Sin?

Chronological Bible Reading Plan: (Day 349: Colossians, Philemon)

"These have indeed an appearance of wisdom in promoting self-made religion and asceticism and severity to the body, but they are of no value in stopping the indulgence of the flesh." Colossians 2:23 (ESV)

We live in the cross-section of the redeemed and the fallen. As the redeemed people of God living in a fallen world, the presence of persistent sin is still possible, falling victim to temptation even though we know its limitations and shortcomings. The question then becomes how one overcomes such sin. Should we submit to the human regulations mentioned by Paul, choosing simply not to handle, taste, or touch objects of temptation? Should we resort to asceticism or self-flagellation? Paul teaches we should not, as such actions may have the appearance of religious behavior but do nothing in terms of stopping the indulgence of the flesh, as anyone who has tried them can attest.

Paul writes that the key to overcoming sin is not focusing on the sin but rather on Christ. Think about it. If all you do is tell yourself to stop doing the sin, then your focus is entirely on the sin most likely leading to temptation. If, however, you avert your attention away from the sin to the satisfying truth of Christ, then suddenly, as the old hymn suggests, the things of this world become strangely dim.

Dear child of God, are you struggling with persistent sin? Do not beat yourself up consistently, living in condemnation. Rather remember who you are in Christ, repent, and refocus on the heavenly things He provides. Having done that, once again recognizing that you have died with Christ, then put to death what is earthly within you, living fully as God's chosen ones, holy and beloved.

~ *Jared*

December 16

The Purpose of the Church

Chronological Bible Reading Plan: (Day 350: Ephesians)

"...so that through the church the manifold wisdom of God might now be made known to the rulers and authorities in the heavenly places."
Ephesians 3:10 (ESV)

As the Church of Jesus Christ, we are called to proclaim the manifold wisdom of God to both creatures on the earth and rulers and authorities in the heavenly places. We are called to unveil God's redemptive plan, forged in eternity past, by which He seeks to unite all things to Him in Christ Jesus, Whose propitiatory work now makes intimacy between God and creation possible. We are revealing the hope of everything!

What an incredible calling we have, and yet so often we lose focus. We make the church experience about us, focusing on how a given church meets our needs or perhaps how it doesn't. We jump from church to church, seeking the most entertainment value or the best childcare. Now, all of these secondary issues are not completely unimportant, but they are just that. They are secondary. In the consumer-driven world in which we live, we must take extra precautions to not fall victim to that mentality in the Church, remembering that our calling to the body of Christ is much larger than a social event. No, it is the hope of the world!

Today, remember the calling of the Church to make known the manifold wisdom of God, and further remember the boldness and confidence that is yours in Christ Jesus to accomplish this calling. Is there someone you know this Christmas who needs this hope? Speak boldly and tell of His glorious worth.

~ *Jared*

December 17

You Work Out As God Works In

Chronological Bible Reading Plan: (Day 351: Philippians)

"Therefore, my beloved, as you have always obeyed, so now, not only as in my presence but much more in my absence, work out your own salvation with fear and trembling, for it is God who works in you, both to will and to work for his good pleasure." Philippians 2:12-13 (ESV)

We are not dependent upon any man, woman, or spiritual mentor in order to grow in our faith in Christ. No, for the Lord is at work within us! The same Spirit of God that raised Christ from the dead is the same Spirit that inhabits us at our salvation, breathing in us new life and allowing us to work out the effects of our salvation. The Holy Spirit shapes and molds us into the image of Christ by revealing truth to us in the Word of God and convicting us over our sin.

He works on the inside of us so that we can work on the outside. As we are shaped into the image of Christ, we must begin to act like Him. Paul calls us later in chapter two to "do all things without grumbling or questioning, that you may be blameless and innocent, children of God without blemish in the midst of a crooked and twisted generation, among whom you shine as lights in the world..." (Phil. 2:14-15 ESV). Obviously, such behavior goes against human nature, but that is precisely the point. We act differently because we are different as a result of the gospel, and our actions testify to its transforming power.

Do you act differently as a result of the gospel? Do you practice the type of humility personified by Christ? Do you do everything without complaining or grumbling? You have been called to live as Christ, but you have also been empowered to do so by the Holy Spirit of God. Live in that power today to put on display the transforming power of Christ within you.

~ *Jared*

December 18

Peace to You

Chronological Bible Reading Plan: (Day 352: 1 Timothy)

"Paul, an apostle of Christ Jesus by command of God our Savior and of Christ Jesus our hope, To Timothy, my true child in the faith: Grace, mercy, and peace from God the Father and Christ Jesus our Lord." 1 Timothy 1:1-2 (ESV)

Typically in Paul's epistles, he greets his reader by wishing upon them peace, a peace that he rightfully acknowledges is only possible with the coming of Christ. This peace provides one of the many things for which we can be thankful on Christmas day, for it is a peace that has been the chief longing of all of creation ever since the fall. The "shalom" or peace written about in the language of the Jewish people was more than simply a cessation of fighting; this word for peace carried with it the idea of completeness or soundness. Peace, then, in the eyes of the Jewish people was a setting right of all creation, which of course was fractured with the introduction of sin. Peace meant a restoration of relationship between God and man; peace meant wholeness.

No wonder, then, we proclaim at this time of year, "Joy to the world. The Lord has come!" Is there any more joyous statement? All of creation feels the tension of sin; all of us feel the separation between us and our Creator, and now we have a way to mend it. Christ came to take upon Himself the weight of our sin and impending punishment. He took the brunt of God's wrath, waging war against the tyranny of transgression, so that you and I could have peace with God the Father through Jesus Christ, His Son and our only hope.

In this beautiful Christmas season, then, fellow brother or sister in Christ, I wish you peace, a peace that is only possible because of the very object of our celebration: Jesus Christ.

~ *Jared*

December 19

TEACH SOUND DOCTRINE

Chronological Bible Reading Plan: (Day 353: Titus)

"But as for you, teach what accords with sound doctrine." Titus 2:1 (ESV)

As the people of God, we have a responsibility to teach His revelation faithfully. The Word of God was given to us to reveal the character of God and His eternal plan to unite all things to Himself in Christ. Scripture is precious, and every follower of Christ should do his or her best to diligently study it and read it, seeking to know Him more as a result. We should be passionate about this pursuit, as in reality it is a pursuit of God. We should desire daily to spend time in Scripture, knowing that in so doing we are spending time with the Lord.

Many today, however, do not make the time to study and meditate on God's word, strengthening their knowledge of doctrine. They believe this kind of practice to be the responsibility of only the "called," and rely upon them to feed them their acquired knowledge, as a caring mother does for her baby. But this is not the mandate given to the Church. Pastors are called to equip, not spoon-feed. Every individual has a unique responsibility to both learn the essentials of their faith and proclaim it to those who do not know.

Do you know the Word of God? Have you allowed scholars to sharpen your understanding of doctrine? Do you seek out trusted perspectives to shed light on issues in Scripture that are hard to understand? Commit today to take ownership of your faith, reading and meditating on truth so that you may be able to follow Paul's challenge to Timothy and teach sound doctrine.

~ Jared

December 20

A People for His Own Possession

Chronological Bible Reading Plan: (Day 354: 1 Peter)

"But you are a chosen race, a royal priesthood, a holy nation, a people for his own possession, that you may proclaim the excellencies of him who called you out of darkness into his marvelous light. Once you were not a people, but now you are God's people; once you had not received mercy, but now you have received mercy." 1 Peter 2:9-10 (ESV)

We have been saved individually, yes, but we have also been saved for a purpose. We have been called to be reconciled to Christ, but we have further been called to be a part of a people, a people fashioned by God for the purposes of God. We are being formed into a royal priesthood to mediate the presence of God upon the earth, interceding for its people. We are being formed into a holy nation, not confined to a geopolitical location but rooted together in the Spirit of God. We are being formed into a people for His own possession, personifying His communicable attributes and displaying His redemptive plan in us for the world to see. We are being formed into a people whose sole purpose is to proclaim the marvelous excellencies of God!

What an incredible privilege it is to be the people of God. We are simply called to brag on this God Who has so radically saved us. The beautiful thing about our calling is that the marvelous excellencies of God never run out. He exists infinitely, meaning there is no limit to all that He is. His goodness is infinite. His love is infinite. His mercy is infinite, and because of this truth, we should never want for material to proclaim.

You have been saved to be a part of a proclaiming people. Today, look back over this past year and see how God has been faithful to you, and as you map out His faithfulness take time to proclaim His marvelous excellencies as displayed in your life as part of this redeemed people.

~ *Jared*

December 21

Jesus is Greater than Moses

Chronological Bible Reading Plan: (Day 355: Hebrews 1-6)

"For Jesus has been counted worthy of more glory than Moses-- as much more glory as the builder of a house has more honor than the house itself." Hebrews 3:3 (ESV)

The whole Bible is about Jesus. From Genesis to Revelation, Scripture is concerned with revealing the glory of Christ, initially in revealing our great need for Him, followed subsequently by His unique role in God's plan of salvation and the anticipation of His triumphant return. Even the great leaders of our faith are meant to point out how Christ was uniquely better than our best. Moses is a great example. Moses did great things for the Lord in leading the people of God out of the bondage of slavery, but even as great as he was, he was still flawed. He was a man who lacked faith in the Lord at times, grew impatient and angry with the people God asked him to lead, and acted impulsively, ultimately leading to his inability to enter the promised land.

The author of Hebrews uses these truths to amplify the glory of Christ for a Jewish audience. Yes, Moses was a great leader. Yes, he was a father of our faith, but he was and is not Jesus. Jesus is greater than Moses, for while Moses was a prophet of God, Jesus is the Word of God incarnate. Jesus is greater than Moses, because although Moses led a specific people out of physical bondage, Christ provides freedom for all people from the bondage of sin and death. Jesus is greater than Moses in that Jesus is the only way to the promised land and will certainly be there when we enter. Jesus is greater and is alone worthy of our worship, praise, and devotion.

As followers of Christ, we must be wary to not fall in love with a leader more than who that leader should be leading us toward. Our devotion must first always be to Jesus, for no leader regardless of his worth on this earth comes close to the glory that is Christ's!

~ Jared

December 22

The Importance of Christ's Deity

Chronological Bible Reading Plan: (Day 356: Hebrews 7-10)

"But when Christ appeared as a high priest of the good things that have come, then through the greater and more perfect tent (not made with hands, that is, not of this creation) he entered once for all into the holy places, not by means of the blood of goats and calves but by means of his own blood, thus securing an eternal redemption." Hebrews 9:11-12 (ESV)

The sacrificial system was always a temporary fix, both in practicality and in God's overarching redemptive design. The sacrifices offered were never able to speak to the fullness of sin's offense, nor compensate adequately in holiness. Yet, the coming of Christ revealed the purpose of the sacrificial system: to establish a process by which Christ could ultimately justify God's offer of salvation and permanently atone for sin. His deity is essential to this provision. If Christ is not infinite, as God alone is, then His sacrifice cannot even remotely account for the entirety of our sin. Secondly, if Christ is not eternal, then that accounting cannot span the expanse of time from the beginning of creation until His return. Christ, then, must be both man and God for Him to be able to secure an "eternal redemption."

For centuries, there have been those who try to minimize the importance of Christ's deity, suggesting that He was simply a good man or a skilled teacher. Make no mistake, though, without the deity of Christ, there is no salvation. If we fail to affirm the fullness of the God-man, then we rob our faith of its power. Defend the teaching of Christ's deity and be thankful that He became sin Who knew no sin so that we could become the righteousness of God.

~ Jared

December 23

Remember the Cloud of Witnesses

Chronological Bible Reading Plan: (Day 357: Hebrews 11-13)

"Therefore, since we are surrounded by so great a cloud of witnesses, let us also lay aside every weight, and sin which clings so closely, and let us run with endurance the race that is set before us, looking to Jesus, the founder and perfecter of our faith, who for the joy that was set before him endured the cross, despising the shame, and is seated at the right hand of the throne of God."
Hebrews 12:1-2 (ESV)

Building upon his list of some of the most faithful people in all of Scripture, the author of Hebrews now challenges us to remain as strong and vigilant as those before us in the face of adversity or temptation. Whatever situation comes your way, know that someone has walked through something similar and has proven faithful. Are you trying to lead a people out of bondage from a powerful empire? Well, look to Moses, who in the face of seemingly insurmountable odds allowed the Lord to work miraculously through him. Have you been called to sacrifice your one and only promised son by the Lord? Look to Abraham, who trusted even when he did not understand, allowing the Lord to deliver his son at the right time. Have you been attacked by a lion lately? Well, look to Samson, whose God-infused power allowed him to tear apart his attacker.

While almost certainly none of us have been in as precarious positions as these, knowing that men just like us stood firm in the face of extraordinary circumstances should give us hope that we can stand when we face obstacles ourselves. Many have gone before us and finished well. Many are proving faithful in our midst presently. There is no reason that you cannot set aside your weights and run this race with endurance. Do not be overcome by thinking that you are the only one. Remember the examples we have and set out to emulate them as you serve our worthy God.

~ *Jared*

December 24

Will You Endure Sound Teaching?

Chronological Bible Reading Plan: (Day 358: 2 Timothy)

"Preach the word; be ready in season and out of season; reprove, rebuke, and exhort, with complete patience and teaching. For the time is coming when people will not endure sound teaching, but having itching ears they will accumulate for themselves teachers to suit their own passions, and will turn away from listening to the truth and wander off into myths." 2 Timothy 4:2-4 (ESV)

Truth is becoming more and more relative, or so it would seem, in our culture today. To say something is absolutely true, especially in religious or philosophical circles, is unpopular at best. Sometimes such statements are even met with anger and animosity. The true follower of Christ, however, should take care to not fall into our culture's trap, recognizing that there are certain things that are absolutely true, including the gospel of Jesus Christ. Because the gospel is absolutely true, we should welcome both its preaching and its proclaiming in our lives. We should welcome its preaching to us because we know that in hearing the gospel, we can become more like Christ. Our purpose is to reject sin and pursue holiness, and we need people in our lives to remind us of the gospel to push us toward that end. We should also welcome its proclaiming in the midst of any circumstance and regardless of consequence, knowing that without it the people around us will perish under the wrath of God.

Does your heart come alive when the Word of God is taught, or would you rather hear the philosophies of man? Do you feel encouraged when the truth of Scripture is spoken over you, even in rebuke? Or do you prefer to be flattered even when it is not genuine? We are not perfect yet and need pruning on occasion; the true follower of Christ welcomes the truth, even when it is inconvenient, in order to achieve that end. Will you endure sound teaching? Will you demand it? Will you teach soundly even when it costs you for the good of those around you?

~ *Jared*

December 25

The Prophetic Word

Chronological Bible Reading Plan: (Day 359: 2 Peter, Jude)

"And we have the prophetic word more fully confirmed, to which you will do well to pay attention as to a lamp shining in a dark place, until the day dawns and the morning star rises in your hearts, knowing this first of all, that no prophecy of Scripture comes from someone's own interpretation." 2 Peter 1:19-20 (ESV)

"Is the calling of Christ worth dying for?" This was the central question on the mind of early Christians as they watched their friends and family be put to death for the sake of Christ. In order to encourage them, Peter reassures them of the certainty of God's faithfulness evidenced in Scripture. Peter's assurance in the worth of this cause rests not in miraculous events nor myths devised by man, but rather the Holy Spirit inspired Word of God.

To make his point in a greater way, Peter takes us on a journey back in time to the Mount of Transfiguration, upon which Peter experienced the glory of Christ unlike any other. He saw the glorified Son of God conversing with Moses and Elijah! What an incredible spectacle! For Peter, though, this event only had significance when placed in the greater narrative of salvation collected in the Prophetic Word. The Prophetic Word, then, is a more sure foundation for our sacrifice than even the Mount of Transfiguration! You don't need a mountaintop spectacle to sure up your faith, for you hold God's full revelation of Himself every day in your hand.

Take comfort, dear friend, in knowing that the Bible (inspired by the Holy Spirit of course) is source enough for our faith, reminding us of God's faithfulness in calling us to redemption and providing a path for that redemption. Treasure this Word for the jewel that it is. Rely upon it in times of distress and call upon it in times of persecution. The Prophetic Word is the most sure instrument we have in reminding us of Christ's great worth and encouraging us to persevere even when times get hard.

~ *Jared*

Decemember 26

Jesus, Our Wrath-Bearer

Chronological Bible Reading Plan: (Day 360: 1 John)

"He is the propitiation for our sins, and not for ours only but also for the sins of the whole world." 1 John 2:2 (ESV)

God perfectly exists. Everything about Him is in perfect balance and harmony, including the make-up of His character. While for us, we may only like to focus on certain aspects of His character that we find comforting, to do so speaks falsely about the fullness of God. Yes, God is loving, but in as much as He is loving, He is also just. In as much as He is merciful, He is also holy. In as much as He is peaceful, He is also wrathful. This last trait is of particular concern in our passage today, as God's wrath is poured out upon that which rebels against His precepts and offends His glory. You see, when you and I choose to find satisfaction outside of God, ignoring His infinite fullness, we offend Him to His core, defeating the very purpose of our creation. This offense demands judgment; God's wrath demands satisfaction.

Jesus became our wrath-bearer. John writes as much when he utilizes the word, "propitiation," which literally means "wrath-bearer." We could not once again experience the fullness of God without our rebellion being accounted for by God's wrath being satisfied. So, in order to save us who were without hope, Jesus came, lived perfectly, and then became our substitutionary atonement on the cross. He lived the life we could not live to take the punishment we could not bear all so that you and I could find abundant and eternal life with God.

As we begin this new year, remind yourself of this overwhelming truth: Christ's perfection allows for your standing before God. He alone gives you the ability to enjoy the fullness of God.

~ *Jared*

December 27

Let Us Support the Work of the Kingdom

Chronological Bible Reading Plan: (Day 361: 2, 3 John)

"For they have gone out for the sake of the name, accepting nothing from the Gentiles. Therefore we ought to support people like these, that we may be fellow workers for the truth." 3 John 7-8 (ESV)

The Church should support its workers. We have been called to be witnesses unto the ends of the earth, and in order to do that we must go into places that do not have local churches established. Our men and women called, then, to these places need means of support. They need to be able to focus on the task at hand of building the Kingdom of God rather than focusing on financial burdens that will prohibit them from their work. Established Churches, then, should seek to partner with those that are called out, so that together we may accomplish our great commission, which is exactly what Gaius and his church had done.

As Baptists, we have the privilege of working with other denominational partner churches in our cooperative program, which funds agencies that do exactly what John is praising here for missionaries all over North America and the world. Through our North American Mission Board and International Mission Board, missionaries are funded every day to do the work of the Kingdom. We are indeed privileged to be a part of such an incredible partnership. Other like-minded denominations, undoubtedly, also have partnerships, reflecting the central truth of this passage: the Church of the living God should acknowledge His calling upon individuals and support them in their efforts whenever possible.

Are you giving to the Lord's work? Are you tithing to your local church, enabling them, then, to give to other ministries? Are you partnering directly with persons or ministers working in proclaiming the gospel and building the Church? Challenge yourself in this new year to be more generous, especially to the work of the Kingdom, for in so doing you become a "fellow worker for the truth."

~ Jared

December 28

Worthy is the Lamb

Chronological Bible Reading Plan: (Day 362: Revelation 1-5)

"Then I looked, and I heard around the throne and the living creatures and the elders the voice of many angels, numbering myriads of myriads and thousands of thousands, saying with a loud voice, 'Worthy is the Lamb who was slain, to receive power and wealth and wisdom and might and honor and glory and blessing!'" Revelation 5:11-12 (ESV)

Why is Christ alone worthy to receive power and wealth and wisdom and might and honor and glory and blessing? Why is He the object of our worship? What is so special about Him that He is the focus of all of Scripture and the climax of God's redemptive plan for all things? In chapter 5 of Revelation, John presents the best of creation surrounding the Lord and responding in worship. God in all of His glory far outshines the greatest collection of the best we have to offer, making Him a worthy object of our affection, and Jesus embodies this truth. Jesus is the incarnate glory of God, revealing to us His nature and His beautiful plan of redemption.

Further, Christ is worthy of our affection and ultimate blessings because of how He secures the glory of God as preeminent by becoming the only source of salvation for creation. Christ's worth is only amplified by His sacrifice, as the saints proclaim that because of His "blood" that was poured out for the people of God, He is worthy to "take the scroll and to open its seals" (Rev. 5:9 ESV). Without His sanctifying work, the glory of God would have demanded our expulsion; yet, because of His work, the glory of God becomes a source of both praise and purpose.

This morning, consider the glory of God and the worth of Christ in making that a source of hope for you rather than a cause for fear. Consider further the power of Christ in your life to remove the seals and secure your salvation. Do not seek to save yourself in your own strength; rather, turn to Him today, behold His glory, and be satisfied.

~ Jared

December 29

Watch and Worship

Chronological Bible Reading Plan: (Day 363: Revelation 6-11)

"Now I watched when the Lamb opened one of the seven seals, and I heard one of the four living creatures say with a voice like thunder, 'Come!'"
Revelation 6:1 (ESV)

John was called up into the heavenlies to behold the reality of our future: unending worship of our worthy God. As the elders, the angels, and even John himself watch the Lord work all things for His glory, they cannot help but proclaim the supreme worth of God. This is the reality of worship: the more we admire the works of the Lord and His supreme worth, the greater we will declare it. As John Piper stated in a sermon, "Our worship is the subjective echo of God's objective worth." When we behold the glory of God, we are to sound forth His worth in worship, and the greater the act of glory we behold or understand, the greater we will declare.

John is living out this truth in Revelation. He is beholding the glory of God, having been led by the Spirit of God, and declaring what He has witnessed in the writing of this book. Our calling is the same. Think about the many ways the Lord has revealed His glory in your life. Think about the gospel of Jesus Christ. Think about the miraculous way that He called you from death into life. Think about the ways He has spoken specifically into your life and called you to a new purpose, having given you a renewed faith. Think about the revelation given to us of His faithfulness in His Scripture. As you consider these things, the spirit within you should feel emboldened to tell of these glorious truths, which is the natural response of the redeemed.

We must continually consider the greatness of God in order to accomplish our purpose of proclaiming the gospel and glory of God to all peoples in all places. Today, watch for the Lord to work and speak, and as He does, for we know with certainty that He will, worship through proclamation to those who need to know.

~ *Jared*

December 30

The Enemy Has Been Defeated

Chronological Bible Reading Plan: (Day 364: Revelation 12-18)

"And I heard a loud voice in heaven, saying, 'Now the salvation and the power and the kingdom of our God and the authority of his Christ have come, for the accuser of our brothers has been thrown down, who accuses them day and night before our God. And they have conquered him by the blood of the Lamb and by the word of their testimony, for they loved not their lives even unto death.'" Revelation 12:10-11 (ESV)

We have been promised certain victory over our enemy and his instruments of sin and death. Yes, Satan was cast out of heaven and given the potential for power here on the earth, and, yes, we in our selfishness rebelled with Him, becoming as guilty as he before the Lord. Yet, when Christ came, He ushered in a new era of promise upon the earth, laying waste to the powers of the evil one and providing for all of creation a glimpse of the glory that is to come in His resurrection from the dead. Christ will overcome every effect of Satan's reign; He will destroy every effect of sin and the sting of death. He has given us hope beyond this life and a certain purpose while living it.

The Church of the living God is empowered to defeat the enemy of God. If we know Christ's resurrection and His second coming to be true, then we must also recognize the power at work within us, further guaranteeing the fulfillment of today's verses that we through the blood of Christ and the word of our testimony will permanently send the enemy and his powers and principalities to their eternal place of worship in judgment.

Take heart, dear friend, today, remembering that in Christ you are more than a conqueror! You have guaranteed victory in Him, and as you find that victory and testify to His faithfulness, slowly and surely you are binding Satan's abilities on the earth and pushing forward the freedom found in the Kingdom of God. Therefore, walk in victory today, because your enemy has been defeated.

~ Jared

December 31

All Things New

Chronological Bible Reading Plan: (Day 365: Revelation 19-22)

"And he who was seated on the throne said, 'Behold, I am making all things new.'" Revelation 21:5a (ESV)

Is there a more beautiful promise in all of Scripture than this from the lips of our glorious Sovereign? In this verse, we see the fulfillment of God's glorious plan for the reconciliation of all things in Christ. Indeed, He will make all things new. In the same way that Christ lived, passed away, and received a glorified body, so too will all things in Christ pass away and be resurrected in glorified form. The earth will pass away but also be made new. Heaven will pass away and be made new. Further, the Lord will restore Jerusalem, His beloved city, and make it a place of meeting that joins both heaven and earth, allowing for fellowship between creation and its Creator, Who will now be with us fully as our God.

The whole of Scripture builds to this moment, as you no doubt have seen through this year together. God created and man fell, but the Lord did not turn His back on us. No! In the midst of our depravity and our descent into darkness, the Lord looked down upon us with loving-kindness and sent His only Son to endure the cross and our shame so that we could be made new.

Hear this today, dear friend: in Christ, you are a new creation; the old has passed away. Do not fall victim to the lies of the enemy, for He has no power over you. Do not fall back into the temptation of fleeting sin, for it has no appeal in the light of God's glorious grace. Do not lose sight of the glorified Jesus, Who provides for you a glimpse of your future reality and that of all things. You are new; may we live like it as we await the completion of that newness in His second-coming.

~ *Jared*

NOTES

NOTES

NOTES

NOTES

NOTES

NOTES

NOTES

NOTES

NOTES